STRESS IN THE DEALING ROOM

High performers under pressure

Howard Kahn and
Cary L. Cooper

London and New York

First published 1993
by Routledge
11 New Fetter Lane, London EC4P 4EE

Simultaneously published in the USA and Canada
by Routledge
29 West 35th Street, New York, NY 10001

Typeset in 10 on 12 point Garamond by
LaserScript, Mitcham, Surrey

Printed and bound in Great Britain by
Biddles Ltd, Guildford and King's Lynn

British Library Cataloguing in Publication Data
A catalogue record for this title is available from the British Library.

Library of Congress Cataloging in Publication Data
Kahn, Howard, 1944–
Stress in the dealing room: high performers under pressure/
Howard Kahn and Cary L. Cooper.
p. cm.
Includes bibliographical references and index.
ISBN 0–415–07375–8
1. Financial institutions – England – London. 2. Job stress –
England – London. I. Cooper, Cary L. II. Title.
HG3000.L82K33   1993
158.7 – dc20   92-23580
CIP

To Valerie and Lily

CONTENTS

FIGURES

TABLES

PREFACE

As the pressure on managers and employees to cope with the radical business changes of the 1990s continues to grow at an accelerating pace, the stress problems associated with high-pressure jobs have become of acute interest. *Stress in the Dealing Room* seeks to determine the sources of stress, and the consequent results of stress in one occupational group, financial dealers operating in the City of London. It also addresses the question of how some dealers manage to cope with the pressures of work in the Dealing Room, and continue to produce high-quality performance. The book will be of value to managers and employees in those organisations which are also subject to high pressure, and where quality performance is required on a permanent basis.

ACKNOWLEDGEMENTS

The authors wish to thank the many financial institutions, dealers and managers who made this book possible. As part of the agreement made with them, no names can be mentioned.

We would also like to thank staff and colleagues at Manchester University, Heriot-Watt University, Edinburgh, and Manchester Polytechnic (now Manchester Metropolitan University), also staff at Routledge for their support and enthusiasm. Special thanks to Graham Lewis, Jim Polson, and Duncan Leuchars for their help with the technical aspects of the book, and to Pamela Hull for her typing and supportive skills.

1

INTRODUCTION

We can trade $100 million in seven minutes or we can do absolutely nothing for seven hours. I let them go to the bathroom then.

(Gray 1983)

These are the reported comments of the manager of a US Dealing Room. What does such an attitude suggest will be the stress levels of the dealers who work in his department?

Since the mid-1980s two topics have regularly found their way into the media, and have been the subject of much discussion, concern, and ill-conceived rumour: occupational stress, and financial dealers.

This book reports on the stress problems faced by those working in the financial institutions of the City of London. It surveys the health of employees working in the UK clearing banks, the London International Financial Futures Exchange, and in merchant banks and foreign-owned banks. They are employed in buying and selling currency, Eurobonds and gilts, trading in stocks, fixed income institutional sales and Swaps, and so on. They provide economic analyses and research for their organisations. These are the people who are generally known as *dealers*. In the book we will highlight the sources of work stress that are the apparent causes of the high levels of mental ill-health, low levels of job satisfaction, and high alcohol intake, of dealers. We will look at the personalities of dealers, and the ways in which they cope, or do not cope, with the stress of their job. Determining whether the attitude expressed at the beginning of this chapter is typical of the management of Dealing Rooms is one of the aims of the investigation we have carried out.

Though we have carried out a study of financial dealers and traders working in the City of London, we believe that the study and the results we describe are as relevant in other areas of the financial sector, and in other countries.

STRESS

Stress has become a major concern both to individuals and to the organisations in which they work in the late twentieth century. This concern is based on two interrelated factors.

Stress and Illness

Firstly, evidence to date supports the proposition that the sources of stress in a particular job, combined with the individual characteristics of the job-holder, can result in job dissatisfaction, mental ill-health, accident occurrence, alcohol abuse, and social or family problems (Cooper 1985): 'Stress is not only a threat to the quality of life, but to physical and psychological well-being' (Cox 1978).

Simply being alive in current society is stressful, and as Kutash, Schlesinger *et al.* (1980) point out:

> each individual not only is beset by the pressures of his or her own daily life but is privy to every disaster in the country and the world through modern news media and communication methods. Perhaps the gains of modern civilisation will be outweighed by the stress-created side effects if we do not come to understand, control, prevent or adapt to stress and anxiety.

Among the behavioural responses to stress are increased cigarette smoking and greater alcohol and drug abuse. Psychological outcomes include family problems, sleep disturbances, sexual difficulties, depression, psychogenic disability, and burnout. Physical outcomes include coronary heart disease, headache, heartburn, backache, and general fatigue (Quick, Horn and Quick 1986). It is the chronic diseases, that is, those which are of long duration and are non-infectious, that are thought to be particularly influenced by the experience of stress (Rabkin and Struening 1976).

The Costs of Stress

Secondly, the costs of stress at national, individual, and organisational levels continue to grow.

Stress at the national level

At the national level, the US Department of Health and Human Services (cited Harvey and Brown 1988) reports that (in the USA) approximately 24 million people suffer from hypertension; more than 20 million are alcoholic; about 650,000 persons die annually from heart attacks (of which almost 200,000 are under 65) and 200,000 from strokes; there are about 200,000–400,000 attempted suicides, of which about one-eighth are successful. Six billion doses of amphetamines, a stimulant drug, are consumed annually in the USA (Ivancevich and Matteson 1987). A large percentage of these figures is directly attributable to stress.

There are many estimates of the costs of stress to the national economy. But whichever is chosen, they all suggest major financial losses. For instance, *The Economist* (April 13 1985) estimates that stress-related illness costs the American economy $100 billion a year, which is ten times more than all labour strikes combined. Higgins (1986) believes that the national cost of stress to US organisations is between 50 and 75 billion dollars each year. Castro (1986) reports that one estimate of the cost to the US economy of alcohol and drug misuse on the job alone is $177 billion, of which Quayle (1983) estimates that $70 billion is attributable to lost production.

Stress at the organisational level

At the organisational level, Cooper and Marshall (1976) note that, from various reports, coronary heart disease and mental ill-health together represent a serious cost for industry in human and financial terms. Evidence from many studies suggests that occupational stress is a major cause of both of these diseases.

Organisations have become increasingly concerned about the impact of stress upon their employees. It may be that the motivation for this is caused in part by recent court decisions (in the US particularly) in favour of plaintiffs seeking compensation for heart attacks and alcoholism allegedly caused by work stress (Harvey and Brown 1988). Some organisations undoubtedly help employees manage stress out of sincere concern for their welfare. Informed and progressive corporations and companies are realising that counting the cost of human resources has tremendous potential benefit (Sutherland 1988), and many organisations are taking the opportunity to 'engage in extensive stress audits' of particular jobs (Cooper and Payne 1988).

The National Institute for Occupational Safety and Health (see Cain 1987) reports that some 60 per cent to 80 per cent of all industrial accidents are related to stress. Estimates suggest that alcohol and drug abuse alone cost US business organisations nearly $40 billion each year. Those employees who abuse drugs show sharply reduced productivity and may account for a large proportion of company thefts (Hollinger and Clark 1983). Drug abuse among high-achieving white-collar workers has been tied to the stress of professional work, where the average working week is now 52.2 hours, compared with 44 hours in 1973 (Hunsaker and Pavett 1988).

Job stress is also related to staff absenteeism and staff turnover. Miner and Brewer (1976) found that poor mental health is a major cause of absenteeism, and other studies have reached similar conclusions. Jamal (1984) notes that there is a positive relationship between stress and absenteeism, employee intention to quit, and actual staff turnover. Steers and Rhodes (1978) have suggested that some absenteeism may be 'healthy' for organisations since it allows employees temporary escape from stressful conditions, so contributing to the better mental health of employees. From a study of 140 former and 143 current managers (in a large southern US electronics firm), Campion and Mitchell (1986) suggest that staff turnover is indeed a very effective, if unfortunate, strategy by which employees handle job stress.

Stress at work has also been linked with coronary heart disease (CHD). French and Caplan (1970) linked quantitative work overload (i.e. being required to do too much work in too little time) with increased cigarette smoking, which in turn is related to CHD. They also found that those employees who had more phone calls to make, smoked significantly more cigarettes than persons with fewer phone calls. Dealers work long hours and are constantly using the telephone.

The direct effects of stress upon work performance are less clear than the effects of stress on mental and physical health. Traditionally, it has been assumed that the relationship between stress and work performance takes the form of an inverted U-shape (see Figure 1.1). Low levels of stress were believed to have little effect upon performance: as stress increased, performance was actually enhanced on many tasks; beyond a certain level stress produced negative effects and so reduced performance (Quick and Quick 1984). However, the relationship between stress and performance may be more complex. Jamal (1984), from a review of many studies of stress and from his own research, concludes that when an

4

employee believes that he or she is stressed (by role conflict, role overload, inadequate resources, etc.), job performance is indeed lowered; but when examining the employee's actual muscle tension, heart rate, etc. the relationship is less clear.

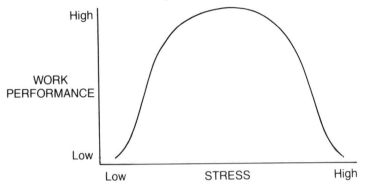

Figure 1.1 Possible relationship between stress and performance

Stress and Compensation Claims

In the United States, stress claims have become the fastest growing category of workers' compensation claims. Hurrell *et al.* (1988) report that claims involving mental disorders caused by stress accounted for nearly 11 per cent of all occupational claims in the early 1980s, and note that among US Social Security Administration disability allowances, mental disorders were the third most disabling condition. More recently, stress claims are reported to account for about 14 per cent to 15 per cent of all occupational disease claims, up from under 5 per cent a decade earlier (*Business and Health*, January 1989; *Journal of American Insurance*, 3rd Quarter 1988). Among the reasons for this are the broadening of the legal definition of stress, the stresses of mergers and acquisitions (which we discuss in Chapter 3), and greater awareness among employees that they can actually get compensation for stress-related illness (*Business and Health* January 1989).

Three other factors are believed to have contributed to the increase in the number of stress-related claims – firstly, a growing number of stress claims from among professional and service-sector workers; secondly, the entrance of more women and younger workers into the workforce; and thirdly, the easier burdens of proof required of claimants (*Small Business Report* November 1987).

Stress disability claims in the US fall into three categories. Firstly, physical–mental, in which a mental disorder brings about a physical one; secondly, mental–physical, in which a mental disorder results from a physical problem; and thirdly, mental–mental, in which a mental disorder results from mental trauma (*Journal of American Insurance*, 3rd Quarter 1988). Because of differing state legislation within the US, it is difficult to obtain overall trends and statistics. For instance, in mental–mental claims, six states require the non-physical cause of the emotional condition to be sudden, ten states require the cause to be somehow unusual if it is gradual, and ten states allow compensation for gradual psychological injury whether or not the stress is unusual (Nugent 1988). Mental–mental claims are reported as making up the majority of stress claims (Bradford 1988). The causes of stress cited most often by claimants include changes in job responsibilities, continual supervisory criticism, additional workload without the consent of the employee, and inadequate communication (*Small Business Report* November 1987).

Comparable British figures are more difficult to obtain, which is a reflection of the differences in the legislative atmosphere and legal positions between the US and UK. However, in May 1989, a secretary won out-of-court compensation from her employers for *tenosynovitis*, a form of repetitive strain injury (Dalton 1989). As other claims of this type increase in the UK, there will undoubtedly be cases brought which are similar to those now common in the United States. For instance, a junior doctor has taken action against his health authority for 'allowing' him to work more than 100 hours a week, claiming that this endangered his own and his patients' health (Cooper and Ferguson 1990).

Currently, it is only possible to speculate on the relevant British figures. On average, in excess of 37 million working days are lost per year in the UK through neurotic disorders, nervous debility, headaches, etc. (Cox 1985). Stress may be costing medium-sized UK companies (those employing around 1,000 staff) £200,000 per year each, or 10–20 per cent of profits (Landale 1989). Overall, stress is considered by the (UK) Health and Safety Executive to cost British industry £4 billion per annum (*The Money Programme*, BBC2, 11 March 1990).

Stress at the individual level

At the individual level, it is believed that stress plays a role in many common illnesses such as headaches and stomach problems (Frese

1985). Many medical experts believe that between 50 and 70 per cent of all illnesses are caused in part by stress (McLean 1980).

Baron (1986) reports that nearly 10 million people in the USA (more than 5 per cent of the total labour force) can be classified as alcoholic (while in another report, by Harvey and Brown (1988), 20 million people in the USA are classified as alcoholic). One US company was so concerned with on-the-job drinking that it bought a breath–alcohol meter to test its employees (*Lincoln Journal* June 11 1983, see Luthans 1989).

Trends in the UK are also causing concern. The major UK alcohol agencies, Alcohol Concern, the Health Education Authority, and the Royal medical colleges, now agree that 21 units and 14 units are the safe weekly limits for men and women respectively: 'The evidence is increasing that there are substantial risks among men who drink more than 21 units a week and women who drink more than 14 units a week' (Alcohol Concern 1987). The risks of getting into serious trouble from alcohol are significantly increased if consumption is between 14 and 21 units for women and between 21 and 35 units for men. American research suggests that if a lifetime view of Britain's post-war generation is taken, 1 in 6 (about 17 per cent) runs the risk of encountering an alcohol problem at some stage. Around 25 per cent of all British men can be expected to experience trouble at some point in their lives due to alcohol.

Dickenson (1988) notes that in terms of personal illness, problem drinking is as widespread a health concern as cancer, and is more than twice as common as diabetes or chronic bronchitis. It is the third biggest killer after cancer and chronic heart disease. Extrapolating figures given by McDonnell and Maynard (1985), Dickenson (1988) suggests that the social cost of alcohol misuse in Britain at 1987 prices would be close to £2 billion per year.

Cooper and Ferguson (1990) report that alcoholism in the workplace in the UK is estimated to cost £2 billion per annum in terms of lost production and sickness absence alone. Cooper (1984) notes that the average senior executive in UK industry is twenty-two times more likely to develop cirrhosis of the liver than the average male, and US figures indicate that workers who have a drinking or drug problem are four times more likely to have an accident, five times more likely to file for compensation, and sixteen times more likely to be absent from work.

DEALERS IN THE CITY OF LONDON

Currency dealers have been the subject of much attention since the mid-1980s. Major changes in the UK financial markets culminated in the 'Big Bang' of 27 October 1986, and the workings of the City financial institutions have been examined by many authors (e.g. Chapman 1988; Hamilton 1986; Webb 1987). The typical customers of a currency trader are foreign mutual funds, off-shore money managers, commodity pool operators, wealthy individuals, and multinational corporations. Some customers are speculators who trade currency like any other commodity (i.e. spot market), while others are 'hedgers' trying to protect foreign profits or lock into current currency prices for some future transaction (i.e. forward market).

In the run up to 'Big Bang', the City went through a series of company mergers and takeovers from overseas as well as UK buyers, all attempting to gain a foothold in 'what promised to be a new global stock market centre in London' (Reid 1988). The growing combines were forced to compete to obtain the skilled staff necessary to run their new computer screen-based operations. As Chapman (1988) highlights:

> salaries rocketed as a game of musical chairs for all but the most mundane jobs got under way. Staffs of merchant banks and broking firms, whose only regular bright spot had previously been the annual bonus payment, suddenly found to their wonderment, that they had taken over from soccer professionals as the group in society most likely to be able to build up earnings without lifting their game.

Reid (1988) indicates:

> age has become less meaningful: chaps of 25 to 27 have made huge sums of money. The young are very screen-literate: some older brokers' talents are now less germane.

There was a massive pay explosion in the City in the mid-1980s as the new 'players' sought to obtain scarce employees, and City terminology such as 'golden hellos', 'golden handcuffs', 'yuppies', and 'marzipan', entered the language. The City environment became one of shirt sleeves rather than dark suits, Porsches rather than Rolls-Royces, and braces rather than belts. The traditional all-male culture of the City was diluted.

8

Premises had to be found with space for large, open-plan offices, which would accommodate a hundred or more dealing staff, with their electronic work units, in one room (Webb 1987). In addition to the development of a Stock Exchange which operated from large Dealing Rooms, and through information technology (i.e. using major installations of computing systems, terminals, telephones, etc.) rather than on a face-to-face basis between jobbers and brokers, other City markets were also revolutionised. The high street clearing banks altered their financial structure, moved into new markets, became far more competitive, and underwent radical changes in culture. Merchant banks, investment and foreign banks have been able, since 'Big Bang', to compete in similar markets. Along with a move towards a 'super league' of financial conglomerates came a switch of attitudes and an obsession with short-term performance.

For many members of the public, any stress problems which might be encountered by dealers were seen as their 'just deserts', of which they were well aware before taking the jobs. Further, the possibility of making large sums of money and 'retiring' at age 35 did not over-enamour dealers with the wider audience. There was (even) disquiet in government circles about the pay explosion:

> It is widely thought within Whitehall that she (the Prime Minister) feels acutely embarrassed that within the de-regulation of the Square Mile, some 25 year-olds are now earning six figure salaries while the dole queue is measured in seven figures.
>
> *(Sunday Times* 16 February 1986)

Public attitudes to dealers, which in turn might affect dealers' behaviour and self-concept, have been formed by newspapers, television series, cinema, and dealers' 'autobiographies'. For example, the ITV 1989 production *Capital City* showed dealers as high earning, neurotic, and amoral. Lewis (1989) writes as an ex-employee of the (then) most powerful international merchant bank, who rose from trainee to $275,000 per year bond salesman within two years. He described Salomon Brothers' trading floor as having minimal supervision and minimal controls. Auletta (1986) describes how greed for power and money brought about the collapse of Lehman Brothers. Bosworth-Davies (1988) presents a picture of major fraud in the City financial markets, and the reasons why it is often not exposed. The 1988 film *Wall Street* set out dealers as motivated by absolute greed, and the influence of the film was such that the anti-hero Gecko's epigrams of 'lunch is for wimps' and 'greed is good' became the international maxims of the late 1980s.

The general public view of City dealers has been summarised by Chapman (1988) as follows:

At lunchtime the best restaurants are usually booked, despite the high prices, while a new breed of City worker may be seen quaffing champagne and munching smoked salmon sandwiches in a brief respite from the desk. These are the Yuppies, despised by the Murdoch 'Sun' and beloved by the Murdoch 'Times', lampooned in the theatre for their avarice and greed and supposed lack of interest in the physical qualities of the opposite sex. Their trademarks are the steel grey sports saloon, the portable phone, and the Filofax. . . . They are at their offices at eight or earlier for the breakfast meeting, make an average 500 or more phone calls a day, write hardly any letters and live centrally. By six-thirty in the evening they are mentally exhausted, and seek solace in the bottle, the brasserie – or the exercise bike. Their elders are not so different, although they tend to commute long-distance from listed country houses, occasionally staying in town when the pressure of work – or home – becomes too great.

The general attitude to many City dealers and to other employees of the City financial institutions appears to be one of distaste, of jealousy, and even of overt hostility.

However, the City of London plays an important role in the British economy and this is a further good reason for examining the group of employees covered by this book. The Bank of England reports that daily money-market transactions average £100 billion (*PM*, BBC Radio 4, 26 September 1989). The importance of the market maker or dealer in the economy was indicated to us by one foreign exchange dealer we interviewed: 'It's a huge, big, global casino. If a government steps out of line they get their currency whacked'.

In addition, the type of work carried out in the City of London, computer- and information-based, highly competitive and market-driven, may be the pattern for much future employment. There is growing concern with the job satisfaction and stress problems of this type of occupational group (see Gale and Christie 1987; Oborne 1985; Zuboff 1988). The City of London has the biggest concentration in the UK of 'knowledge workers', individuals who possess intellectual skills and higher educational qualifications, and who use discretion to make decisions on non-routine tasks. They are paid for their expertise, but only while it is relevant. The increasing sophistication of work throughout the economy means that knowledge workers will predominate across a much broader spectrum of business and industry (Golzen 1989). For instance, Gray (1983) reports a New York currency trader whose study at home is a duplicate of his work environment, with video screens and telephone sets. In future, more traders and other knowledge workers may choose or be required to work at home in a similar work environment. This is another reason why the findings reported in this book will be of value to many employment areas in the banking, finance, and information-dependent sectors.

So far as can be determined, no investigation similar to the present one has been carried out, examining the potential stress problems and the consequent health effects faced by those working in 'Britain's glossy, modern-style stock market' (Reid 1988). Two reports are worth mentioning, however. Firstly, in the United States, Hunsaker and Pavett (1988) placed a one-page questionnaire in the trade magazine of the US brokerage industry. Approximately 3,000 individuals completed the questionnaire. They report that 65 per cent of respondents said that they had never used drugs, 3 per cent used drugs whenever they felt like it, and 28 per cent used drugs outside the workplace only. Fifty-four per cent of respondents reported consuming alcohol during the workday, but only 2.3 per cent did so on a daily basis. Sixty per cent disagreed with the statement that it was easy to obtain drugs at work. Forty-eight per cent of brokers cited alcohol as the most serious problem at their place of employment. Eleven per cent said their co-workers had an alcohol problem. The authors consider that these results do not support the stereotype of the coke-sniffing, marijuana-puffing stockbroker, and compare their data with US norms indicating that 65 per cent of the 18–25 year-old population had used illicit drugs. Many features of their study are open to criticism, but their data provide background to the present investigation.

Secondly, in a study in Norway, Rodahl (1989) has compared the work of the foreign exchange trader with that of air traffic controllers. Both require the capacity to deal with several problems simultaneously and the ability to make quick decisions. The heart-rate reaction of a foreign exchange trader was monitored through a two-hour period, which included first buying $17.4 million and selling $9.9 million, and then buying $19.7 million and selling $10.1 million. The heart-rate of one trader was seen as 'surprisingly moderate, and not unlike the reactions observed in a number of air-traffic controllers' (Rodahl 1989). Some degree of stress, however, was shown by the heart-rate of a dealer who had bought $10 million, sold $6 million, and was awaiting the establishment of the new exchange rate for the dollar. During our interviews with dealers, one told us: 'Before the figures come out it's nerve racking, you feel sick. You can't go in laid back, it's like trench warfare. Everything happens so quickly. When it's busy it's stressful. There's not eight hours of stress'.

Is the work of a dealer particularly stressful in comparison with other jobs? Wilby (1985) reports a rating by 'stress experts' of various jobs on a ten-point scale (see Table 1.1). From this list seven occupations may seem, superficially, to be similar to that of a dealer, namely, pilot (civil aviation), management, marketing/export, sales and retailing, stockbroker, accountancy, and banking. Of these occupations, it is considered that though the job of a dealer takes place within a banking environment, it is quite unlike that of a bank clerk. Some of the activities of an accountant may be found within the sphere of dealing. There are major elements of the job of a stockbroker inherent in that of a dealer, e.g. dealing with investments, the requirements to make a profit, and the need to recognise potential gains and losses. There are many management activities in the job of dealing, and the work concerns the marketing, exporting, selling, and retailing of financial commodities. At a simplistic level, as we have seen, the work of a dealer may be similar to that of a pilot. Both experience alternative periods of relative boredom and high activity. Both groups depend upon computer technology, and an incorrect decision or action can have major effects. Both command high salary income but little career development and potential. It is not thought prudent to exaggerate the comparability of any two occupations, but Table 1.1 indicates that the dealer's job contains many elements in common with other professions which have been rated as attracting above-average stress. In this study we will attempt to answer the question posed at the beginning of the paragraph.

Table 1.1 Stress experts' ratings of various occupations

Financial areas:		Prison officer	7.5
Accountancy	4.3	Ambulance service	6.3
Banking	3.7	*Health:*	
Building societies	3.3	Chiropodist	4.0
Insurance	3.8	Dentistry	7.3
Actuary	3.3	Dietetics	3.4
Stockbroker	5.5	Environmental health	4.6
Commerce/management:		Doctor	6.8
Advertising	7.3	Nursing midwifery	6.5
Management	5.8	Occupational therapy	3.7
Marketing/export	5.8	Optician	4.0
Market research	4.3	Osteopath	4.3
Personnel	6.0	Pharmacist	4.5
Public relations	5.8	Vets	4.5
Purchasing and supply	4.5	Physiotherapy	4.2
Sales and retailing	5.7	Radiographer	4.0
Secretary	4.7	Remedial gymnast	3.5
Company secretary	5.3	Speech therapy	4.0
Work study/O and M	3.6	*Environment:*	
Arts and communications:		Farming	4.8
Art and design	4.2	Forestry	3.7
Broadcasting	6.8	Horticulture	3.8
Journalism	7.5	Nature conservancy	3.2
Museums	2.8	*Public administration:*	
Photographer	4.6	Civil service	4.4
Publishing	5.0	Diplomatic service	4.8
Musician	6.3	Local government officer	4.3
Actor	7.2	Town and country planning	4.0
Film production	6.5	Sports/recreation admin.	3.5
Professional sport	5.8	*Personal service industries:*	
Librarian	2.0	Catering/hotels, etc.	5.3
Uniformed professions:		Travel	4.8
Armed forces	4.7	Hairdresser	4.3
Pilot (civil aviation)	7.5	Beauty therapy	3.5
Merchant navy	4.8	*Public service industries:*	
Fireman	6.3	Post and telecomms	4.0
Police	7.7	Gas	4.0

Table 1.1 Continued

Electricity	4.6	*Professional services:*	
Water	4.0	Architecture	4.0
Public transport	5.4	Barrister	5.7
		Solicitor	4.3
Caring professions:		Surveyor	3.7
Nursery nurse	3.3	Estate agent	4.3
Social worker	6.0		
Teacher	6.2	*Industrial production:*	
Youth and community	4.2	Ceramic technology	4.0
Church	3.5	Food technology	4.0
Psychologist	5.2	Printing	5.6
		Plastics and rubber	4.5
Technical specialities:		Textiles/clothing techn.	4.5
Biologist	3.0	Timber/furniture techn.	4.3
Chemist	3.7	Leather/footwear techn.	3.8
Computer	3.8	Mining	8.3
Engineer	4.3	Construction/building	7.5
Geologist	3.7	Brewing	4.0
Lab technician	3.8		
Metallurgist	3.8		
Operational research	3.8		
Packaging	3.8		
Patent work	4.2		
Physicist	3.4		
Biochemist	3.6		
Statistician	4.0		
Linguist	3.6		
Astronomer	3.4		

Average scores for each occupational group:

Uniformed professions	6.4	Public services	4.5
Commerce/management	5.3	Professional services	4.4
Arts/communication	5.3	Public administration	4.2
Industrial production	5.1	Financial areas	4.0
Caring professions	4.7	Environment	3.9
Health	4.6	Technical specialities	3.7
Personal services	4.5		

Source: Sloan and Cooper (1986)

'BIG BANG' AND THE CITY OF LONDON

Some said it was bound to enhance the City's languishing international competitiveness: others, that it would open the gates to foreign giants who would stride in and eat the natives alive. A few feared that it would have the effect of destroying the valued club-like intimacy and integrity of City professionalism: most admitted that these qualities had already been eroded by increasing cosmopolitanism and the impact of new technology.

(Webb 1987)

Three factors came together in the period preceding 'Big Bang': changes in information technology, the international attitudes adopted by the banks, and the expansion of the banks' securities operations (Webb 1987).

The traditional methods of the City institutions (i.e. the Stock and other Exchanges, discount houses, insurance companies, commercial banks and merchant banks, etc.), were generally based upon self-regulation, informal sanctions, personal relationships, i.e. the old 'club' atmosphere of the City. With the movement to the City of many foreign banks, the development of short-term money markets, a more international outlook in the City, and the revolution in communications, it was clear that these methods were unsuitable:

Under the 'Big Bang', the Old Guard knew, everything would be different. Those who wanted to survive would have to behave like Chicago future dealers. Life would become just like a job on the money or commodity markets, where young men and women would arrive to a room full of telephones and computer terminals at 7.30 every morning, scream at them and at each other for at least 12 hours, and leave exhausted in the evening. This was a world where the mid-life crisis came at the age of 26.

(Chapman 1988)

In addition, the threat to the City of London of competition from the US and Japan was clear: 'The Stock Exchange had become stagnant, complacent and introverted, and would need dramatic restructuring if it was ever to become internationally competitive again' (Webb 1987).

The mandatory separation between the functions of the stockbroker and the stockjobber had been abolished in the 1980s.

Traditionally, a client would go to a broker who in turn would approach a jobber who, in competition with other jobbers, bought and sold stock and lived on the difference between the buying and selling prices. In 1986, jobbers were permitted 'to broke'. Brokers became dealers and market-makers. Minimum commission was abolished. It is irrelevant to dealers whether prices go up or down. So long as prices are moving, dealers have the possibility to make profits. If prices are not moving, no-one is trading, but the large financial institutions can use their power to force markets to move.

Major advances in computer technology meant that any financial centre which had the will to install the latest computer systems would find itself, for a time, technically ahead of the world. London became the technological pace-setter:

> The City (of London) is placed to bridge the (time) gap between New York and Tokyo – at present New Yorkers are still asleep when trading stops on the Tokyo Stock Exchange, but the new dealing systems mean that it is no longer necessary for trading to take place as a result of dealers gathering in a hall to shout at each other, like farmers at a cattle auction.
>
> (Chapman 1988)

Market-makers no longer compete face-to-face on the Stock Exchange (trading ceased on the Stock Exchange floor on 31 January 1992, when members of the London Traded Options Market moved to new premises in the City of London) or other 'floor', but by computer screen and by telephone. Computers and the screen have become not mere adjuncts of dealing, but the indispensable tool. The technology which supported 'Big Bang' is now an essential part of the dealer's job:

> In 1984–86 a typical major securities firm would have invested some £30m on a totally new electronic system, without which after 27 October 1986 it would neither be able to make a market competitively nor settle the formalities of its deals at all.
>
> (Webb 1987)

The computer systems used by firms engaged in brokerage and/or market-making carry out four major tasks:

(a) to deliver comprehensive information on the state of the market;

(b) to reflect all relevant deals as they occur;

(c) to provide a mass of lateral and background data to meet what might be called 'risk management'; and

(d) to cope with the administrative aftermath of accounting and settlement, the vital 'back room' operation.

(Webb 1987)

It is possible to integrate these four systems, but it has usually been necessary to install them separately.

Employers' attitudes to their Dealing Room staff are not readily available. Two City financial institutions are considered to be among the 'best' companies to work for in the UK. These are James Capel, agency brokers and market-makers in gilt, and Phillips and Drew, stockbrokers (Reynolds 1989). The Personnel Director of James Capel considers that there is no James Capel type:

there are 1500 types who work here, with backgrounds ranging from Eton to the East End. All we look for is enthusiasm – controlled extroverts and self-starters.

(Reynolds 1989)

Phillips and Drew tend to recruit three different types of employee:

specialists like arbitrageurs, whose main function is to spot opportunities in the market; salesmen who tend to be more extroverted and enjoy presenting ideas; and analysts who tend to be more introverted.

(Reynolds 1989)

A dealer told us:

The dealer's job is changing from 'seat of the pants' to 'analyst'. The 'seat of the pants' people, and the East Enders, they eat and sleep dealing, and they eat and drink, and so on, a bit more. The analysts have a classical education, wider interests, sport, other outlets. They treat stress differently.

Another dealer in a small Dealing Room said:

A good gilts dealer needs a good memory, reticence – because of insider trading – sharp reflexes, must be numerate, have an active mind, and keep his cool and not get excited. He needs to make quick decisions, be literate and accurate. It's not essential to be extrovert. Quiet aggression. Extrovert type to be a jobber. To be a broker, introvert or extrovert. You've got to be able to cope with working by yourself. A good client dealer

17

needs to be sharp, have a good knowledge of the market from experience, and have a knowledge of dealers. You need a sense of humour, you mustn't lose your temper.

Phillips and Drew, like James Capel, look for staff who are quick on their feet, have an agile brain, and a resilient personality. The need for resilience was emphasised by a spot dealer who told us:

Some days when you've done well, you feel on top of the world, or some days your chin is on your chest, you feel a right idiot. You can swing from high ecstasy to degradation in a couple of days.

A sterling dealer emphasised style:

What makes a dealer? Your manner of speech, selling yourself, being confident, being sure of yourself. Being flexible, a risk-taker, knowing when to take a loss.

A Dealing Room manager put a composite picture of 'the successful dealer':

What makes a successful dealer? They're group oriented, they need judgement, and a good environment. They can follow their own judgements and management leads. They need to handle defeat sensibly and to understand risks. You've got big dreams.

Phillips and Drew encourage staff to come in between 6.30a.m. and 7.00a.m. – they get a full English breakfast in the Director's dining room and are at their desks by 8.00a.m. Among 100 companies examined by Reynolds (1989), only Phillips and Drew formally note that stress is an important factor, and the company has produced a video outlining the work, which employees can take home to their families. The importance of family support is clearly recognised. Reynolds (1989) quotes the chief personnel manager of Phillips and Drew as considering that the pressure of dealing is so high that traders are reputed to burnout at 29: 'I've heard of some going off to set up market gardens but in reality most of them slip quietly into management'.

SUMMARY

Work-related stress is a contemporary and growing problem at the national, organisational, and individual level, and City dealers ostensibly work in an environment which would appear to attract a high level of stress. Recent rapid changes in the City, and public attitudes to the work, to the job-holders, and to the associated rewards, might be expected to add to any stress inherent in the job. Nor are the changes of the 1980s completed: 'As for the City as a whole . . . "Big Bang" . . . is . . . a legal, structural and economic revolution. It is still rumbling on, and no one can with certainty predict its duration or its outcome' (Webb 1987).

It is the purpose of our study of dealers to find whether they are more stressed than other employees, and what the sources and effects of these stresses are. We will look at the mental and physical health of dealers, and will suggest how individual dealers and their employers can recognise and deal with the sources and symptoms of stress. While our study was conducted within the Dealing Rooms of the City of London, there are many reasons to believe that our results are relevant to other professional groups.

In the following chapters we will provide an outline of the concept of stress and how it is relevant to those working in the financial markets and in other similar occupational groups. We will explain the methods we used to obtain the information we were seeking about dealers. We will present the results of our study as they affect dealers and the implications for the management of Dealing Rooms. We are sure that our book will be of value not only to those who work in the City, but to all who are concerned about the health of their staff and of themselves.

2

THE CONCEPT OF STRESS

THE PROBLEM OF DEFINING STRESS

A major problem which the general reader faces is the way in which the term 'stress' is used in the media (and by authors of books on the subject!). It has taken on different meanings which are sometimes contradictory and often confusing. Many people use the word 'stress', but fail to define precisely what they mean by stress, how they visualise stress, and how they consider that the mechanism of stress operates. This is very confusing, and makes it difficult to obtain an overall picture of current thinking about stress.

In this chapter we will examine the various ways in which stress has been conceptualised, and put forward our own view of stress. Two terms associated with stress which are generally not under dispute are 'stressor' and 'strain'. These are used fairly consistently by most writers on stress (Beehr and Franz 1986). 'Stressor' refers to those things in the environment (i.e. outside the individual) which might result in the triggering of 'stress'. 'Strain' refers to the way in which the individual responds to 'stress', whether that reaction is physical, psychological, or related to an individual's behaviour. These responses indicate the ill-health or well-being of an individual. We might summarise by stating that job stressors occur in the workplace and cause strain.

Researchers into the topic of occupational stress have variously used the term stress to denote environmental factors pressing on the individual (like the use of the word 'stressor' above), or the immediate or long-term effects of stress (as the word 'strain' is mostly used), or the individual's reactions. Thus, stress is understood by some people to be a source, or an outcome, or related to an individual's personality. Cummings and Cooper (1979) believe that: 'This

20

confusion . . . makes it difficult to compare the results of different studies or to understand the . . . relationships reported in the research'.

Similarly, Cooper and Marshall (1976) note that 'stress' is often used to denote pressure on the individual, or the effects of this pressure, or an individual's reactions. To add to the complications, stress is seen by some people as an individual perception. Advocates of this view believe that an event is stressful only if the individual perceives it as such.

So 'stress' has been used essentially in four fundamentally different ways, and these are well summarised by Kasl (1983):

a) as an environmental condition
b) as an appraisal of an environmental situation
c) as the response to that condition; and
d) as some form of relationship between the environmental demands and the person's ability to meet the demands.

It is interesting to consider why the term 'stress' is used so confusingly. There appear to be four main strands in the development of the concept of stress as it is used today, as noted by Briner (1986). Firstly, the biological and biochemical ideas found in the nineteenth-century work of Bernard, and in Cannon (1935) and Selye (1956). Secondly, the psychoanalytic ideas of Freud, which led Hartman (1939) and Menninger (1938) to look at the potential role of the ego in stress. Thirdly, the application of applied psychology to the military and industrial sectors, with the aim of designing tasks to obtain the most efficient worker performance. Fourthly, the relationship between stress and illness, where stress is seen to refer to lifestyles, occupations, particular events, individual personality, and so on.

The way people use the term 'stress' will depend upon which of these viewpoints is selected. However, there are yet other ways in which the concept of stress has been based, for instance, learning and behavioural, developmental, sociological, ethological, physiological, and neuro-biological (Kutash, Schlessinger et al. 1980).

Briner (1986) notes that one of the most common views of the stress mechanism is based on the argument that our ancient antecedents evolved in a way which enabled the body to be employed physically in the struggle for survival. Briner (1986) points out that the threat of attack by an animal would automatically evoke nervous and hormonal reactions in preparation for a physical response to the attack. Pulmonary ventilation increased, as did heart-rate and cardiac output, and blood volume shifted from the gut and skin to the muscles. Stress hormones caused stored energy to be released as glucose and fatty acids. The excreted stress hormone cortisone provided fuel for the working muscles. As soon as the attack and the effort associated with it were over the same regulatory mechanisms brought the excited organisms back to a state of rest. However, Briner (1986) also points out that this ancient scenario suggests that early humans went round all day scared of, and reacting to, attack, which may not have been the case.

In the modern human, stressful situations may produce the same stress reaction, but there is rarely an opportunity for a physical outlet for the stress response, such as 'fight' or 'flight'. This may cause organic changes in individuals over time, which may turn out to be pathological in nature (Rodahl 1989).

Historically, interest in stress stemmed from its potential role in causing illness. Stressors were (and often still are) seen as adverse events, and stress is seen as a negative outcome. However, stress can be considered in other ways. Stress can certainly be viewed as negative, but it can also be seen as positive and valuable. The near or complete absence of stress may itself be a negative condition for most people. A certain amount and quality of stress may be beneficial, since in moderate amounts it can stimulate people to work harder and accomplish more (Vecchio 1991). This kind of positive stress is termed eustress (from the Greek 'eu', meaning 'good'). There is an optimum amount of stress which is 'good' for people, and below and, more commonly, above this optimum level, the health and work performance of individuals are affected.

While stress can be regarded as an inevitable factor in life, there is nothing inevitable about the negative outcomes of stress, i.e. distress (Quick and Quick 1984). The aim should be to maximise eustress and minimise distress, and to strike a balance between the destructive forces of both hypostress (too little stress) and hyperstress (too much stress). Figure 2.1 shows the four basic variations of stress which should be balanced by the individual. It is because of the difficulty of maintaining such a fine balance that many people fall prey to the negative effects of stress.

MODERN VIEWS OF STRESS

There have been three main views of stress during the twentieth century, and in order to determine where we have reached today in our understanding of stress, the next section will briefly describe these three views. The section develops the ideas stated earlier in this

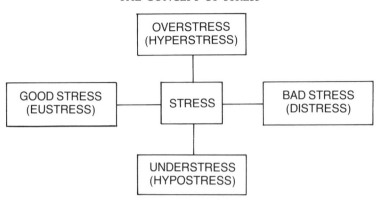

Figure 2.1 The four basic variations of stress
Source: Selye (1980)

chapter, and will show how the different uses of the term 'stress' have developed. The three most common views of stress see stress as i) a response to a threat, ii) the threat itself, and iii) internal to the individual.

Stress as a Response

Those who consider stress as a response to events are basing their views on the work of Cannon (1932). Cannon was probably the first modern researcher to apply the concept of stress to humans, in the way in which it had traditionally been used in physics and engineering. Humans, as seen by Cannon: 'are in some ways analogous to physical objects such as metals that resist moderate outside forces but that lose resiliency at some point of great pressure' (Hobfoll 1989).

Cannon was interested in the effects of cold, lack of oxygen, and so on, upon living beings. Though the initial impact of a stressor, or its continuation at low levels could be withstood, he concluded that prolonged or severe stressors eventually lead to a breakdown of the individual's biological systems.

Cannon's work was developed by Hans Selye. Selye, while searching for a new sex hormone, discovered that virtually all stressful stimuli result in tissue damage, and entitled this occurrence the General Adaptation Syndrome (Selye 1956). The syndrome has three stages: alarm, resistance, and exhaustion. In the alarm stage, the internal stress system of the body is activated by an external stressor, and this results in a number of physiological and chemical reactions, e.g. increases in pituitary and adrenalin secretions, heart-rate, blood pressure, and a general heightening of the senses. If the external stressor should continue, the resistance stage is entered, when the body 'calls upon the needed organ or system to deal with the stressor' (Luthans 1989). Should the stressor persist, the adaptive systems brought into use in the resistance stage may become drained, and the tertiary stage, exhaustion, occurs. When this happens, the cycle may commence again with the alarm stage, when another organ or system is activated to deal with the stressor or, ultimately, death occurs.

In developing the General Adaptation Syndrome, Selye concluded that living beings have a pattern of stereotyped responses that become evident in response to stimuli. Whatever the particular stimulus, the body responds in a predictable way. Selye (1983) points out that a variety of dissimilar situations are capable of producing stress, and that it is consequently difficult to pinpoint any one as the cause of the stress reaction.

Selye's (1936) formulation of stress was largely responsible for popularising the concept in the scientific vocabulary, and: 'it initiated an era of research and theoretical development conducted with accelerating enthusiasm on an international scale in numerous branches of the medical and later the social sciences' (Rabkin and Struening 1976).

Stress as the Threat Itself

Stress has been commonly used to refer to the *external* conditions which result in an individual experiencing 'discomfort', 'tension', etc. In this context, the term 'stress' refers to the presence of various stressors, i.e. external sources of pressure (Baron 1986). Brief, Schuler and Van Sell (1981) have compiled a list of potential job-related stressors organised into three basic categories:

   (i) organisational characteristics and processes
  (ii) job demands and role characteristics
 (iii) individual characteristics and expectations.

Each variable in the list (see Table 2.1) has been found to result in stress and therefore to affect job behaviour (Saal and Knight 1988). The nature of the relationship between stress and job behaviour, however, is not at all clear.

Whereas the response-based approach to stress was developed from a base founded in medicine, the view of stress as the threat itself, with its emphasis on the sources of stress, was a reflection of the growth of industrialisation. The aim of those researching stress from this viewpoint was to produce working conditions which would optimise production. Thus, attention was paid to items such as temperature, noise levels, crowding, the speed of the assembly line, workload, etc.

While industrialisation brought working conditions which resulted (and still do result) in disease, the emphasis in recent years has been upon the psychological effects of work stressors, particularly those relevant to the new technologies. For instance, in relation to the operation of desktop computers, researchers have examined 'office ergonomics', e.g. the dimensions of desk height, seat design, nearness of other operators, illumination, acoustic and thermal environments (Oborne 1985). The relationship between environmental demands and operator performance has been a major concern of those who have emphasised this model of stress. They are particularly interested in where maximum operator performance is achieved. The individual's internal responses to external stressors are of less concern to them. Performance is seen to be directly related to the stressors which are present.

Given the realities of the kind of research outlined above, often conducted in commercial organisations which are perhaps keen to obtain speedy results, it is not surprising that individual differences are not examined in any detail, despite the acceptance that any two individuals may react differently to the same 'stressor'. It is argued by some researchers that an event is only stressful if the individual perceives it as such (Lazarus 1966), and subsequently there has in recent years been a move towards providing the individual with the ability to create their own, personal, work environment. For instance, adjustable workstations, chairs, and desks, recognise variations in the human frame and individual needs.

Stress as Internal to the Individual

Once it was accepted that individuals differ in their responses to stress, attention moved to why this is so, and what determined these differences. Research has concentrated upon many possibilities, and Table 2.2 shows a partial list of potential mediators of stress and one scheme for organising them, developed by Elliot and Eisdorfer (1982).

Table 2.1 Potential job-related stressors

ORGANISATIONAL CHARACTERISTICS AND PROCESSES
  Organisational policies
    Inequitable or inadequate performance evaluations
    Pay inequities
    Ambiguous or arbitrary policies
    Rotating work shifts
    Frequent relocation
    Idealistic job descriptions before hiring
  Organisational structure
    Centralisation; low participation in decision making
    Low opportunity for advancement or growth
    Increased size
    Excessive formalization
    Excessive specialization and division of labour
    Interdependence of organisational units
  Organisational processes
    Poor communication
    Poor or inadequate feedback on performance
    Ambiguous or conflicting goals
    Ineffective delegation
    Training programmes
JOB DEMANDS AND ROLE CHARACTERISTICS
  Working conditions
    Crowding
    Lack of privacy; poor spacial arrangements
    Noise
    Excessive heat or cold
    Lights; inadequate, glaring, or flickering
    Presence of toxic chemicals
    Safety hazards
    Air pollution, including radiation

Table 2.1 Continued

Interpersonal relationships
    Inconsiderate or inequitable supervisors
    Lack of recognition or acceptance
    Lack of trust
    Competition
    Difficulty in delegating responsibilities
    Conflict within and between groups
Job demands
    Repetitive work
    Time pressures and deadlines
    Low skill requirements
    Responsibility for people
    Underemployment
Role characteristics
    Role conflict
    Role ambiguity
    Role underload/overload
    Role-status incongruity
INDIVIDUAL CHARACTERISTICS AND EXPECTATIONS
Career concerns
    Under/overpromotion
    Midcareer crises
    Obsolescence
    Unmet expectations and goals
    Job insecurity
Individual characteristics
    Type A behaviour pattern
    Anxiety
    Intolerance of ambiguity
    Flexibility/rigidity
    Introversion/extroversion

Source: Brief, Schuler and Van Sell (1981)

Table 2.2 Potential mediators of the relationships between stress and illness

PERSON FACTORS

Personality (personality traits, coping dispositions)

Personal resources (intelligence, special skills, motivation, some personality variables)

Temperament (beliefs, attitudes)

Past history (past experience, repertoire of skills, previous psychiatric history)

Socio-demographic variables (age, sex, race, socio-economic status)

Genetic variables (biological predispositions to illness)

Biological variables not genetically transmitted (physical condition, diseased organs)

PROCESS FACTORS

Cognitive appraisal (meaning of an event, significance for well-being)

Coping (strategies used to react to or negate the effects of an event)

ENVIRONMENTAL FACTORS

Interpersonal factors (social networks, social supports)

Other external factors –

    Physical setting (geographic and architectural characteristics)

    Organisational factors (institution size and structure)

    Human aggregate (characteristics of the persons inhabiting a particular environment)

    Social climate (social prejudices, social expectations)

    Cultural factors (cultural belief systems, institutionalised methods for dealing with change)

    Other environmental stressors (war, economic upheaval)

Source: Elliot and Eisdorfer (1982)

Recognising the importance of individual differences in stress outcomes, it has been suggested that it would be better to view the concept of stress as related to the drive towards 'homoeostasis', or maintenance by living systems of a steady state. When forces threaten to disrupt this balance, the individual must act (or cope) to restore its steady state. A stress, then, is any of these forces and there are obviously many potential stresses.

This homoeostatic idea of stress incorporates many of the views of stress we have already mentioned. That is, it recognises the importance of: the sources of stress, which may be internal to the individual (e.g. their needs and desires), or external; the resources which are available to the individual, both internal (skills) and external; the ways in which the individual appraises the potential discrepancy between the perceived demands on them and the perceived resources they have available; the methods the individual uses to cope with the discrepancies (by their actions); and the negative aspects upon health of failure to cope. These negative aspects may be physiological responses (e.g. physical illness) or psychological responses (e.g. fear, anxiety, tension). A third response to stress by the individual may be to adopt behaviours to cope with the stress (e.g. by dealing directly with the sources of stress, by drinking, drug-taking, or self-persuasion that the threat is not major).

It is this idea of stress which is used in the present study of dealers. It has the support of those who conceptualise stress as a state which results from a misfit between the skills of the individual and the demands made upon him or her, i.e. what has been called the 'person–environment fit'. Stress will occur when a person appraises a given relationship with the environment as taxing or exceeding the person's resources and so having the potential to result in distress. McGrath (1976) summarises this view as follows:

> There is a potential for stress when an environmental situation is perceived as presenting a demand which threatens to exceed the person's capabilities for meeting it, under conditions where he expects a substantial difference in rewards and costs from meeting the demand versus not meeting it.

As we have noted earlier, stress occurs not only when the demands on a person exceed their capability, but also when their capabilities exceed demand (Glowinkowski and Cooper 1986).

The view of stress we have taken is also based on the suggestion that people seek out and are satisfied by those situations, environments, and jobs, which best fit their personalities, and avoid those that do not. A good fit results in high performance and satisfaction and low stress, while a poor fit results in decreased performance and satisfaction, and high stress (Furnham 1981). The individual brings to their particular working situation certain needs which the organisation may or may not meet by providing career opportunities, adequate salary, recognition, etc. when stress will be reduced.

Van Harrison (1978) has suggested two kinds of person–environment fit: firstly, the extent to which an individual's skills and abilities match the requirements of the job; and secondly, the extent to which the job environment provides the resources to meet the needs of the individual.

As might be expected, there is disagreement about these ideas. For example, Holland (1973) is critical of the person–environment proposal, and suggests that it is a person's personality type (which could be realistic, investigative, artistic, social, enterprising, cultural, etc.) and their background which lead them into certain occupations. However, Mount and Muchinsky (1978) consider that certain jobs are more satisfying than others whatever the personality of the job holder.

Even though the present study uses the term 'stress' basically to refer to something internal to the individual, it is clear that new ways of looking at and refining the concept and study of stress 'will go on forever, as long as biology and medicine exist, alongside the study of psychology and sociology' (Selye 1983).

3

SOURCES OF STRESS AT WORK

In this chapter we look at the potential causes of stress in individuals who work in the financial markets. In a later chapter we determine the actual sources of stress in the Dealing Room which result in job dissatisfaction, mental ill-health, and increased alcohol consumption.

The previous chapter has indicated the concept of stress which supports the present study of dealers. The underlying premise of this idea of stress is of a 'mismatch' between the individual and his or her job (Sloan and Cooper 1987). The stress associated with the lack of 'fit' between the person and the job will lead to job dissatisfaction, anxiety, and depression, and to organisational problems such as absenteeism and high labour turnover. This model also takes account of differences between individuals including their personality, their behaviour patterns, the social support used by them, their age, sex, etc.

BURNOUT

A great deal has been written in recent years about stress: 'Of all the areas of industrial and organisational psychology, the literature relating to occupational stress continues to be one of the fastest growing' (MacKay and Cooper 1987).

In addition, the concept of burnout has attracted an increasing amount of attention since the mid-1970s (Gillespie 1983), and thinking about stress and burnout has progressively overlapped. *Job burnout* refers to the negative effects of working conditions when job stress seems unavoidable to an individual, and sources of satisfaction or relief appear unavailable (Moss 1981). It results in physical, emotional, or mental exhaustion, and appears to be most common among professionals who deal with other people, such as lawyers, accountants, managers, nurses, police officers, social workers, and teachers. Dealers and others working in the financial markets also fall into this category. For instance, not only do dealers have to work closely with their colleagues, they also have to communicate with dealers and brokers elsewhere in their own organisation and in other companies, with customers, with members of the public (and with investigators such as the present authors), etc.

Rodgers (1984) estimates that about 20 per cent of business owners, managers, professionals, and technical people in the USA suffer from job burnout. In contrast with the characteristics of people who may (only) encounter the problems associated with job stress, those who are likely to experience job burnout experience a great deal of stress as a result of job-related stressors, are perfectionists and/or self-motivating achievers, and often seek unrealistic or unattainable goals (Harvey and Brown 1988). Consequently, they cannot cope with the demands of their job, and their willingness to 'try' drops dramatically. Dealers might be expected to meet many of these criteria for developing burnout.

The objective of this chapter is to examine those sources of stress and burnout which might be expected to be particularly relevant to dealers and to the other professionals working in the financial sector. The potential sources of stress are discussed under two headings. Firstly, sources of stress at work, and secondly, those individual characteristics which might in some way affect an employee's response to these potential sources of stress.

Readers who seek more information about the areas mentioned are encouraged to examine the references provided.

SOURCES OF STRESS AT WORK

Six major categories of potential sources of stress at work have been identified by Cooper (1986) as shown in Figure 3.1. They are stressors intrinsic to the job, the role of the individual in the organisation, career development, relationships with others at work, organisational structure and climate, and the interface between home and work. This last source of stress could be regarded as extra-organisational (Sutherland and Cooper 1988), but because of the strong relationships between events at home and at work it is included here with the other five categories. Each of these potential sources of stress at work will be examined in turn. Later, we will determine how much of a source of stress each item actually is to the dealers who are the subject of our study.

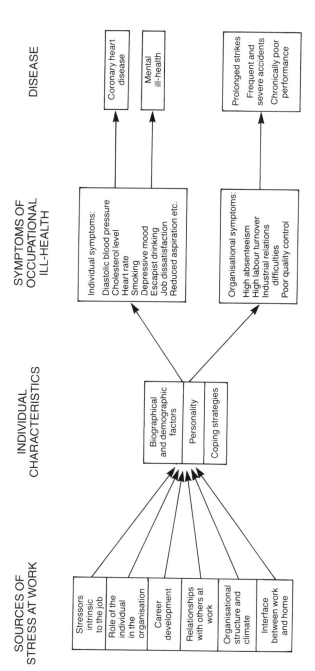

Figure 3.1 The major categories of stress at work
Source: Cooper (1986)

STRESSORS INTRINSIC TO THE JOB

Within this category are included both the physical demands and the task demands of a job. Every job is thought to have a set of unique factors which job holders identify as sources of pressure, but the major recurring themes reported by employees are physical working conditions, shift-working, work overload and underload, occupational level, repetition of and boredom with work, and the 'person–environment' fit. The physical demands of the job of dealing discussed here relate to working conditions, and the stress factors relevant to modern, open-plan, technology-driven offices. Task demands seen as particularly relevant to dealers are work overload and underload, and working long hours.

Working Conditions

There appears to be clear evidence of a positive relationship between stress and physical factors such as noise, extreme temperatures, and pollution (Staw 1984). This stress is in turn related to reduced performance. Fine and Kobrick (1978) have also shown that working conditions which are perceived as unpleasant can be sources of stress. In addition to extremes of heat and cold, and noise, these include crowding, shift work, and also flexible working hours. Within the office environment, stress has also been linked with office ergonomics, automation, air conditioning, ventilation, artificial lighting, natural lighting and view, visual and acoustical privacy, and physical safety (Wineman 1982).

French and Caplan (1972) associate stress with jobs which have little influence and responsibility, while in contrast Cooper and Payne (1978) have found jobs with substantial responsibility to be stressful. Kornhauser (1965) shows that poor mental health is directly related to, among other things, excessive and inconvenient hours. Simply getting to work on time can be stressful (Rodahl 1989).

Information Technology

More and more jobs are being replaced or supported by information technology products, i.e. computer terminals, communication systems, database management systems. While the initial impact of information technology was on shop floor work and in the manufacturing sector, in recent years more attention has been paid to installing computer systems in the office, and this is particularly true of financial institutions.

The modern international stock markets are almost totally dependent upon information technology. There have been many reports of those office workers who use a Visual Display Unit or Terminal (VDU or VDT) suffering negative psychological and physiological effects (e.g. Bennett *et al.* 1984; Dainoff *et al.* 1981). However, no detailed studies of users similar to those under examination in this book have been carried out, i.e. users who are near-totally dependent upon a computer system, but whose job, while centred around the computer system, has many other elements. Thus the potential negative effects of VDUs upon white-collar office staff may not be capable of extrapolation to Dealing Room staff.

The relationships between computer usage and stress are complex. Indeed, it has been noted that:

> developments in the technology of the electronic workplace are running ahead of developments in our understanding of the human at work.
>
> (Gale and Christie 1987)

Frese (1987) suggests that:

> it is necessary to ask whether there are new psychological stressors relating to working with a computer and/or whether some well-known stressors become more pronounced in computer work.

Nevertheless, it appears that using information technology products might result in four potential stress problems for dealers:

i) *system response time and breakdowns.* For dealers and others working in the financial markets, it would appear that the fastest possible response time, and the speediest update of data which the computer can provide (i.e. data providing the prevailing market positions), are desired. Schneiderman (1986) however, warns that very short response times add to feelings of being rushed (and so adds to this particular stressor). It may well be that it is the variability of the response time (i.e. predictability) that is the more stressful. In addition, dealers are paid partially by results, and their retaining their jobs may also depend upon high performance, so that a slow response time and/or equipment breakdowns are potential stressors.

ii) *feelings of being rushed and of high concentration.* Johansson and Aronsson (1984) consider these factors as particularly relevant to clerical workers using VDUs. As Frese notes: 'The cursor constantly blinks, signalling readiness for further input'. Although this aspect of the technology may be less relevant to dealers, nevertheless there are features of the job which mean that dealers are 'hurried' by the computer system.

iii) *supervision by the computer*. Clerical workers (e.g. word process operators) can have their performance monitored in terms of the number of keystrokes made per hour or day, and this may lead to stress outcomes (Smith 1984). The activities of dealers can also be logged by the computers they use (in addition to the recording of telephone calls to and from their clients, colleagues, etc.). Stress may result from this aspect of the supervision of dealers.

iv) *abstractions of work*. Hacker (1985) considers that there may be a natural need in humans to handle things (paper, folders, numbers) in a concrete way, and this disappears in computer work. Stress may result from this loss of concreteness.

Frese (1987) has also noted that lack of concreteness may lead to a feeling of unreality towards the objects (manipulated on the VDU screen), and though Frese's (1987) study relates to those playing war games, the effects of abstractedness upon Dealing Room staff may be similar, that is, for some individuals, the feelings of 'unreality' may extend beyond the Dealing Room walls and into their lives outside.

The overall stress effects of the technology upon dealers are uncertain. It is probably dependent upon the particular organisational context in which the work is done. Kahn and Cooper (1986) suggest that management attitudes to the implementation of computer-based systems, that is: 'proper management in selection of equipment . . . in its installation, testing, maintenance, operation etc., and appropriate involvement of the staff who will be affected by the changeover', is a major determinant of the stress outcomes on user staff. Within the financial organisations which are the subject of the present study, little user involvement in these terms was detected, and equipment was often installed hurriedly to meet the needs of 'Big Bang'.

There is certainly evidence that VDU work is demanding on the eyes and that this, plus a workplace with little control and high stressors, can lead to eye-strain.

Other (psycho) somatic reactions to the VDT workplace have been described as headaches and backaches.

(Cakir 1981)

Backaches

> may be a function of bad ergonomic design that forces the
> worker to lean forward, thus not having a support of a
> chairback.
>
> (Frese 1987)

In the Dealing Rooms, traders spend much time slumped in chairs,
looking at multiple screens. Physical stress may therefore result.

In a study of 109 clerical employees who use computer workstations, Sutton and Rafaeli (1987) found that there was evidence of
negative health effects upon employees caused by intrusions from
others. The authors suggest that open-plan offices, such as are found
in financial institutions, have generally negative effects on
employees' reactions. They believe that intrusions from others may
be stressors:

> because they hamper control and decrease predictability of
> important events. Interruptions from noisy co-workers, noisy
> machines, ringing telephones, and people walking in and
> around a work-station may be impossible to predict and may
> thus lead employees to perceive that they have little cognitive
> control over important events.
>
> (Sutton and Rafaeli 1987)

Interruptions may be potent sources of unpredictability and lack of
control, and density (i.e. the number of people working physically
close together) may also increase unpredictable interruptions and
decrease perceived control. Lack of control over work and lack of
predictability are certainly stressors (see e.g. Sutton and Kahn 1987).
However, it has also been noted that interruptions may *enhance*
well-being for managers, since managers typically seek the live
action created by telephone calls and unexpected visitors (Mintzberg 1973), and interruptions can produce task variety and create
opportunities for friendships.

Overworked employees may concentrate even harder on their
work than other employees and ignore intrusions stemming from
their physical environment (called the 'detachment' hypothesis).
Perhaps people perceive occupational stressors hierarchically: 'if
they are under relatively severe stress they may not notice or react
to relatively minor threats' (Sutton and Kahn 1987).

Abdel-Halim (1981) reports a study which included eighty-one
managerial and non-managerial personnel working in banks in

complex, high-scope jobs, using mediating technology. High levels of role stress in this situation were found to be disturbing and dissatisfying for role incumbents, and he suggests that this is due to such employees often being 'involved in external boundary-spanning activities, functioning as information processors and filters ... as representatives of the organisation, and as formal and informal agents of the organisation who influence the customers or clients' (Abdel-Halim 1981).

Abdel-Halim (1981) found that such employees face role requirements involving relatively high risk and excessive or chronic stress, resulting in substantial health costs: 'Low levels of role ambiguity and overload (perhaps through adherence to the organisation's rules) would be a source of relief and satisfaction for these individuals' (Abdel-Halim 1981).

The work of dealers, and other financial employees, appears to be similar in many ways to that of the staff described above, and the potential outcomes might be expected to be similar.

In white-collar, routine, intellectually undemanding, high speed work (only partially comparable to the work of dealing), those using a computer terminal for the major part of the day were found by Frankenhaeuser and Johansson (1986) to have slightly higher adrenalin excretion levels (a source of potential illness) and took longer to unwind after work. (This may also be related to Tension Discharge Rate, discussed later in this chapter.)

To summarise the potential effects of using information technology, Amick and Ostberg (1987) believe that evidence is emerging that links certain *work characteristics* (heavy workload, routine and repetitive work, low control and little social support) with the development of stress-related disease, and that certain applications of office automation appear capable of exacerbating these characteristics. For instance, Martin and Wall (1989) investigated 'attentional demand' (concentration, close inspection of work, quick reactions) and 'cost responsibility' (responsibility for valuable products and machinery) as causes of strain in blue-collar workers, and found that where both factors are present high psychological strain results: 'employees working under these conditions reported greater job-related anxiety, more pressure, and worse general mental health than their counterparts in jobs characterised by other combinations of these independent variables' (Martin and Wall 1989).

Though these results may not be widely generalizable, they have implications for dealers. Dealers use information technology products, are required to demonstrate high attentional demand, and their decisions have major cost implications. Overall, it may be reasonable to suggest that the use of Information Technology would be a source of stress for dealers.

Work Overload and Work Underload

Both quantitative and qualitative work overload can lead to high levels of stress. Quantitative overload refers to those situations in which an individual is asked to do more work than can be completed in the time available. Qualitative overload occurs when an individual feels a lack of the skills and abilities needed to perform a given job. While the picture of work overload as a cause of stress appears relatively obvious, French and Caplan (1972) have shown that the opposite situation is also relevant. Both quantitative and qualitative underload lead to stress:

> Quantitative underload refers to the boredom that results when employees have so little to do that they find themselves sitting around much of the time . . . qualitative underload refers to the lack of mental stimulation that accompanies many routine, repetitive jobs.

> (Baron 1986)

The results of studies investigating such job characteristics including work overload (French and Caplan 1972; Friedman, Rosenman and Carroll 1958; Margolis et al. 1974; Sales 1969) in a variety of settings with various types of subjects seem to indicate that these job characteristics do fairly consistently relate to the experienced stress of the participants. For instance, Sales (1969) found that work overload and work underload, even when they were not perceived by the employee as such, resulted in increases in the individual's serum cholesterol, and Friedman et al. (1958) found that objective quantitative overload led to elevations in blood cholesterol levels. Margolis et al. (1974) report that work overload is related to significantly increased escapist drinking. French and Caplan (1970) relate work overload to increased cigarette smoking.

It has also been found (Frankenhaeuser and Gardell 1976) that high levels of pressure, competition and work load (all of which dealers might be expected to encounter) and a monotonous, unchallenging environment lead to physiological symptoms of stress (e.g. catecholamine secretion), disruptions of behaviour (e.g. a high level of psychosomatic complaints), and psychological disturbance (absenteeism, poor work performance, feelings of alienation, and hostility).

Cooper and Marshall (1976) note that several studies have reported an association of qualitative work overload with cholesterol level, which is regarded as a factor in heart disease. However, it should be recognised that both quantitative and qualitative overload may be related to the individual's personality, for instance achievement orientation (Brooks and Mueller 1966). We would expect many of those working in the financial markets to be highly achievement oriented and actively searching for more work to do.

Working Long Hours

Working long hours can lead to health problems. Russek and Zohman (1958) found, in an early study of 100 young adult coronary patients, that 45 per cent had been working 60 or more hours per week. Similarly, Breslow and Buell (1960) observed that, for workers in light industry, aged under 45 years, those who spend more than 48 hours per week at work have twice the risk of death from coronary heart disease than those working 40 or less hours per week. Dealers, as we shall see, work extremely long hours.

Spruell (1987) notes that the corporate culture (discussed later in this chapter) can result in 'workaholism', and points out that people can get drawn into workaholism, particularly if senior managers believe that work addiction is the preferred behaviour in the organization. A recent MORI poll of 200 senior managers in a range of companies found that 1 in 6 starts work before 7.30a.m., 1 in 4 don't leave work until substantially after 6.30p.m., and 1 in 4 works most often at weekends (Taylor Made Films 1992). Additionally, the feeling of having to work harder and harder can stem from individual attitudes. The threat of mergers, which is very relevant to the economic climate of the early 1990s, may prompt people to work late, and to work long hours.

THE ROLE OF THE INDIVIDUAL IN THE ORGANISATION

Here we consider the demands made upon the individual as a consequence of their job role, which has been shown to be a major source of work stress. Role conflict and role ambiguity are the most widely examined sources of stress in (managerial) stress research (Beehr 1985). Being 'responsible' for the work of others is also included within this category of potential stressors. Role shock, and the stress associated with managerial roles are also considered relevant to dealers.

Role Conflict

Most people play several different roles simultaneously at any one point in their lives, for instance parent, child, manager, subordinate, etc., and different behaviours are required from an individual in each of these roles. Often, the needs and expectations of those encountered in each role are difficult or impossible to reconcile. Katz and Kahn (1978) consider this as an example of role conflict.

Greenhaus and Beutell (1985), in an examination of stress research, conclude that: 'work schedule, work orientation, marriage, children, and spouse employment patterns may all produce pressures to participate extensively in the work role or the family role'. Stress occurs when the time demands for the work role and the family role are incompatible; when the strain from participating in one role makes it difficult to fulfil the requirements of another role; and when the behaviours required by one role make it difficult to fulfil the requirements of another role.

The increasing tendency for men and women to occupy roles at both work and at home has led to many studies of the consequences for role conflict. For instance, pressures to spend long hours in the office may conflict with demands or expectations from family members to spend time at home. Burke and Greenglass (1987) report two studies (i.e. Greenhaus and Kopelman 1981, and Pleck, Staines and Lang 1980) which indicated that large minorities of males believe that their job and family lives do interfere with each other. Work–family conflict was greater when all children were pre-schoolers, and also was greater for men whose wives were employed in managerial/professional positions.

Role conflict also exists when an individual has to carry out tasks which are not perceived as part of the job (Sutherland and Cooper 1988).

Role conflict and role ambiguity (which is discussed below) are strongly related (Burke 1988). However, both have unclear relationships with stress outcomes and are stronger for measures of attitudes such as job satisfaction, than for behaviourally- or clinically-based measures such as accidents, poor work quality, or illness (Kasl

1978). Nevertheless, French and Caplan (1970) have found that role conflict is related to physiological stress, and Kahn *et al.* (1964) relate role conflict to negative health outcomes. Shirom *et al.* (1973) found in a study of various occupational groups that for white-collar workers there was a significant relationship between role conflict and coronary heart disease.

Kahn (1989) has identified four types of role conflict:

(i) intra-sender conflict – different prescriptions and pro-scriptions from a colleague may be incompatible;
(ii) inter-sender conflict – pressures from one person oppose pressures from another person;
(iii) inter-role conflict – membership in one organisation is in conflict with membership of other groups;
(iv) person-role conflict – where role requirements violate moral values, or needs and aspirations lead to behaviours unacceptable to one's colleagues.

Surprisingly, it has been suggested that role conflict and ambiguity are, in some cases, essential to mental and physical well-being. Kreitner *et al.* (1985) point out that financial or administrative officers (who face no physical dangers at work as compared with, say, police officers) would possibly feel trapped from a career-opportunity standpoint, and be more stressed than police officers by too *little* role conflict and role ambiguity.

Role Ambiguity

McGrath (1976) reports that from 35 to 60 per cent of employees indicate experiencing role ambiguity to one extent or another. Role ambiguity occurs when an individual is uncertain about his or her job role, for instance the latitude of their authority and responsibilities, or the ways in which work performance is evaluated. This may be due to the inadequacy of training received to do the job, poor communication systems within the organisation, or the deliberate withholding or distortion of information by a colleague.

A number of studies have indicated that stress is an outcome of role ambiguity. For instance, in a survey of the nursing service (57 per cent female) in a US Veteran's Administration Medical Center, Bedeian and Armenakis (1981) found that role ambiguity and role conflict were associated with high levels of job-induced tension. They also found that both of these items are directly related to low levels of job satisfaction, and 'have an even greater indirect effect on job satisfaction through their effect on tension'. Szilagyi *et al.* (1976) show that: 'high levels of role ambiguity and role conflict were both associated with lower levels of work-related job satisfaction across multiple occupational levels in a hospital and a manufacturing firm'.

Other studies, in a variety of research settings and with different types of subjects, indicate that role ambiguity does fairly consistently relate to the experienced stress of the participants (e.g. Caplan and Jones 1975; French and Caplan 1970; Margolis *et al.* 1974).

Responsibility for Others

Responsibility at work may refer to 'things', e.g. buildings, machinery, money, but it is responsibility for 'people' which appears to carry the greater risk to health (Cox 1978). Individuals who are responsible for others at work, and so must motivate, reward, and admonish them, etc., generally experience higher levels of stress than those who have no such responsibilities (McLean 1980). The former group is more likely to report feelings of tension and anxiety, and to show the overt symptoms of stress. Two of the reasons for this are related to the interpersonal aspects of a manager's or supervisor's job. Those in charge of other people at work have to face the human results of the decisions they make, which may cause an individual to be sacked, or not promoted, or not given a bonus, etc., and managers and supervisors often have to deal with personality conflicts between members of staff, and intervene in disputes, etc. Yet they must also promote co-operation and leadership. French and Caplan (1970) found that responsibility for people was significantly related to heavy smoking, diastolic blood pressure, and serum cholesterol levels.

Role Shock

Role shock is explained thus by Minkler and Biller (1979): ' . . . the stresses and tensions manifested as discontinuity are encountered when moving from familiar to unfamiliar roles. These unfamiliar roles may constitute totally new roles, or familiar old roles which are played differently in a new situation'.

It is not difficult to imagine that those who have entered the world of high finance (as, for instance, dealers) experience role shock; and even those dealers who have been in the job for some time will, in the 1990s, have to face the problems of reduced profits and bargains, and work harder in order to maintain their competitive position.

Syme *et al.* (1966), cited by Minkler and Biller (1979) discuss: 'the increased occurrence of coronary heart disease associated with what they term "cultural mobility" or "the changes in customs, values and beliefs" as movement takes place from one "social world" to another'. Many dealers will be culturally mobile, and will encounter major cultural changes when joining financial institutions. Perhaps such encounters are faced each new day in the Dealing Room.

Stress and Managers

Stress was originally viewed as a hazard relevant to executive-level organisational staff (Levinson 1964), and seen only to apply to those in senior management positions. For instance, at the management level, Brummet *et al.* (1968) report that managers suffer extreme psychological symptoms of stress at work. Stress is now seen to be just as pertinent to those in manual work (Cooper and Smith 1985), and in white-collar professional work (Cooper and Marshall 1980).

Cooper and Melhuish (1980) note that managers identified as being candidates for a heart attack usually had four common characteristics:

(i) personalities that were extremely competitive, aggressive, and impatient, with feelings that they were under constant time pressure (i.e. Type A personalities, which we shall discuss later in this chapter);

(ii) a recent job change that placed demands upon time and relationships;

(iii) a job with an organisation with poor organisational climate and little social support;

(iv) involved in a situation where personal values were in conflict with those of the organisation.

While it is often assumed that as one climbs the managerial ladder stress increases, it appears that middle-level managers are particularly prone to stress, and Ivancevich *et al.* (1982), who studied 339 managers, either owning their own firm or working for business/industrial organisations, note that middle managers report higher quantitative work overload, lack of career progression, and other environmental stressors compared with other levels of managers.

This may be due to problems particular to this group, such as reporting relationships, work flow, and communications.

In a comparison of the perceived causes of stress in managers in Canadian and US organisations, Rogers (1983) reports that for Canadian managers, high stress is often precipitated by inadequate or inappropriate organisation design, while for US managers it is due to anxiety related to decision-making. Differences may be due to variances in organisational culture. Whereas US organisations are seen as more highly bureaucratised, with more emphasis on managerial accountability, and show a lack of trust between supervisor and subordinate, Canadian organisations are marked by inadequate or ambiguous definitions of managerial scope, authority, and responsibility, i.e. poor organisational design, and more paternalistic patterns of interaction. These differences may also be true of British-, US-, and European-owned City of London financial institutions, and our findings in this area will be discussed in Chapter 7.

Glowinkowski (1985) summarises the effects of stress upon managers:

> While stress can be short-lived it can represent a continuous burden leading to short term outcomes such as tension, increased heart rate, or even increased drinking or smoking ... stress may increase smoking and cause over-eating, which are also high risk factors in coronary heart disease.

CAREER DEVELOPMENT

This category of stressor refers to the impact of under-promotion, over-promotion, status incongruence, lack of job security, thwarted ambition, etc. (Cooper and Marshall 1976). Career development also encompasses the need for retraining, and for a total change of career.

In addition, a number of work stressors have emerged in recent years which reflect changes to national and international economies, particularly since the depressive economic effects of the oil-price rises of 1973. These appear to have particular effects on career progress and prospects. Burke (1986), noting that work stressors change over time, if not in fact at least in potential interest to both stress researchers and job incumbents, suggests that: 'four of these work stressors have begun to receive increased recent attention during the last few years: mergers and acquisitions, retrenchment and budget cutbacks, job future ambiguity and insecurity, and occupational locking-in'.

Here we note the potential stress effects of over- and under-promotion, job security, mergers and acquisitions, retrenchment and cutbacks, and occupational locking-in, all relevant to dealers and many other occupational groups.

Over-promotion and Under-promotion

Both over-promotion and under-promotion have been shown by Brook (1973) to result in mental illness. Over-promotion (when an individual has responsibilities beyond his or her capabilities, and which situation may be exacerbated by lack of further promotion prospects) and under-promotion (when an individual has not been given responsibilities commensurate with his or her actual or self-perceived abilities) may result in minor psychological or major psychosomatic symptoms.

Job Security

Job security, that is, the level of the threat of job loss or un-employment, is associated with health problems including ulcers, colitis, and alopecia (Cobb and Kasl 1977), and with increased muscular and emotional complaints (Smith *et al.* 1981). These outcomes may be aggravated when no suitable employment alternatives appear to be available, or when retraining is necessary to obtain a new position. Sutherland and Cooper (1988) point out that where an individual who is concerned about potential job loss is middle-aged, the concerns will be increased by the recognition that learning seems to take longer, energy is more scarce, opportunities are less, and by the threat of a keen, younger workforce competing for jobs. The predominantly 'ageist' culture associated with British and US employment attitudes would be expected to further the impact of this stressor.

Mergers and Acquisitions

In a survey carried out in 1988 by the London Business School and Egon Zehnder, of forty acquisitions of British organisations not one acquiring company had carried out an audit of the acquired company's human resources (reported by Cartwright and Cooper 1989). In these cases there was reason to suspect 'cultural incompatibility' between many of the acquiring and the acquired organisations, and consequent psychological impact upon the latter's workforces. Many London financial institutions were acquired by other, particularly foreign-based organisations in the 1980s, and Marks and Mirvin (1986) note that corporate takeovers affect not only executives who see their career progression as negatively affected, but also office staff who recognise that their jobs are likely to be reviewed on the basis of how they fit into the new company, and not upon their past record.

Wahlund and Nurell (1978) report that stress among white-collar workers during reorganisations is due to concern for the future. The major cause of the inevitable stress which results from the 'merger syndrome' is seen to be a clash in corporate cultures. Cartwright and Cooper (1992) found that the level of culture shock among managers, and how companies attempt to introduce a new culture, largely determine the degree of success in merging companies.

Retrenchment and Cutbacks

The national and international economic problems of the 1970s, 1980s, and 1990s have resulted in the drive by many organisations to become more financially sound. Typically, to achieve this, each department or section within an organisation becomes a 'cost centre' and is required to achieve a 'balanced budget'. This is obtained by budget cuts, changes in goals, reduction in organisational slack, and so on. Jick (1983) believes that individuals in such organisations may be subject to a number of sources of stress including role confusion, job insecurity, work overload, career plateauing, poor incentives, office politics, lack of participation in decision-making, tense organisational climate, ideological disagreement, and job and personal life conflicts.

Occupational Locking-in

Occupational locking-in occurs when an individual has minimal opportunity to move from his or her present job. This may be due to lack of suitable employment alternatives in the marketplace, or to the inability to obtain a different job within the current organisation. In the context of highly-paid white-collar professionals working in the financial institutions, such as dealers, a major locking-in factor may be the financial commitments they have undertaken. Those who have to meet high mortgage payments, and who seek to maintain a particular life-style, may find that they have little opportunity to move to other suitably rewarded employment in a period of economic contraction.

The feeling of being trapped in a job leads to job dissatisfaction and reduced mental well-being (Sutherland and Cooper 1986). Wolpin and Burke (1986) found that those professionals who reported being 'locked into' their job endured extreme costs. They had lower feelings of self-worth, more negative encounters in their marriages, and less marital satisfaction, and reported more depression, poorer physical health, and less life satisfaction.

RELATIONSHIPS WITH OTHERS AT WORK

It is clear that the presence of relationships at work can be both a stressor and a source of support (Sloan and Cooper 1987). The major aspects of interpersonal relationships which have been the subject of recent investigation include status incongruence, social density, abrasive personalities, leadership style, and group pressure (Quick and Quick 1984). The stress effects of relationships at work have also been examined by viewing relationships on a hierarchical basis, viz. relationships with immediate boss, with colleagues, and with subordinates. Heavy demand for co-operation with superiors and subordinates has been shown to be stressful for white-collar workers (Wahlund and Nurell 1978). Folkman (1982) found that the largest proportion (60 per cent) of stressful events occurring in paid work involved interactions with a colleague.

We examine here two particular stressors, namely relationships with immediate boss, and status incongruity. Social support is both a source of stress and a moderator of stress, and will be considered later in this chapter.

Relationships with Immediate Boss

Cooper and Marshall (1976) point out that, concerning work relationships: 'very little empirical work is available on the medical side on how this particular stressor may contribute to physical and mental ill health'.

Buck (1972) found, however, that those workers who felt their boss was low on 'consideration' reported feeling more job pressure.

Managers and those managed interact with each other, and some studies have indicated that subordinates affect leaders as much as leaders affect subordinates. In one study it was found that in newly-formed groups, as most Dealing Room teams are, leaders may adjust the amount of support they give staff (i.e. their supportive behaviour) in response to the level of group cohesion and arousal already present (Greene and Schriesheim 1980). Leaders who are unable or unwilling to adjust their leadership style to the group norms can be expected to suffer psychological problems. In support of this view, Seltzer and Numerof (1988) found that individuals who rated their supervisor high on consideration also reported low burnout.

Savery (1988) looked at 158 employees working in the staff head-quarters of a major local government employer in Western Australia and examined several sources of support – immediate manager, peers, subordinates, spouse/partner, friends and relatives, and union officials. He found that the employee's immediate manager was perceived as the most useful in reducing stress, followed by their peer group, and then by their friends and relatives. Spouse support was not a major source of stress relief. Job satisfaction was also most influenced by immediate manager and peers. Team working, which might provide more social support from all organisational levels for the individual, is a major factor in Japanese management theory, and has become important in contemporary management practice in the United Kingdom and the United States.

Status Incongruity

When success in adulthood forces a person to physically and psychologically abandon his 'roots' – ties with his friends, activities, styles of behaving, and neighbourhood – the negative psychological and physical effects of this change can range from alcoholism and schizophrenia to coronary heart disease. . . . This condition frequently imposes costs severe enough to force a high-powered achiever to choose between his health or his career.

(Berglas 1986)

This situation is 'status inconsistency' and it appears to be similar to the issue of 'status incongruity' cited by Cooper and Marshall (1976) as 'the incongruity between an individual's social status and that of his parents'. It is not difficult to imagine that many dealers have achieved a status quite different from that of their parents and/or

49

erstwhile childhood friends, whether measured in strictly financial terms, or in the life-style which their earnings allow them to adopt. Berglas (1986) notes that status inconsistency is particularly relevant to women approximately in the 30 to 36 age group, when they are forced by corporate goals either to forego childbearing or lose potential advancement at work.

ORGANISATIONAL STRUCTURE AND CLIMATE

This source of occupational stress includes such factors as office politics, lack of effective consultation, no participation in the decision-making process, and restrictions on behaviour (Cooper and Marshall 1976). These stressors originate from the structural design and process features of the organisation, though organisational climate will embrace individual perceptions of both these features (Cooper, Sloan and Williams 1988).

Organisational structural stressors also include the effects of the interdependence of departments and a high degree of departmental specialisation and formalisation, and little opportunity for individual advancement. Other 'process'-related stressors include poor communication, poor or inadequate feedback about performance, inaccurate or ambiguous measurement of performance, and unfair control systems (Brief, Schuler and Van Sell 1981). Factors we consider here within organisational structure and climate are participation in decision-making, performance appraisal, and organisational culture.

Participation in Decision-making

Participation has been defined in this context as involving subordinates with their superiors in the managerial decision-making process (Tannenbaum and Massarik 1989), where decisions are made in order to organise, direct, or control responsible subordinates to the end that all service contributions are co-ordinated to achieve the purpose of the enterprise. Miller and Monge (1986) found from an examination of many studies of participation that extensive participation in decision-making produced large increases in staff performance and job satisfaction. Participation may also increase the quality and quantity of output, reduce staff turnover, absenteeism, and lateness, improve industrial relations, improve employees' readiness to accept change, permit better management of subordinates, and improve the quality of managerial decision-making.

In a study of employees working in a hospital outpatient department, those members of staff who were provided with opportunities and encouragement to participate in the redesign of their own jobs reported lower levels of stress (in terms of emotional strain) than colleagues who were given no such opportunities and encouragement (Jackson 1983). The former group also reported higher job satisfaction, and lower levels of role conflict. French and Caplan (1970) found that people who reported greater opportunities for participation in decision-making reported significantly greater job satisfaction, lower job-related feelings of threat, and higher feelings of self-esteem.

Margolis *et al.* (1974) conclude that non-participation is the most consistent and significant predictor of strain and job-related stress. They found that 'non-participation was significantly related to . . . overall poor physical health, escapist drinking, depressed mood, low self-esteem, low life satisfaction, low motivation to work, intention to leave job and absenteeism from work' (Cooper and Marshall 1976).

Participation is beneficial because it gives staff discretion and influence over aspects of their work. High demand coupled with low discretion produces the highest incidences of job dissatisfaction, pill-taking, absence, and reports of exhaustion (Janman *et al.* 1988).

Performance Appraisal

Being evaluated by others can be a stressful experience. This is particularly true where such an evaluation has important effects upon career prospects (Baron 1986). Dealers' performance will determine salary and promotion prospects. Irving *et al.* (1986) report that: 'higher levels of stress, lower levels of satisfaction and a deterioration in relations with peers, supervisors and senior management have been reported by clerical workers using computers with performance monitoring systems'. As already noted, transactions conducted via the computer systems, telephone systems, etc. used in Dealing Rooms are recorded (perhaps a modern extension of the 'My word is my bond' Stock Exchange motto and tradition).

Organisational Culture

Organisational culture is generally concerned with shared values and norms, and has been defined by Schein (1985) as:

> a pattern of basic assumptions – invented, discovered, or developed by a given group as it learns to cope with its problems of external adaptation and internal integration – that has worked well enough to be considered valuable and, therefore, to be taught to new members as the correct way to perceive, think and feel in relation to those problems.

Organisational culture has emerged as a major force used for organisational change in recent years. The more important aspects of organisational culture are generally agreed to be observed behavioural regularities (e.g. use of common language), norms of behaviour, dominant values (e.g. high product quality), philosophy (e.g. the ways in which clients are treated), rules, and organisational climate (the overall 'feeling' of the organisation) (Luthans 1989).

For instance, in work there is often a gap between what the rules say should be done and the expectations that people have developed for themselves. The rules might say that an employee should work till five o'clock, when actually colleagues expect an individual to work only until ten minutes to five (Payne 1979). Personal relationships with the work group may deteriorate if this expected norm of behaviour is not adopted by an individual. Stress may occur when the organisational culture is not accepted by the individual.

THE INTERFACE BETWEEN HOME AND WORK

This category of potential stressor consists of those events which occur outside the specific work environment but which affect the individual's behaviour at work, and so must be considered when assessing sources of occupational stress. These include life events, issues relating to the family including the conflict between company and family demands, financial difficulties, and conflicts between personal and company beliefs. It has been noted previously that relationships at work can be both a stressor and a source of support mitigating the effects of stress. Similarly, personal life events and family relationships may mitigate or exacerbate the effects of organisational stressors. Here, we mention the stress associated with dual career couples, relationships between work and family, life events, and the stress associated with high achievers.

Dual Career Couples

The problems of dual career couples are centred around the conflicts which arise in a society which may still tend to regard the traditional family as the norm. These conflicts include sex role, identity, work overload, role cycling dilemmas, lack of role models, and dilemmas of equality within the couple relationship. The most well-documented pressures for dual earners are overload and role conflict, due to long working hours, non-standard or inflexible work schedules, and multiple roles. Lewis and Cooper (1987), in a study of 152 couples, found that couples expecting their first child reported high pressure from work overload and greater difficulty in being flexible at work than childless couples (but less so than couples who were already parents). However, there were no greater manifestations of stress in the former group. Mothers reported lower levels of job satisfaction than all groups, and fathers reported less job satisfaction than childless men, but more somatic symptoms than other men. Overall, however, Lewis and Cooper (1987) found that multiple roles, if handled well, can be satisfying.

Relationships between Work and Family

General family-based strains may result from four potential sources. Firstly, role pressure or overload (e.g. due to homemaking); secondly, interpersonal conflicts (between husbands and wives, parents and children); thirdly, role captivity (where people are bound by one role, but would prefer to be in another); and fourthly, the restructuring of family roles through time (Pearlin and Turner 1987).

Bromet et al. (1988) suggest that they have detected a positive association between occupational stress and marital stress which lends some support to the 'spillover' hypothesis of Glowinkowski and Cooper (1985). The spillover hypothesis characterises a relationship between work and non-work that results in similar experiences and reactions as desired (or found) by the individual in the two domains, and is usually contrasted with 'compensation', a process in which an individual seeks opposite experiences and satisfactions at work and at home in order to make up for deficiencies in one of the settings (Gutek et al. 1988).

As an example, Cooke and Rousseau (1984) found in a study of teachers that, though the demands of the teacher's family might conflict with the demands of work, the family also provided comfort and support to the teacher, and so apparently enabled the teacher to overcome some of the more harmful physical effects associated with stress (e.g. headaches, loss of sleep) better than single teachers. However, the overall life-style of unmarried teachers might be expected to differ in many ways from that of married teachers, and so the relationship between marital status and stress outcomes is probably quite complex.

It has also been found by Bromet *et al.* (1988) that, for men, marital stress did not result in any subsequent physical and psychological outcomes, disorders, or alcohol problems. These researchers believe that family environment factors are less strongly associated with mental health in men than in women. Wives at home raising children, however, may grow to resent what they perceive to be the glamorous or committed life of the (dealer) husband.

Life Events

Many studies indicate that when individuals undergo stressful changes in their lives, such as dealers have in recent years, their personal health suffers (e.g. Ganellen and Blaney 1984). The purpose of life events research, therefore, is to demonstrate an association between a recent increase in the number of events requiring the individual to make social adaptations, and the consequent onset of illness. The more life events, the greater the effect expected. These events give rise to what has been called 'social stressors', defined as any set of circumstances the advent of which signifies or requires change in the individual's ongoing life pattern (Holmes and Rahe 1967). A serious, stress-inducing life event is defined as such because it affects homoeostasis (see Chapter 2). Negative stress stems from such events as loss or injury, either psychological or material, real or imagined, and is the result of the change to self-image that is induced by a major life event (Horowitz 1979).

Johnson and Sarason (1979) report that life stress events have been found to be related to sudden cardiac death, myocardial infarction, pregnancy and birth complications, the seriousness of chronic illnesses, major health and less serious physical problems, anxiety and depression, and work performance. It appears that life stress events may increase an overall susceptibility to illness rather than being related to a specific disorder.

Holmes and Rahe (1967) have listed and weighted some forty-two of the life events that produce such negative effects (see Table

3.1). Findings from research studies suggest that where an individual experiences more of these stressful life events within a given period of time, they are more likely to develop serious illness. Those who report life events which score a total on the Holmes and Rahe (1967) scale of 150 to 300 points within a twelve-month period, have a 50 per cent chance of becoming seriously ill during the subsequent twelve months. Where a score in excess of 300 points is found, a 70 per cent chance of ill-health is indicated. Results reported by McClelland and Jemmott (1980) also suggest that the frequency of life changes is associated with physical illness reports.

The type of life event change, whether it involves power, affiliation, or other stressors, together with individual differences, appears to moderate the resulting outcome of illness. Individuals high in the need for power, high in inhibition (i.e. in expressing the power motive, and in controlling their assertiveness in a civilised way), and high in power stress (i.e. life events which challenge the individual's ability to perform powerfully or impress others) have been found to be more illness prone (McClelland and Jemmott 1980).

It appears that life events defined as 'exits' (e.g. separations, deaths) result in psychiatric illness, while life events defined as 'entrances' (e.g. reconciliations, birth, marriage) do not; and 'loss' events result particularly in depression, while 'danger' events produce anxiety.

Interestingly, in view of what we have said about changes over time in work stressors, problems at work are reported (MIND 1992) to have replaced what used to be regarded as the principal 'life events' causes of stress in the UK. The biggest contributing factors to life events stress are said to be 'pressure to perform', 'fear of redundancy', and 'the recession'.

High Achievers

The consequences of success have been noted by Berglas (1986) as analogous to a two-bladed sword. There are positive and negative consequences that follow upon the attainment of a significant achievement, victory, or goal. With success come rewards such as material wealth, fame, prestige, power, control, and influence. However, successful individuals are required to demonstrate largesse, 'give' to others, 'nurture' others, and tolerate the envy of others. Berglas (1986) defines this 'success syndrome' as:

Table 3.1 Life events rating scale

Life event	Scale value
Death of spouse	100
Divorce	73
Marital separation	65
Jail term or similar	63
Death of a close family member	63
Major personal injury or illness	53
Marriage	50
Being fired from work	47
Marital reconciliation	45
Retirement	45
Major change in health or behaviour of a family member	44
Pregnancy	40
Sexual difficulties	39
Gain of a new family member	39
Major business readjustment	39
Major change in financial state	38
Death of a close friend	37
Change to a different line of work	36
Major change in number of arguments with spouse	35
Mortgage or loan for major purchase	31
Foreclosure on a mortgage or loan	30
Major change in responsibilities at work	29
Son or daughter leaving home	29
Trouble with in-laws	29
Outstanding personal achievement	28
Spouse begins or stops work	26
Begin or end school	26
Change in living conditions	25
Revision of personal habits	24
Trouble with boss	23
Change in work hours or conditions	20
Change in residence	20

Table 3.1 Continued

Life event	Scale value
Change in schools	20
Change in recreation	19
Change in church activities	19
Change in social activities	18
Mortgage or loan for lesser purchase	17
Change in sleeping habits	16
Change in number of family get-togethers	15
Change in eating habits	15
Vacation	13
Christmas	12
Minor violations of the law	11

Source: T. H. Holmes and R. H. Rahe (1967)

the condition that develops when the rewards of success expose an individual to a variety of psychologically stressful situations; these render him vulnerable to disorders ranging from depression and drug abuse to self-inflicted failures and even suicide. . . . The distinctive feature of an individual who is victimised by the Success Syndrome is the causal link between his experience of success and his subsequent suffering.

Berglas (1986) suggests that success (in America) is seen as more than merely attaining what one wants; it is attaining a desired outcome that provides both a high level of material wealth and public recognition, and few of those driven by success care about the fact that success causes stress and loneliness. The denial and distortion of real problems arising from success can lead to many psychological disorders. Berglas (1986) states that 'the stress derived from success is inevitable and can be expected to touch virtually every corner of an individual's life'.

In an examination of high achievers, Garfield (1986) suggests that they feel most alive when engaged at full throttle (i.e. exhibiting Type A behaviour). He considers that they share six attributes:

• missions that motivate: the call to action, the click that starts things moving;

- results in real time: purposeful activity directed at achieving goals that contribute to a mission;
- self-management through self-mastery: the capacity for self-observation and effective thinking;
- team-building playing: the complement to self-management – empowering others to produce;
- course correction: mental agility, concentration, finding and navigating a critical path;
- change management: anticipating and adapting to major change while maintaining momentum and balance within an overall game plan.

Dealers would certainly seem to fit this description of 'high achievers'.

In a related view, of 'high fliers', Boyatzis (1982) has said that 'peak performers':

> can be seen working long hours when it is needed. They can maintain a high quality of performance through 14-hour days and 70-hour weeks. Throughout such a prolonged or arduous task, they maintain their usual degree of attention to detail ... have energy and resistance to stress .. remain relatively calm and patient . . . engage in activities specifically chosen to reduce the effects of the stress or fatigue.
>
> (cited Garfield 1986)

Derr (1986) considers that, based upon her study of the career patterns of successful US naval officers at mid-career, and from her career counselling activities, she is able to formulate five definitions of career success. These are: firstly, 'getting ahead', where the individual gains promotions or advancement in a status system, often associated with large organisations; secondly, 'getting secure', where individuals exchange dedication, loyalty, and service for financial benefits, job security, and reciprocal appreciation; thirdly, 'getting free', where an individual prefers a marginal position where there is personal autonomy, 'space', loose supervision, and personal responsibility for outcomes; fourthly, 'getting high', where individuals seek positions of excitement, action, and total engagement in work – they find it difficult to separate themselves from their work; and fifthly, 'getting balanced', where some career-centred individuals are preoccupied with balancing work, relationships, and self-development.

For each of these orientations both opportunities and problems, particularly with relationships, present themselves. For instance, the 'getting ahead' stage is characterised by 'gamesmanship', competition, and action-oriented, superficial activities. Relationships at work and home can suffer, especially where a get-ahead husband or the dual career couple are concerned. Where a 'get-high' careerist is concerned, there may be little time or energy left over for relationships. Work comes before other aspects of life.

If dealers are regarded as high achievers, peak performers, and successful careerists in the terms described above, it may be reasonable to suppose that relationship stressors will be high, and that they will exhibit many of the behaviours noted in this section, behaviours that can lead to illness.

INDIVIDUAL CHARACTERISTICS OF DEALERS

We have examined above the major sources of stress at work which might affect dealers. However, we pointed out in Chapter 2 that an individual's personality affects their responses to stress and their methods of coping with stress. The relationship between personality and stress has been classified in at least three ways. Firstly, an individual's personality is regarded by some as a precursor to a stress-related health outcome, i.e stress is determined by personality. Secondly, personality is seen as a moderating variable which helps determine the strength of the stress reaction. Thirdly, and conversely, personality is directly affected by stress (Sloan and Cooper 1987). Thus, it is less than simple to determine what the true relationships between stress and personality are.

The individual differences which we believe might affect stress have, again, been selected on the basis of their relevance to the dealers who are the subject of our study. The most significant variables are seen to be the psychological dispositions of Type A behaviour, introversion/extraversion, neuroticism/stability, and locus of control; and the sociodemographic variables of the individual's sex, age, work experience, and level of ability. The role of social support and of other stress coping techniques, and other potential moderators of stress, will also be considered in this section.

Type A (Coronary Prone) Behaviour

Two American physicians, Friedman and Rosenman (1974), believe that they have isolated two main types of behaviour pattern, which they term Type A and Type B. Most of the research examining these behavioural patterns and the links with ill-health (usually coronary heart disease, CHD) has concentrated on Type A personalities.

Rosenman and Friedman (1983) define Type A behavioural pattern (TABP) as:

> a particular action-emotion complex that is exhibited or possessed by an individual who is engaged in a relatively chronic and excessive struggle to obtain a usually unlimited number of things from his environment in the shortest period of time or against the opposing efforts of other things or persons in the same environment.

Brief *et al.* (1983) describe Type As as those individuals who work long, hard hours under constant deadline pressures and conditions for overload; often take work home at night or on weekends and are unable to relax; constantly compete with themselves, setting high standards of productivity that they seem driven to maintain; tend to become frustrated by the work situation, to be irritated with the work efforts of others, and feel misunderstood by superiors. Dealers and many other financial workers would appear at first sight to possess Type A personalities.

Of particular relevance to the present study of dealers, Payne (1988) notes that Type A is higher amongst those of higher socio-economic status and education, and that these people tend to occupy more demanding jobs, i.e. with more responsibility, greater supervising load, higher workload, and involving more difficult tasks.

Particularly susceptible Type A individuals tend to be professional/technical and managerial, aged between 36 and 55 years of age, living in urban environments (MacKay and Cooper 1987). Blumenthal *et al.* (1980) suggest that the most coronary-prone individuals are those who have pent up aggression or anxiety, or who struggle to gather as many possessions as possible in as short a time. Derevenco *et al.* (1988) report that industrial managers show a marked prevalence of Type A behaviour, and office workers with less occupational responsibility show significantly less TABP.

Dealers tend to work in groups and are dependent upon each other for support, and there is a potential source of stress in this dependency, since Baron (1986) points out that: 'Type As prefer to work by themselves rather than with others. They are definitely "loners" rather than "team players".'

Type As lose their tempers more frequently, and are more likely to lash out at others for even slight provocations (Holmes and Will 1985). Perhaps these factors explain why Type A individuals have consistently been shown to obtain significantly higher scores on life events stress inventories (see earlier in this chapter).

Ortega and Pipal (1984) have reported that Type As seek more challenge in their work and in their lives in general than Type Bs. Their study indicates that Type As prefer more difficult problems than Type Bs, and this difference increases in magnitude as the Type As continue to work harder than Type Bs, i.e. the more effort they expend on working, the more challenge for which they feel the need. Type Bs appear to react in the opposite direction. Therefore, it seems that Type As can become caught up in an ever-increasing maelstrom of work.

Froggatt and Cotton (1987), in a study using 118 undergraduate students, found that Type A individuals are no more likely to *feel* stressed by role overload than Type Bs. Because the Type As felt that *less* work was being demanded of them the authors suggest that Type As may gravitate to jobs and situations that are actually *more* demanding, and this has implications for financial organisations with Dealing Rooms, and for other high pressure environments. They believe that their results effectively challenge the notion that Type A individuals are more likely than Type Bs to perceive a given situation as stressful, at least with respect to short-term, qualitatively simple tasks. All this means that Type As may not realise that they are under severe pressure or stress.

House (1972) also suggests that Type A personalities may gravitate into those occupations which allow them freedom to utilise this particular personality disposition, and to achieve the rewards of status and recognition which society offers those who compete and strive aggressively.

Type As have been found to exhibit significantly more overt Type A behaviour than Type Bs where a task is regarded as moderately uncontrollable (such as dealing), and Type As have been shown to display greater levels of Type A behaviour when exposed to highly uncontrollable stressors (Benight and Kinicki 1988).

The increasing urbanisation of and technological changes in Western society, where special rewards are available to those who can think, perform, and communicate, and generally live more rapidly and aggressively than their peers, is seen to encourage the growth of TABP.

Type A Behaviour and Ill-health

Having examined some of the thinking behind the idea of Type A behaviour, we can now look at evidence of the effects of Type A behaviour on health. In a review of the literature on Type A behaviour pattern, Rosenman and Friedman (1983) conclude that 'the data indicate that the concept of TABP has construct validity and that it does not reflect the distinguishing characteristics of personality traits or psychopathology that are measured by standard psychometric inventories'.

TABP appears to be a cause of coronary heart disease and the severity of coronary atherosclerosis in both males and females. Rosenman and Friedman (1983) support their arguments by reference to a statement by fifty 'eminent scientists' assembled by the National Heart, Lung and Blood Institute in order critically to examine the evidence for the association between TABP and coronary heart disease:

> the Review Panel accepts the available body of scientific evidence as demonstrating that Type A behavior . . . is associated with an increased risk of clinically apparent CHD in employed, middle-aged US citizens. This increase is over and above that imposed by age, systolic blood pressure, serum cholesterol, and smoking and appears to be of the same order of magnitude as the relative risk associated with any of these factors.

In an examination of the reasons why Type A behaviour might lead to CHD, Ganster et al. (1986) suggest that Type As may either really be exposed to more objective stressors at work or they may be simply more apt to appraise their work as more demanding; or Type As may select more stressful environments, or make them more stressful; or Type As may be inherently physiologically hyper-reactive to real or imagined stressors than Type Bs.

In a three-year long-term study of some 300 managers, Howard et al. (1976) found that over 61 per cent were classified as Type A. Extreme Type As reported more stress symptoms, showed higher blood pressure, higher cholesterol, and higher triglyceride levels. More were cigarette smokers. Type As reported less participation in exercise than Type Bs. For moderate Type As, no conclusive findings were made. Howard et al. (1976) believe that it is the difference in the job environment which results in moderate Type As becoming extreme Type As.

When exposed to stressful conditions, Type As often show larger increases in psychological arousal (e.g. heart rate, blood pressure) than Type Bs (Pittner et al. 1983; Holmes et al. 1984). Type As also tend to be more likely to experience feelings of helplessness when confronted with stress which they feel they cannot control (Brunson and Matthews 1981).

Type As also appear to employ different strategies than Type Bs for coping with work-related stress. Type As tend to deny that they are upset by the stress, and so are not able to come to terms with the stress outcomes, and expose themselves to more of it for longer periods of time (Baron 1986).

In a study of the associations between Type A personality and stress symptoms and sales performance in a real estate company, Herried et al. (1985) found that where a great deal of autonomy is afforded individuals, the Type A person is likely to do well, but if commitment to a particular company, ability to co-operate with other organisational members, or willingness to accept control from within the company are necessary, Type A orientation may have more negative implications. Thus, the organisational culture experienced by dealers will affect the stress and the stress outcomes they encounter.

A study of 1,949 male and female adults by Rime et al. (1989) suggests that the positive relationship between Type A behaviour and coronary heart disease is not particularly specific. They found that Type A behaviour is also significantly associated with reports of peptic ulcer, thyroid problems, asthma, and rheumatoid arthritis. Although a number of studies have failed to replicate the relationship between Type A behaviour and coronary heart disease, the results of an examination of many studies by Booth-Kewley and Friedman (1987), led them to conclude that the association between Type A behaviour and coronary heart disease is 'highly reliable and non-trivial'.

Rosenman et al. (1975) have also stated that those individuals diagnosed as Type A persons are more than twice as likely to experience heart disease than are Type Bs.

Extroversion/Introversion

Eysenck (1981) claims that the two personality traits of firstly, extroversion/introversion, and secondly neuroticism/stability (which we discuss below) are universal across cultures, and within cultures across time. Other researchers have confirmed that these factors are enduring personality characteristics, and Eysenck and Eysenck (1964) believe that while other important factors might exist, these two factors contribute more to a description of personality than any other set of factors.

Eysenck and Eysenck (1963) describe the extrovert as follows:

> The typical extrovert is sociable, likes parties, has many friends, needs to have people to talk to, and does not like reading or studying by himself. He craves excitement, takes chances, often sticks his neck out, acts on the spur of the moment, and is generally an impulsive individual. He is fond of practical jokes, always has a ready answer, and generally likes change; he is carefree, easy-going, optimistic, and likes to 'laugh and be merry'. He prefers to keep moving and doing things, tends to be aggressive and lose his temper quickly; altogether his feelings are not kept under tight control, and he is not always a reliable person.

Much of this description would suggest that dealers might be expected to be extroverts.

The same authors describe the introvert as follows:

> The typical introvert is a quiet, retiring sort of person, introspective, fond of books rather than people; he is reserved and distant except to intimate friends. He tends to plan ahead, 'looks before he leaps', and distrusts the impulse of the moment. He does not like excitement, takes matters of everyday life with proper seriousness, and likes a well-ordered life. He keeps his feelings under close control, seldom behaves in an aggressive manner, and does not lose his temper easily. He is reliable, somewhat pessimistic, and places great value on ethical standards.

> (Eysenck and Eysenck 1963)

Eysenck (1967) notes that successful businessmen tend to be stable introverts, and Hockey (1972), from a summary of many studies of introversion/extroversion, suggests that extroverts prefer and work best in noisy environments while the opposite is true of introverts. Dealing Rooms are found to be very noisy environments.

When attempting to explain *why* extroverts actively seek 'exciting' situations it is often suggested that inactivity and boredom can be highly arousing physiologically for extroverts, and result in uncomfortable subjective effects. The levels at which they become 'aroused' may be higher for extroverts than for introverts (Hamilton 1979).

Extroverts have also been shown by Furnham (1981), in a study of students, to seek out stimulating social situations which involve assertiveness, intimacy, and competition, more than introverts, while neurotics (see below) tend to avoid situations involving competition or social interaction, and enjoy reading. Kahn *et al.* (1964) found that extroverts were more highly reality-oriented and adaptable than introverts.

When we look at the relationships between extroversion/introversion and health, we find that Eysenck (1985) detects a link between extroversion and myocardial infarction, and Eysenck and Eysenck (1964) suggest a link with cancer. For instance, Coppen and Metcalfe (1963) found that a group suffering from cancer had significantly higher extroversion scores than two control groups. (Nevertheless, (Eysenck 1985) suggests that extroversion may be connected with a particularly well-functioning immune system, in that colds are less prevalent in extroverts!)

Eysenck (1965) has suggested that extroverts are likely to consume more alcohol than introverts, and Allsopp (1986) found that beer consumption among 18–21 year-old male craftsmen and students was significantly correlated with extroversion, but not with neuroticism.

There is also a significant trend for extroversion to decline with advancing age (Eysenck and Eysenck 1964).

Neuroticism/Stability

The two dimensions, extroversion and neuroticism, are conceptualised as being unrelated and independent dimensions of personality. Neuroticism (sometimes called emotionality, or anxiety, or instability) can be acquired in many different ways (Bootzin and Max 1980). Payne (1988) noted that stress research had largely ignored neuroticism in the preceding 25 years, despite the fact that the 'man in the street' would recognise the importance of the disposition to be anxious as an important stress factor.

Anxiety is seen by Bootzin and Max (1980) to consist of

> verbal reports of apprehension, impending danger, inability to concentrate, feelings of tension, and expectations of being unable to cope; . . . attempts to avoid the situation, impaired

speech and motor co-ordination, inhibition of ongoing behavior, and performance deficits on complex cognitive tasks; and . . . muscle tension, increased heart rate and blood pressure, rapid respiration, dryness of the mouth, drop in resistance in galvanic skin response, coldness in the extremities, nausea, diarrhoea, and frequent urination.

Early work which examined the relationships between work and the incidence of neurotic illness found that it was most prevalent among those who found work boring, were engaged in assembly, bench inspection, and tool room work, or performed jobs requiring constant attention (Wall and Martin 1987). This led to poor job adjustment, and frequent absence from work (Cooper and Payne 1967). Cox (1978) reports that in a study of the health of Australian telegraphists, those described as neurotic exhibited higher incidents of peptic ulcers, dyspepsia, occupational cramps, and chronic eczema.

It is not clear what produces these physiological effects of anxiety, though the discovery in the 1960s that benzodiazepines reduce anxiety provided impetus for studies of brain systems that might be involved (Elliott and Eisdorfer 1982).

Kets de Vries and Miller (1984) believe that organisations, too, can be neurotic, and give examples of paranoid, compulsive, depressive, schizoid, and dramatic organisations. Similarly, Frost (1985) suggests three types of 'sick' organisation – neurotic, psychotic, and sociopathic – where symptoms can manifest in individuals or the organisation as a whole. The initial 'carriers' of stress are usually at or near the top of the structure, i.e. make major decisions and shape the company's culture.

Individuals who combine neuroticism and introversion have been found to be more susceptible to fatal heart disease (Jenkins 1971) and to angina pectoris (Baaker 1967; Lebovits *et al.* 1967; Finn *et al.* 1969).

The anxieties and stress-related reactions towards working with new technology have been described as 'cyberphobia', and this condition is seen to result in such characteristics as rapid heart-beat, nausea, diarrhoea, sweating, etc. General fears surround the belief that the technology strips people of freedom and privacy (Shotton 1989).

The use (and consequent abuse) of alcohol as a relief from anxiety and stress has a long history, and has been associated with the development of habituation and addiction. However, Powers and Kutash (1980) report that in experimental drinking studies it has been discovered that alcohol frequently *increases* rather than decreases anxiety and stress levels. The authors suggest that anxiety and stress relief are not the sole factors in the use and abuse of alcohol, but are especially important ones. It may be that the first drink taken to reduce anxiety is successful, but new stressors, such as guilt about drinking, are created, and an individual may continue to drink in response to these additional stressors, leading to habituation and addiction.

Neuroticism, like extroversion, declines with age (Eysenck and Eysenck 1964).

Locus of Control

Locus of control is the expectancy that the rewards and major events in one's life are controlled either by one's own actions (internality) or by other forces such as fate, luck, or powerful others (externality). In organisational settings, rewards or outcomes include promotions, favourable circumstances, salary increases, and general career advancement (Spector 1988). Locus of control is regarded as a relatively stable personality characteristic (Rotter 1966).

Whether the working environment is viewed as generally unmanageable and hostile, or as supportive and readily subject to control, will determine the consequent emotional impact on the individual. Those who believe that they *will* be able to master most demands by doing what is necessary, or discovering what to do and how to do it, would seem less likely to be threatened or helpless or hopeless in stressful situations. This is in contrast with chronically anxious individuals who believe that they are incapable of mastering the situation (Folkman *et al.* 1979).

The personality trait of control has been broken down by Thompson (1981) into four types: *behavioural control*, where an individual believes that they can make an appropriate behavioural response in order to gain relief; *cognitive control*, where a coping strategy such as ignoring or distracting oneself from the stressful event can be used; *informational control*, which refers to some type of communication or message (e.g. warning signals) given to the potential recipient of a stressful event; and *retrospective control*, which involves attributing causes to events that have already occurred.

Locus of control as a personality trait may overlap with neuroticism and with anxiety, but Payne (1988) has concluded that there is sufficient evidence to indicate that locus of control does moderate the relationships between stressors and strain. Spector (1982) argues that locus of control is related to job motivation, effort, performance, job satisfaction, perception of the job, compliance with authority, and supervisory style.

In general, people with 'internal' locus of control are more satisfied (Furnham 1987). 'Internals' would indeed be expected to indicate greater job satisfaction than 'externals', and for four reasons. Firstly, dissatisfied 'internals' will quit dissatisfying jobs. Secondly, 'internals' tend to achieve higher rewards due to their better performance. Thirdly, 'internals' tend to achieve more frequent promotions and salary increases. Fourthly, individuals who have sufficient control to leave the stressful situation and who chose to stay will evaluate the job situation as satisfactory (Spector 1982).

Spector (1982) also notes that 'internals' may actually seek situations in which they have control, and this may carry over into leisure activities. As noted above, 'externals' tend to be more anxious than 'internals'. 'Internals' would be expected to better perform those tasks (such as dealing) which necessitate complex information collection or processing, and those tasks or organisational demands which require initiative and independence of action.

There is compelling evidence that control, even the belief that one has control, is associated with a myriad of positive outcomes, and lack of control is associated with various forms of ill-health (Perrewe and Ganster 1989). From a study of family physicians, Revicki and May (1985) suggest that individuals with a strong sense of personal control (internals) mobilise their support systems in the presence of stressful situations. However, 'internals' may display more anxiety in situations not perceived to be within their control (Sutherland and Cooper 1988).

Marino and White (1985) found that among hospital employees, for those who were 'internals', 'job specificity' was positively related to job stress, while for 'externals' there was a negative relationship. Job specificity refers to organisations with very mechanical structures, precise role prescriptions, standardised operating procedures, formal work roles, and centralised lines of authority (such as bureaucracies). Other structural factors, hierarchy of authority, job codification, and lack of participation in decision-making, were not found to interact significantly with either internal or external control to affect stress.

Arndt, Feltes and Hanak (1983), cited Oborne (1985), report that secretaries who used word processors and had 'external' locus of control were more reluctant to use the equipment. This suggests that, in the work situation, 'externals' are less willing to adopt new ideas and methods of working, particularly new technology. New technology may be seen to be associated with centralisation of decision-making and with closer control over staff, with consequent stress effects (see earlier this chapter).

Mention has already been made of the stress problems associated with occupational locking-in. Burke (1982) found that among 127 administrators, occupational locking-in was more perceived by those employees with 'external' locus of control.

Hardiness

Related to locus of control is the personality resource of 'hardiness'. Hardiness comes from a strong sense of being 'on course'. It is a personality style which uses a form of coping that includes keeping specific stressors in perspective, knowing that one has the resources with which to respond to stress, and viewing stressors as potential opportunities for change rather than as threats (Kobasa 1988).

Jamal (1984) considers that organisational and professional *commitment* (the extent to which a worker identifies with and is attached to an organisation and profession), which would appear to be related to hardiness, moderates the effects of stress. Less confident co-workers spend significant amounts of their energy hiding behind pronouncements of 'policy' and 'higher authority' and manoeuvring to protect their skins, which tend to be thin (Garfield 1986).

It has been suggested by Cavanagh (1988) that stress can also be self-created by people who adopt social imperatives (e.g. 'people must treat me fairly'), or who stretch attitudes which are virtuous to the point where they become vices (e.g. 'I don't like it when anything goes wrong'). In these cases, however, it may be that stress has preceded a change to the individual's personal philosophy.

People who thrive in high-powered jobs approach life with specific attitudes that Kobasa and Puccetti (1983) have defined as an openness to change, a feeling of involvement in whatever they are doing, and a sense of control over events. This latter point also indicates a relationship between hardiness and locus of control.

The hardy personality is less likely to become ill during periods of life stress (Kobasa 1988). Kobasa and Puccetti (1983) found in a study of 204 business executives that those high in hardiness reported fewer symptoms of ill-health than those low in hardiness, no matter the level of stressful life events (see earlier this chapter). They also report that for those low in hardiness, the more social support received from their family, the poorer their health. One interpretation of this relationship is that this group (those low in hardiness) does not attempt to, or is rendered less able to cope with the stress encountered *because* of their family's support. We shall look at this interesting relationship in dealers later.

Gender – Professional Women

In addition to the stressors which are common to both sexes, the professional woman has to deal with a unique set of stressors (though they are encountered, if less often, by men). These include discrimination against women (e.g. traditional discrimination, their special career planning needs, lower salary, a comparative lack of advice and support), stereotyping (e.g. of particular personality traits), the marriage/work interface (e.g. childcare, career/family conflicts), and their social isolation (to avoid the 'mother, seductress, pet, fair maiden' role entrapment) (Nelson and Quick 1985). Chusmir and Franks (1988) add the 'token woman' stressor to this list of stressors, and that of power differences with men.

Women managers, particularly those in high management, are more likely than equivalent men to fall victim to ulcers and high blood pressure and may rely more on drugs to relieve tension. Professional women may also be at greater risk of mental ill-health and decreased job satisfaction (Davidson and Cooper 1983). A high degree of job insecurity, such as fear of being laid off, office politics, competition, lack of teamwork and mutual support, is seen as a particular source of stress for women managers (Cooper and Davidson 1982).

Despite these negative views of female employment, Lourie (1981) suggests that women executives, if they can survive the initially stressful periods of being conspicuous exceptions in unfamiliar roles, are significantly more likely to stand stressful situations than men. This may be due to women having higher tolerance levels and being more in touch with their feelings, and so being better able to deal with their emotions. Perhaps those individuals who withhold emotions are more likely to become ill from the effects of stress, especially men who will not show sadness, anger, or fear because they do not wish to appear effeminate. Men may be more bodily stressed by internalising emotion (Taylor and Cangemi 1988). Those women who have developed coping strategies that suppress emotions are two or three times more likely to develop breast cancer than women who 'break down' (and cry, for instance) under stress (Cantacuzino 1989).

In studying the evidence for sex differences in stress, Jick and Mitz (1985) found that women did indeed report higher rates of psychological distress and minor illness, and that men are more prone to report severe physical symptoms and illness. This is not to say that this is evidence that the differences between the sexes are 'real'. In considering reports of stressful events, it appears that women rate events that they have experienced very much higher than men (Cox 1978) and this needs to be noted in any analysis of occupational stress data. For instance, Taylor and Chave (1964) note that in a large-scale study of anxiety in the community, women report neurotic symptoms about twice that of males.

Using data from a major American study of health, the Framingham Heart Study (FHS), Haynes and Feinleib (1980) found that working women: 'experienced more daily stress, marital dissatisfaction, and ageing worries and were less likely to show overt anger than either housewives or men', but they had a lower incidence of coronary heart disease than working men. Further data from the FHS shows that working women who score high on Type A are twice as likely to develop coronary heart disease than their male counterparts (Cooper 1983).

There is some evidence that females have smaller zones of personal space (i.e. invisible boundaries surrounding a person's body into which uninvited others should not enter) than males (Liebman 1970). Females have been shown to prefer slightly warmer environments than men (Oborne 1985). So, in modern, open-plan, environmentally-controlled offices, both women and men may see different aspects of the working environment as a stressor.

The stress problems faced by women can be summarised as follows:

The generally accepted fact that depression and suicide are more frequent in women, especially those with high education levels and high social achievement, can be interpreted as a reflection of their not being able to reach their aspirations.

(Moulton 1980)

Age, Experience, and Level of Ability

Both the age of the individual, and the experience the individual possesses of a particular working environment, are moderators of the stress-strain relationship, and are clearly interrelated.

Physical and psychological changes which occur with ageing may increase vulnerability to the adverse consequences of stressors. As people age, major life events will occur (loss of spouse, parents, marriage, etc.). Some chronic conditions may be tolerated well until these added stressors, or the ageing process itself, depletes coping resources (Elliott and Eisdorfer 1982). To balance this, it might be expected that with age comes experience in coping with a stressful, or potentially stressful, situation. For instance, in a study of MBA students, Seltzer and Numerof (1988) found that the number of years experience within an employing organisation was negatively related to burnout, i.e. the longer the individual had been employed in the organisation, the less burnout recorded. Older white-collar workers have reported stress due to their inability to match the pace of younger colleagues, and due to the lack of shared values (Wahlund and Nurell 1978). This may be the situation in Dealing Rooms.

The level of ability of the individual is also a moderator of the response to stress, since it would be expected that an able employee would be able to complete a work task where an employee with less ability would not. The success of the former and failure of the latter will affect evaluation of self and self-esteem and consequently the stress outcome. Through training, the individual may decrease strain by adapting his or her abilities, and can simultaneously increase performance and productivity (Rohmert and Luczak 1979).

Social Support

It has already been noted that the degree and nature of support from others within and outside the work environment can moderate the effects of job stress. Supervisors (often) have to give support, co-workers do not. Ganster et al. (1986) and Kaufmann and Beehr (1986) found that support from a supervisor did indeed lower stress levels in staff (cited Smithers 1988).

However, there is no clear agreement as to the definition of social support or how it alleviates stress (MacKay and Cooper 1987). The present study of dealers takes 'social support' within the organisational context to mean helpful and comforting activities by other members of the organisation. Research clearly shows that where an individual can count on a high degree of support from others when facing potential stress-making situations, they are better able to cope with the situation. Caplan *et al.* (1975) and Kobasa and Puccetti (1983) suggest that social support may act as a buffer between the individual at risk and the stressor. Lin *et al.* (1979) found that social support is often used as a coping strategy, i.e. those facing stressful conditions at work actively seek to strengthen their relationships with others at work. Social support can derive from social, organisational, and/or family networks and the effects on stress of each type may not be equal. LaRocco *et al.* (1980), cited Sutherland (1988), found that co-worker support was more effective than either supervisor or home support against the impact of stress on depression and somatic complaints.

Cobb (1976), cited Savery (1988), has identified three types of social support: firstly, *emotional support*, which makes the recipient feel cared for; secondly, *esteem support*, which makes the recipient feel valued; and thirdly, *network support*, where the person feels connected to a social network of mutual obligations. House (1981), also cited Savery (1988), lists four acts by which individuals show social support: by emotional support (esteem, affect, trust, concern, and listening); by appraisal support (affirmation, feedback, social comparison); by informational support (advice, suggestion, directives, information); and by instrumental support (aid in kind, money, labour, time, modifying environment).

Several studies have reported an increased risk of coronary heart disease (Herd 1988), and higher levels of symptomatology (Cobb 1976), among people with weak social support. House (1981) suggests that supportive social relationships can directly enhance health by supplying the individual with the basic human needs for affection, approval, social contact, and security, and also by reducing interpersonal tensions and anxieties. These are the main effects of social support, operating directly upon the outcomes of stress.

Social support may also have a 'buffering' or 'interactive' effect on stress in that it modifies the effects of stressors upon strain, and is clearly seen in environments of high stress. For instance, family support, both social and emotional, has been found significantly to reduce the impact of high occupational stress on depression.

Social support networks may not always be supportive, however. Relationships with others may not only create a potential for conflict, but inhibit independence and personal growth (Elliott and Eisdorfer 1982). Working in groups is also a cause of conflict, e.g. conflict of personal and group goals, needs, and values, and Ivancevich and Matteson (1980) note that this can be a source of stress.

Threats to an individual's self-esteem may be the most serious of stressful events, and it may be that this type of stress is the most important that social support can counter (Cohen 1986).

A variation on these views of social support is presented by Seers et al. (1983), who found that job satisfaction was positively related to social support for those employees in a large US government agency who reported high levels of stress, but not for those who reported low levels of job stress. Though these results are open to a number of interpretations, it may be that those facing potentially high stress make more use of social support as a coping mechanism. Where the design of a particular job denies an individual the chance to work within a group, or where an individual is shut out from a group, social support is not available.

Marcelissen et al. (1988) examined 2,034 employees of twenty-one Dutch companies at levels they say are comparable to those of the general population, over a period of three years. They found that though an employee's co-workers tended to provide more support than supervisors, social support by supervisors was felt to be more important to the individual than support by colleagues. Further, they assert that only for persons at the lower end of the occupational hierarchy does the social support provided by the supervisor play an important role in eliminating and reducing stressful circumstances at work. This may be due to the lower degree of autonomy and greater dependency upon the supervisor in these jobs.

When an individual exhibits strains (e.g. anxiety, anger, and depression), this appears to reduce the social support made available by co-workers. This may be due to the reluctance of people to approach individuals who have problems; to the fact that those who are tense, are easily angered, are often depressed, or are nervous, are less attractive to others; and to the possibility that social support is inversely related to variables such as neuroticism and pessimism (that is, the more the person is neurotic or pessimistic, the less social support he or she receives). Persons high in strain may often report *lowered* levels of social support because they are embarrassed by their feelings, and prefer not to discuss them and seek help, and because these negative feelings of anxiety, depression, and anger may hinder the use of the social skills required for asking and obtaining social support.

Weiss *et al.* (1982), in a study of forty-four persons attending management development seminars at Purdue University, found that stressful events at work within the previous twelve months resulted in a significant increase in individuals engaging in on-the-job search behaviours (searching for support), e.g. asking a colleague to comment on their work. They suggest that this will lead to better job performance, in the short-term at least.

A characteristic which has been suggested as an influence on social support is the gender of the recipient. Males may benefit from work-based sources of support, while females rely on family and non-work sources (Leavy 1983). Holahan and Moos (1981) found that for employed women, both support from her family and at work were associated with decreases in depression and psychosomatic symptoms. For men, only support at work was related to decreases in both health outcomes. Fusilier *et al.* (1986) found that though women and men might receive similar amounts of support from co-workers, friends, and family, social support from family and friends improved on life satisfaction and reduced depression on men, but not on women. They also found that social support from co-workers reduced anxiety in women but not in men, and that no gender differences were found regarding the effects of social support on either (somatic) health outcomes or job satisfaction. These findings suggest that organisations should attempt to improve non-work support for men (e.g. paternity leave) and improve work-based support for women.

Cooper (1981) concludes that social support (the individual's work group and social group) can mitigate some of the effects of stress, and suggests that shared decision-making, group affiliations, corporate identity, group counselling, etc., are examples of forms of organisational social support.

In summary, Payne and Jones (1987) conclude that evidence from many studies is good enough to allow them to claim with reasonable confidence that social support, however measured, can affect the psychological outcomes and probably the long-term physical effects of stress.

Stress Coping Techniques

Individual well-being is influenced not only by an individual's personality, but by how the individual copes with the actual or potential stress they experience. Coping resources can be drawn from within the individual, or from the environment. Four approaches to stress coping have been summarised by Edwards (1988). Firstly, psychoanalytical approaches to coping, where coping is defined in terms of thinking realistic thoughts and taking actions which solve the problems facing the individual. Secondly, coping is characterised in terms of particular personality traits or coping styles, such as locus of control and Type A behaviour. Thirdly, coping is regarded as a series of stages through which the individual passes, and which occur in a specific sequence. Fourthly, coping has been conceptualized either in terms of specific methods of coping or according to the target of the coping effort.

Five categories of coping resource have been identified by Folkman *et al.* (1979): using personal health, energy, and morale; problem-solving skills; social networks; utilitarian resources (money, social agencies, etc.); and general and specific beliefs (e.g. self-efficacy, the belief in some higher natural order).

An alternative view of the mechanisms used to cope with stress is presented by Epstein (1986). Individuals may ignore or avoid the implications of a threatened event, distort the perception or interpretation of the event, or modify their self-concept to assimilate the new information. The tendency of Type A individuals to employ denial, and thus to endure stress longer and/or at higher levels than Type B individuals, is noted by Chesney and Rosenman (1983).

Osipow and Davis (1988) examined 175 veterinary students to determine the role of coping resources in moderating the effect of stress on strain. Their study included six sources of job stress, namely, role overload, role insufficiency (i.e. inadequate skills, education, etc.), role ambiguity, role boundary, responsibility (for others), and physical environment; four strain outcomes, namely, vocational strain (problems with work quality or output), psychological strain, interpersonal strain, and physical strain; and four personal resources for coping with stress, namely, recreation, self-care, social supports, and rational/cognitive coping (e.g. organising one's work load, establishing priorities). All coping resources were effective in reducing strain. High levels of social support reduced all the impacts of the stressors except for those from the physical environment, and high levels of recreation moderated the impact of role overload, role ambiguity and responsibility on strain. High levels of self-care reduced the impact of role overload, ambiguity, and boundary, and responsibility. Cognitive/rational coping moderated role overload and responsibility. More interestingly, in some cases, *low* use of a coping resource was *more* effective in reducing the stress. The four coping resources were effective in reducing the four strain outcomes individually. Thus, we can conclude that almost any form of coping, including social support, can reduce the effects of strains.

Tension Discharge Rate

Tension discharge rate (TDR) has been suggested as both a potential moderator of stress and a technique for coping with stress (Rose, Jenkins and Hurst 1978). Tension discharge rate is the rate at which the individual dissipates job-related tension. The underlying assumption is that those individuals who can leave the job-induced tensions behind at the end of the workday will be healthier than those who bring their psychological baggage home with them and dwell on it (Matteson and Ivancevich 1983). Tension discharge rate has been shown to be predictive of health status in air traffic controllers (Rose, Jenkins and Hurst 1978).

Matteson and Ivancevich (1983) obtained feedback from medical technologists. They measured a number of aspects of personal health (e.g. use of drugs, tranquillisers, cigarette smoking, alcohol consumption, visits made to the doctor) in the preceding six months, and also measured tension discharge rate. Those who were low in the ability to dissipate job-related tension reported poorer health than those who were able to do so. Dailey *et al.* (1986), from a study of three employee groups, believe that tension discharge rate is a valid measure across diverse samples.

Cottington *et al.* (1986), in a study of male hourly workers, found that hypertension was greatest among those men who suppressed their anger (i.e. had a low TDR) and simultaneously reported more job stress in the areas of job future ambiguity and dissatisfaction with co-workers and promotions. They also note that hypertension was also high among those who were satisfied with their co-workers but who were also more likely to express their anger at work.

The potential of cathartic discharge (e.g. shouting) as an effective method of coping with stress has been advanced (Evison 1988), and would appear to be related to tension discharge rate.

Other Moderators of Stress in the Individual

Other individual characteristics have been shown to influence the impact of stress. For instance, ethnicity (membership of a particular racial and/or minority group) and physical condition. The need for power has been examined by McClelland (1975), who followed up Harvard graduates who had scored high on the need for power, after twenty years. He found 58 per cent to have high blood pressure or to have died from heart failure.

Among personality variables which have been the subject of recent investigation is dispositional optimism. Scheier and Carver (1985), cited Kobasa (1988), found that students who were highly optimistic were less likely to report physical symptoms than students who were initially less optimistic.

CONCLUSION

As we saw in Chapter 1, the sources of occupational stress are extensive and vary for each individual. They may be related to the work or home environment of the employee, or to features of their personality. The interplay of all these factors means that the outcomes in terms of ill-health, job dissatisfaction, etc. will be different for each person. The remainder of this book is concerned with determining if and why dealers in the City of London are stressed, what the effects of this stress are, and what can be done to reduce or eliminate the potential negative outcomes of stress.

4

WHO ARE THE DEALERS?

GAINING ACCESS

In this chapter we indicate how we went about finding the information we needed concerning City dealers. In order to meet the aims of our study, we were required to gather a great deal of data about dealers. We were particularly interested in their demographic details, what they see as the sources and levels of stress in their lives and at work, their personalities, the effects of stress on them, and how they attempt to cope with stress. In this chapter we will present basic data about dealers, i.e. their backgrounds and their personalities. In the next chapter, we will present our findings about dealers' stress levels, job satisfaction, and how they cope with stress.

To find out all the information we needed in order to achieve the requirements of our study, it was essential in the first instance to gain access to a sufficiently large number of Dealing Room employees. This would provide us with a valid sample of dealers.

Since this study is probably the first detailed examination of the stress levels of financial dealers we had to find organisations and individuals who were willing to support the study and provide entry to the Dealing Rooms. Approaches were made to the personnel or human-resource managers of a number of City-based financial organisations in the hope that they would support the project and obtain access for us to Dealing Room staff. There were three reasons why it was believed that this group of managers would be supportive of a study of the stress problems encountered by a section of key personnel within their organisations. Firstly, as senior company executives, they themselves would be likely to be subject to high levels of stress, and would be sympathetic to other functions' stress problems. Secondly, human resource managers have direct, major responsibilities for subordinates with stress problems. Thirdly, this group of executives would seem to be in the appropriate position within their organisations to detect potential stress sources and outcomes, to provide advice, and to be interested in initiating policies to prevent and manage stress.

It should be pointed out that while many of the managers we contacted were only too willing to participate in the study, a number of managers were less supportive. The reluctance of some personnel managers in particular, and managers in general, to support investigations of stress in their employees has been encountered by many other researchers. An explanation for this reluctance has been put forward by Giles (1987) who points out that some Personnel Directors have awarded *themselves* between 7 and 10 points on a 10-point stress scale (where a higher score indicates higher perceived stress), and awarded their average member of staff 3 or 4 points. Personnel Managers justify these ratings by arguing that lower-level staff do not have the same weight of responsibilities as themselves, and though their subordinates might *feel* more stressed they were not so in reality. From the previous chapter, we know that stress is most definitely not restricted to the executive and managerial levels in an organisation.

In addition, Giles (1987) found that some personnel managers lacked awareness of their own stress, and of the impact of their behaviour upon people around them. They showed less sensitivity than might be desirable to the stress of lower-level staff, and believed that, since *they* could cope with stress by their 'in-built' qualities, *others* should do the same. These managers saw no role for stress training or counselling in their organisations. However, research shows that executives do not necessarily suffer more stress than other people (Cooper and Marshall 1980), since higher-level staff can balance pressure by the ability to delegate work, and by high levels of involvement, status, and job satisfaction.

Finally, some of the managers of financial institutions simply may not care about the stress problems of their staff (as one personnel manager told us, 'they are well-paid to do the job, they know the demands that will be made of them'), or they may be unwilling to face the implications which might follow from a study of the stress problems of their staff. Of course some managers were, quite naturally, particularly concerned about both the confidentiality aspects of the project, and the staff time which might be involved.

We decided that the participation of ten financial organisations would provide us with an adequate sample of dealers with which to work. Examples of the ways in which we obtained the support of three of these organisations follow. Firstly, the local (Manchester, UK) manager of a major European bank referred one of the researchers to the General Manager of the London headquarters of the Bank. The General Manager immediately agreed to support the project by allowing the researchers to interview four dealers. Secondly, a dealer in a bank with headquarters in the USA asked to be sent a copy of a 'typical' stress questionnaire, and to be informed of the benefits which her bank might gain by supporting the project. Thirdly, the head of Capital Markets at one institution agreed to participate on condition that the study would also provide him with feedback about how long his organisation could expect to retain Dealing Room staff, since he believed that there were few opportunities for the promotion of dealers into management: he was also concerned about how career concerns might affect dealers' performance. We were happy to agree with these requirements.

The way in which the researchers gained entry into one US-owned bank is shown below.

Timetable of Contacts with a US-Owned Bank

4 March	– obtain phone number of contact
8 March (i)	– line engaged
8 March (ii)	– contact busy, researchers asked to call following day
9 March (i)	– contact not available
9 March (ii)	– line engaged
10 March	– leave telephone number for contact to phone researchers
16 March	– speak to contact – agreed that researchers should write with details of the project
18 March	– letter sent to bank
28 March	– contact phones researchers with approval – researchers can interview i) chief dealer ii) deputy chief dealer, and iii) three traders Researchers asked to contact chief dealer

11 April (2.30pm) – phone chief dealer – not available
11 April (3.30pm) – phone chief dealer – at meeting
11 April (4.30pm) – phone chief dealer – make contact.
                     Agreed researchers can visit bank on
                     19 April to carry out interviews, and
                     to write with details
19 April   – researchers visit bank, spend 8.30am –
                     7.30pm in Dealing Room
27 April   – researchers write to bank
                     Vice-President
10 June   – researchers write to bank
                     Vice-President
13 December   – researchers write to bank
                     Vice-President

PARTICIPATING BANKS AND FINANCIAL INSTITUTIONS

Of the ten financial institutions participating in the study, five were British-owned, that is, two of the 'Big Four' UK clearing banks, one of the major Scottish clearing banks, one smaller clearing bank which offers a conventional banking service, and one chartered accountant with a Dealing Room. There were also two major European International banks, one each from within and outside the European Community (EC), and three very large US-owned international commercial banks which maintain a presence across, and indeed dominate, all categories of banking business. These were the ten organisations which form the basis of our study of dealers.

The conditions laid down by these organisations are indicative of the caution of financial institution executives. For example, one participating bank, which is generally regarded as a traditional, relatively conservative, financial institution agreed to co-operate only if a number of constraints were accepted. Firstly, interviewing of Dealing Room staff would be done in a 'quiet room' off the Dealing Room, and not in the Dealing Room itself. Secondly, the bank insisted that *they* would select those members of staff who might be interviewed, and the dealer's agreement to this would be paramount. Eventually the names of the 'volunteers' were drawn from a hat by a senior manager.

INTERVIEWING DEALERS

Having gained the support we needed for the success of the project, it was decided that a number of interviews with dealers should be conducted. In advance of the interviews, a letter was sent to the appropriate contact at each institution for distribution to interviewees. This outlined the purposes of our study, and indicated briefly the proposed content and the aims of the interviews, stressing their confidentiality.

The researchers' purposes in carrying out the interviews were:

(i) to obtain information about the job of dealing and the environment in which dealers work;

(ii) to determine which aspects of the dealer's job might be stressors, and the behavioural outcomes of stress in dealers, and

(iii) to establish adequate relationships with Dealing Room staff and their employing organisations, so that the project would gain credibility and encourage institutions to co-operate in other stages of the project, particularly in the distribution of questionnaires to Dealing Room staff.

A total of twenty-six interviews were carried out with dealers. Sixteen of these interviews were recorded, with the agreement of the interviewee, on audio-tape, and four interviews were conducted without recording, all in rooms adjacent to the Dealing Room floor. Six interviews were carried out with dealers at their desks, as they worked.

Initially, a schedule of structured interviews was adhered to. In these cases, questions were drawn up formally in advance of the interview. As more information was gained by the researchers, this gave way to a semi-structured interviewing technique, and latterly to a near-conversational encounter, with information being recorded graphically on paper, using the Mind Map method (Buzan 1982). All of the information collected, no matter which method was employed, was written up in note form immediately after the interview.

While interviewees were selected by varying methods – 'voluntarily', by a member of management, by drawing names from a hat, by who was available at a particular time – it appeared to make little difference to the attitudes adopted by the dealers interviewed. So long as total confidentiality was assured, interviewees seemed, to the researchers, to be honest and forthcoming.

Each interview lasted between the half-hour which was scheduled, and one hour or more. Indeed, a number of dealers were content to continue with the interview for as long as was practical. This may be because the vast majority of dealers noted that this was the first occasion on which they had been asked about their attitudes to their job. While many managers and company executives were reticent, dealers themselves were particularly supportive.

In talking about the subject of interviewing, Garfield (1986) has noted that:

> formal question-and-answer interviews too often lead to conditioned cliches, particularly when the topics are such loaded ones as personal success and performance on the job. . . . A more inviting way of eliciting information has been sharpened into a fine art by investigators such as Studs Terkel in oral histories like 'Working' who asks the kind of questions you would ask while having a drink with someone.

Terkel (1972) himself considers that this method of interviewing leads to talk that is 'idiomatic rather than academic'. This informal approach was the method adopted by the interviewers in most of the interviews, and consequently provides support for the validity of the results we present.

Each interview commenced with a brief outline of the project by the researcher. Each interviewee was asked to describe their background, education, and employment history, and then their current job within the Dealing Room. Other topics then covered included those features which dealers saw as the attraction of dealing, the factors which were seen as determining the success or failure of a dealer, the effects of the job on home and social life, their training and future employment prospects, and their work-life expectancy. The subject of stress, its sources and manifestations, was introduced later in the interview, and was generally related by the interviewer to points raised earlier in the interview by the dealer.

SURVEYING DEALERS: THE STRESS INVENTORY

At the completion of the schedule of twenty-six interviews, we designed a questionnaire to obtain the data which would meet the requirements of the project. The questionnaire was based upon the view of stress we have adopted (see Chapter 2), and by points raised during the interviews. The questionnaire (see Appendix 1) consisted of a number of different sections or inventories, the aim of which was to produce a complete, non-threatening, and efficient package, that would provide us with the information we required for the investigation. The questionnaire consisted of eight sections.

Section One obtained biographical data about dealers. Section Two was concerned with the mental health of the employee (two different measures were used here). Section Three examined the stress or coronary-prone behaviour of the dealer. Section Four measured the dealer's perceived locus of control. Section Five measured the dealer's job satisfaction. Section Six covered those aspects of work which the dealer saw as potential sources of stress in the job. Section Seven obtained two measures of the dealer's personality, namely extroversion/introversion and neuroticism/stability. Section Eight was developed to find the ways in which dealers attempted to cope with any stress they encountered. These sections are now explained in turn.

The first mental health scale used was the 18-question mental ill-health scale of the Occupational Stress Indicator (OSI, Cooper *et al.* 1988). Employees are asked to rate each question on a scale of 1 to 6. This provides a single overall score for each respondent, ranging from a minimum possible 18 (low mental ill-health) to a maximum 108 (high mental ill-health). It provides an insight rather than a clinical diagnosis of mental health (Cooper, Sloan and Williams 1988).

The second measure of mental well-being used consisted of three separate scales of the Crown-Crisp Experiential Index (Crown and Crisp 1979). Each scale consists of eight questions, giving a twenty-four-item questionnaire designed to assess three specific areas of behaviour, namely:

(i) Free-floating anxiety
(ii) Somatic concomitants of anxiety
(iii) Depression

The higher the score on the three scales, each of which can range from 0 to 24, the more mental ill-health is indicated.

Coronary-prone or Type A behaviour was measured using the fourteen-question scale of the OSI (Cooper, Sloan and Williams 1988), which has been designed for completion by a management and management-level audience. Respondents score each question on a scale of 1 to 6. The scale yields a total score ranging from 14 to 84, the higher scores being indicative of more coronary-prone behaviour.

Locus of control was measured by the twelve-question inventory of the OSI (Cooper, Sloan and Williams 1988). Here, dealers were asked to rate each question on a scale of 1 to 6. This produces a single score which represents a broad view of the control which the individual feels he or she has over the things at work which concern them. The possible score for an individual on this scale ranges from 12 (perceives greater control) to 72 (perceives less control).

A fifteen-item inventory designed by Warr, Cook and Wall (1979) was used to assess the overall job satisfaction of the dealer with both the intrinsic and extrinsic features of their job. Each of the fifteen questions is rated on a scale of 1 to 7. Total scores on this inventory can range from 15 to 105, and the higher the score the higher the job satisfaction indicated by the respondent.

The sources of stress in the dealer's job were measured using an eighty-seven-item inventory, based upon the six sources of stress identified by Cooper (1986) (see Figure 3.1 in Chapter 3), namely stress associated with

   (i) aspects intrinsic to the job
  (ii) the managerial role
 (iii) relationships with other people
 (iv) career and achievement
  (v) organisational structure and climate, and
 (vi) home/work interface

This inventory also included additional sources of stress specifically relevant to the job of dealing, items which were generated from the interviews. Each item is rated on a scale of 1 to 6. The higher the score in each item, the more stress is indicated.

Extroversion/introversion and neuroticism/stability were each measured by twenty-four questions from the Eysenck Personality Inventory (Eysenck and Eysenck 1964). Scores on each measure range from 0 to 24, where higher scores on each scale indicate more extroversion and more neuroticism, respectively. The inventory also includes a nine-question 'lie scale' which has been developed to indicate whether the respondent may have been 'faking', i.e. providing what he or she considers to be 'acceptable' answers to this and, by extension, to the other inventories. The higher the score on these nine questions, the more the respondent may be suspected of 'lying'. Thus, the inventory overall consisted of fifty-seven questions yielding three separate scores.

In order to determine the ways in which dealers attempt to cope with the stresses relating to their work, a thirty-item inventory was included in the questionnaire. Dealers were asked to rate each item on a scale of 1 to 6. This inventory was based on the stress coping inventory of the OSI (Cooper, Sloan and Williams 1988), and yields six scores, each indicating a separate strategy for coping with stress, namely.

   (i) social support
  (ii) task strategies
 (iii) logic
 (iv) home and work relationships
  (v) time
 (vi) involvement

Sections One, Three, Four, Six, and Eight of the questionnaire aim to uncover basic data about dealers, their personalities, how they perceive the job of dealing in terms of the potential sources of stress, and how they attempt to cope with these stresses. Sections Two, Five, and Seven of the questionnaire seek to determine how dealers react to working in the Dealing Rooms, in terms of the effects on their mental health and job satisfaction. In addition, we also asked dealers in Section One to indicate how much they smoke and drink, as these are also indicators of work stress.

The eight-section questionnaire was assembled into a twelve-page A-4 size booklet, including a title page which described the project and stressed the anonymity and confidentiality of each reply, and indicating how the questionnaire should be completed and returned to the researchers.

A three-character code which would indicate the organisation to which the questionnaire had been sent was entered manually in the top right-hand corner of the questionnaire by the researchers before distribution. On return of the questionnaire it would then be possible to analyse results from each organisation separately, and provide each with their own results, which was a requirement of many of the supporting organisations.

Questionnaires were delivered in appropriate bundles to a contact at each of the ten participating institutions for onward distribution to dealers. Each dealer was asked to return the completed questionnaire to the researchers in a franked, addressed envelope supplied by the researchers. Out of over 600 distributed, 237 questionnaires were returned to the researchers (a near 40 per cent response rate). Data from the 225 usable questionnaires were then analysed by computer.

WHO ARE THE DEALERS?

In the following pages of this chapter we present our findings about dealers' personal and work profiles, and their personalities. A summary of our results can be found in Kahn and Cooper (1990).

BIOGRAPHICAL DATA OF DEALERS

Sex

It can be seen from Table 4.1 that a total of 186 males (84 per cent) and 36 females (16 per cent) returned completed and usable questionnaires. These figures reflect the sex bias in the job of dealing, which unlike other City of London institutions, e.g. accounting, banking, and similar professions, is almost totally dominated by males. Traditionally, City work has confined females to the stereotypical tasks of secretary, typist, etc. Only within recent years have women moved into the long-established, though now radically changed, City function of dealing.

Table 4.1 Sex of dealers

	n	%
Male	186	83.8
Female	36	16.2

Enquiries made by the authors at the ten institutions participating in the study showed that the ratio of males to females, the ratio of graduates to non-graduates, and the average age of dealers in the returned stress-questionnaires is a representative sample of the whole population of City dealers from which the sample has been taken.

Age

As shown in Table 4.2, the group of dealers forming the sample is older than might be expected, given that it is believed by the general public that dealing is a profession dominated by young people. Only 8 per cent are aged 23 or younger, and the percentages across the 24–26, 27–29, and 30–34 age bands are similar (21 per cent, 19.2

per cent, and 22.3 per cent respectively). A total of 27.3 per cent of dealers are aged 35 to 50, but few dealers (2.2 per cent) are aged over 50 years. This latter feature may well be due to the stressful nature of the job, so that stressed dealers leave at a relatively early age, or to the early retirement policies of employing organisations, or to promotion or transfer to other functions, etc. The mean age for the whole group was 32 years.

Table 4.2 Age distribution of dealers

Age range (years)	n	%
23 or younger	18	8.0
24–26	47	21.0
27–29	43	19.2
30–34	50	22.3
35–40	30	13.4
41–50	31	13.9
51–60	5	2.2

Nationality

A specific item was included in the questionnaire on nationality, so that we might determine whether foreign nationals, working in British Dealing Rooms, experience different sources and levels of stress than their British colleagues. However, few respondents fell into the former category, only twenty-one or 9.5 per cent (see Table 4.3). Because of the low numbers, further investigation of this group was not pursued.

Table 4.3 Nationality

	n	%
British	200	90.5
Non-British	21	9.5

Marital Status

Table 4.4 shows that over half (53.8 per cent) of dealers are currently married, 29.1 per cent are single, and 13 per cent co-habiting. Few respondents are divorced (3.1 per cent) or separated (0.9 per cent). These figures indicate that the traditional view of dealers as single or divorced is not confirmed. The majority of dealers, therefore, will have domestic commitments to balance against their work role, and the figures may underestimate the number who have these commitments. For instance, many dealers will be responsible for elderly parents and relatives, etc.

Of the 120 married dealers, 18 (15 per cent of all married dealers, or 8 per cent of the total sample) indicated that they have been married previously. Therefore, divorced, separated, and re-married dealers constitute 12.1 per cent (n = 27) of the total sample. The view that dealing and City work, and the environments associated with them, result in marital breakdown, is not substantiated by these figures. Nevertheless, one Foreign Exchange dealer told us:

> If the divorce rate among dealers is high, it's because of the very social atmosphere you work in. You go out at night into the City, and after a hard day's work you go for a drink. You get home after 9 p.m. and that can lead to problems.

Table 4.4 Marital status of dealers

Marital status	n	%
Married	120	53.8
Single	65	29.1
Divorced	7	3.1
Separated	2	0.9
Co-habiting	29	13.0

Dealers' Partners' Jobs

One hundred and twenty-five dealers (55.6 per cent of the sample) replied to a question asking for details of their partner's job. This compares with the 149 (66.8 per cent) who are married or co-habiting. Seventy-seven of these (61.6 per cent) gave details of their partner's work, of which 12 (9.6 per cent) were in the 'housewife' or 'mother' category. A percentage breakdown of the replies given by dealers is shown under seven groupings in Table 4.5.

Table 4.5 Dealers' partners' jobs

Job	%
White-collar	33.8
Finance/Banking/Accounting	23.4
Housewife/mother	13.0
Arts-related	10.4
'Helping' professions	9.1
Blue-collar	5.2
Other/Unemployed	5.2

Jobs included lift engineer, economist, bar person, midwife, opera singer, diplomat, milliner, artist, and nurse. It is noticeable that almost one quarter of replies indicate a 'City' type job, e.g. banker, investment banker, dealer. The general impression Table 4.5 gives is that dealers' partners fill white-collar/professional work. Since many dealers failed to give details of their partners' employment (perhaps to ensure that they could not be identified), the data gathered should be considered as indicative only. It suggests that many dealers have partners in jobs of high responsibility, who themselves may be stressed by their work environment, thus potentially adding to any stress problems faced by dealers.

Dependent Children

In addition to domestic commitments, almost one-third of dealers (72) have children aged under 18, for whom they may be expected to have some responsibility (see Table 4.6).

Level of Education

It might be expected that those working in Dealing Rooms would be required to have high standards of education. Indeed, a number of personnel managers told us that they currently recruited only

Table 4.6 Dependent children

No. of children aged under 18	n	%
No children	152	67.9
One child	28	12.5
Two children	30	13.4
Three children	12	5.4
Four or more children	2	0.9

graduates. Table 4.7 indicates that almost half of our sample (49.5 per cent) had a degree, and very few (3.2 per cent) had no formal academic qualifications.

Table 4.7 Level of education of dealers

Level	n	%
No formal qualifications	7	3.2
O-level or equivalent	47	21.2
A-level or equivalent	58	26.1
Degree level or equivalent	78	35.1
Higher degree level	32	14.4

Talking about the selection of staff, a junior foreign exchange dealer told us:

> There's a certain something about you. You either make it or you don't. You have to be quick at making decisions and quoting prices, be fairly intelligent. You can't be quiet. You have to shout or you won't be heard. You've got to be loud.

Perhaps personnel managers look for these attributes in staff.

JOB DEMOGRAPHICS

Length of Service in Present Job

The expansion in the numbers employed by the financial institutions in Dealing Rooms during the mid-to-late 1980s is reflected in the statistics in Table 4.8. The sample shows a group of relatively new employees. Of the total, 48 per cent have less than three years', and 67 per cent less than four years' experience of dealing. A sizable minority, 21 per cent, have experience of six or more years.

Table 4.8 Length of service in present job

Length of service	n	%
1 or less year	52	23.5
2 years	54	24.4
3 years	42	19.0
4 years	16	7.2
5 years	11	5.0
6–10 years	30	13.6
11–27 years	16	7.2

Number of People for Whom Responsible at Work

The sample of dealers we examined comprises two distinct groups. Table 4.9 shows that 46 per cent have no responsibilities for other people at work, while the remaining 54 per cent are responsible for others at work. Four respondents have major staff responsibilities for between 400 and 700 others, indicating that they are in charge of a Dealing Room or Treasury. The preponderance of respondents who indicate that they have responsibilities for other personnel suggests that the sample may over-represent this group of staff, or dealers believe that they have more authority than they do in fact possess.

Table 4.9 Number of people for whom responsible at work

Number of people	n	%
0	101	45.7
1–5	70	31.7
6–10	20	9.0
11–30	16	7.3
31–75	10	4.5
400–700	4	1.8

Expected Next Promotion

Table 4.10 shows that 56 per cent of our sample expected to be promoted within one year. This contrasts with the comments made by one manager, that there were few opportunities for promotion in dealing. In addition, many City of London organisations have reduced their numbers of Dealing Room staff: 'There are too many players chasing too few trades. By the end of 1989, around 50,000 jobs will have been lost in the City, (*Sunday Times*, 16 October 1988).

Table 4.10 Expected next promotion

Length of time	n	%
Within 1 year	119	56.4
1–5 years	66	31.3
Over 5 years	2	0.9
Never	24	11.4

It was not possible to determine how realistic were the views of dealers concerning their promotion prospects, but a long time gap before an expected or desired promotion has been shown to be significantly related to psychiatric illness and job dissatisfaction (Arthur and Gunderson 1965; Cooper, Sloan and Williams 1988). Threat of job loss has been noted as associated with a number of health problems, including ulcers, colitis, and alopecia (Cobb and Kasl 1977), and with an increase in muscular and emotional complaints (Smith *et al.* 1981).

Number of Hours Travelled to/from Office

The average time dealers spend travelling to and from work is approximately nine and a half hours per week. The increasing congestion in London (and in other urban areas) suggests that travel time may be expected to increase from this figure. A breakdown of the answers given to this question is shown in Table 4.11. More than 20 per cent of the sample spent upwards of 15 hours per week travelling to and from work.

Table 4.11 Number of hours travelled to/from office

Number of hours per day	n	%
1	81	36.7
2	93	42.1
3	41	18.6
4–5	6	2.8

Number of Hours Spent at Work/in Office

The number of hours spent by dealers at work or in the office is shown in Table 4.12. Of the sample 34 per cent indicate that they spend 51 hours or more per week at work or in the office. Since some of the technology associated with dealing can be used at home or while travelling, it is very probable that the number of hours dealers spend working will increase as the technology becomes more ubiquitous, and competition between financial institutions for scarce deals increases further. A number of dealers interviewed noted that they worked from home, so data may underestimate actual hours worked in many cases. One dealer commented: 'You can take the equipment home if you've got a position. You're always thinking about the job. You go for a beer after to wind down'.

Table 4.12 Number of hours spent at work/in office

Number of hours per week	n	%
40 hours or less	33	15.1
41–50 hours	111	50.7
51–55 hours	54	24.6
56–80 hours	21	9.6

HEALTH DEMOGRAPHICS

Exercise Activity

Three questions were asked about the exercise activities of dealers, and results are shown in Tables 4.13 to 4.15. Body weight is of concern to 48 per cent of the sample, but a majority (61 per cent) take 'planned exercise' only when possible or less often, and even more (73 per cent) manage an 'ideal' exercise programme 'sometimes' or less often. The importance of exercise is pointed out by Sutherland (1988): 'intuitively it seems that an unfit or ill (physically or mentally) employee may be less tolerant and more vulnerable to other stress at work'.

The job of dealing, as with so much work in the financial and other sectors, is essentially sedentary.

Table 4.13 Maintenance of desired body weight

Frequency	n	%
Almost all the time	116	52.3
Sometimes	53	23.9
Never	53	23.9

Table 4.14 Taking planned exercise

Frequency	n	%
Always	36	16.1
Usually	52	23.2
When possible	41	18.3
Occasionally	42	18.8
Not usually	19	8.5
Rarely	34	15.2

Table 4.15 Managing an 'ideal' exercise programme

Frequency	n	%
Always	26	11.8
Usually	34	15.4
Sometimes	39	17.6
Not usually	47	21.3
Never	75	33.9

PERSONALITY DEMOGRAPHICS OF DEALERS

Coronary-Prone Behaviour

Type A coronary-prone behaviour is made up of a cluster of traits, and is characterized by extremes of competitiveness, impatience, aggressiveness, and feelings of being continuously under pressure from time and from the challenge of responsibility.

(Hingley and Cooper 1986)

The fourteen-question scale used to measure this aspect of an individual's personality shows that dealers indicate higher coronary-prone behaviour than national norms. Dealers have scores similar to those other groups which might be expected to exhibit high coronary-prone behaviour (namely, middle managers, management consultants, and board directors).

Figure 4.1 shows dealers' scores and how they compare with the scores of other occupational groups on the OSI coronary-prone scale used in the study. Dealers show higher coronary-prone behaviour scores than middle and senior managers, occupational psychologists, blue-collar factory workers, and nurses dealing with the mentally handicapped, and it is clear that dealers as a group exhibit more coronary-prone traits than the average population. One reason for this is undoubtedly that of self-selection, i.e. individuals who exhibit high coronary-prone behaviour are attracted to and are selected by managers for the kind of jobs found in Dealing Rooms, that is, jobs high in responsibility and power, where the decisions made by the individual dealer have far-reaching effects. In addition, it is probably true that individuals low in coronary-prone behaviour do not succeed in the Dealing Room environment and either are perceived as failures by their superiors and 'let go', or decide for themselves early on in their careers that they do not wish to continue in the job. Whatever the reasons, we found that 63 per cent of dealers scored higher on the measure (and so indicated higher coronary-prone behaviour) that the mean score of the general population.

Locus of Control

Dealers score significantly higher on the locus of control scale than normative data. This indicates an 'external' locus of control and thus less perceived control over events (lower scores indicate more per-

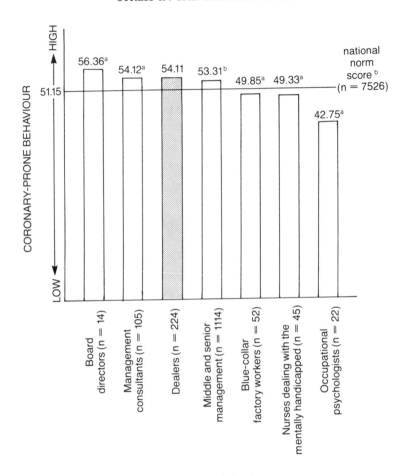

Figure 4.1 Coronary-prone or Type A behaviour scores
Sources: [a] Cooper, Sloan and Williams (1989); [b] NFER-Nelson (1992)

ceived control over events). Figure 4.2 shows that dealers have higher locus of control scores than middle and senior managers, management consultants, board directors, and occupational psychologists, and lower scores than blue-collar factory workers and nurses dealing with the mentally handicapped. It appears that dealers feel that they have less control over events than those in managerial positions. Consequently, it may be expected that dealers are more anxious and less able to deal with frustrating events: they would also be expected to be less psychologically healthy than those in management positions.

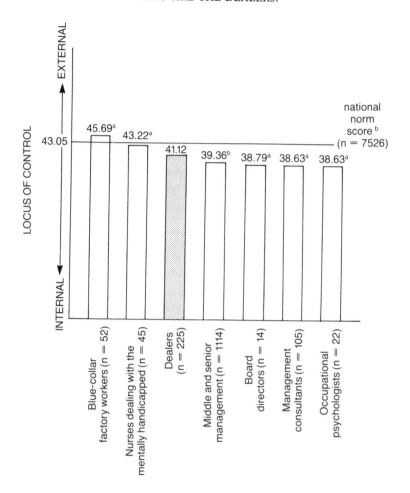

Figure 4.2 Locus of control scores
Sources: [a] Cooper, Sloan and Williams (1989); [b] NFER-Nelson (1992)
Note: External locus of control means less control over events. Internal locus of control means more control over events

The lack of control which dealers have was pointed out to us by one foreign exchange dealer: 'It's rumours that drive the market'.

However, not all dealers feel this way, as one forward deposits dealer said: 'This bank is steeped in tradition. I am my own boss. I can wheel and deal to my heart's content. My parameters are generous. I can make instant decisions here, and stand or fall by them'.

Extroversion

Comparison of dealers' extroversion scores with those of the normal population are shown in Table 4.16. This indicates that dealers are significantly more 'extrovert' than average. Indeed, only three out of twenty-two employment groups who were examined by the originators of this test (Eysenck and Eysenck 1964) are found to be more extrovert than dealers (namely, salesmen, whose mean score was 13.63, apprentices, 13.70, and student occupational therapists, 13.43). One spot dealer told us: 'The job makes you extrovert. It's not necessary for the job, but you get hyped up sometimes'.

Table 4.16 Extroversion scores

	n	Scores	Significant differences
Dealers	211	13.37	
Normative data[a]	2000	12.07	(p <0.001)

[a]*Source*: Eysenck and Eysenck (1964)

Neuroticism

Dealers score higher on the neuroticism scale than the normative population, but the difference is not statistically significant (see Table 4.17). Dealers are no more neurotic (as described by Eysenck and Eysenck 1964) than the average person.

Table 4.17 Neuroticism scores

	n	Scores	Significant differences
Dealers	218	9.12	
Normative scores[a]	2000	9.07	

[a]*Source*: Eysenck and Eysenck (1964)

Lie Score

The scores of dealers on the lie scale are as shown in Table 4.18 and this indicates that there is little difference between this group and the normative population. The results of the present study, at least in terms of the probable honesty of the answers supplied by dealers on the questionnaires, are given credibility by these data.

Table 4.18 Lie scores

	n	scores	significant differences
Dealers	221	2.30	
Normative scores[a]	651	2.26	

[a] *Source*: Eysenck and Eysenck (1964)

DEALERS – FACT OR FICTION?

Do the results presented in this chapter support the publicly-held view of dealers?

** 'Dealers are predominantly single yuppies'.
FICTION.
Most dealers are married, though only one-third of them have children.

** 'Only young people can make a success of dealing'.
FICTION.
More than 70 per cent of dealers are aged over 26, and more than half are aged 30 or above.

** 'Dealers are uneducated'.
FICTION.
About half of dealers have a degree, and 3 per cent have no formal academic qualification.

** 'Most dealers are new to the job'.
FACT.
More than two-thirds of dealers have been in their current job less than 3 years, and almost half for less than 2 years.

** 'Dealers don't think of the long term'.
FICTION.
Almost 90 per cent of dealers expect to be promoted within 5 years, and more than half within 1 year.

** 'Dealers live in the City of London, close to the Dealing Rooms'.
FICTION.
About two-thirds of dealers spend 2 or more hours travelling to get to work every day, and 20 per cent spend more than 3 hours.

** 'Dealers spend long hours at work'.
FACT.
About one dealer in three works more than 50 hours per week, and almost 10 per cent spend more than 56 hours a week working.

** 'Dealers spend a lot of time "pumping iron" to keep fit'.
FICTION.
Under 40 per cent of dealers take regular planned exercise, and under 30 per cent manage an 'ideal' exercise programme.

** 'Dealers are hard driving, achievement oriented'.
FACT.
Dealers have above-average Type A personalities, the type of personalities that are time-conscious, pushy, hard-driving, and excessively ambitious.

** 'Dealers are real "extroverts"'.
FACT.
Dealers are significantly more 'extrovert' than the average person.

** 'Dealers are neurotic'.
FICTION.
They are no more neurotic than the average.

** 'Dealing makes you a liar'.
FICTION.
Not according to our results.

In summary, the publicly-held perception of dealers as young, single, under-educated, and relatively new to the job, is only partially substantiated by our study. Dealers are predominantly male (84 per cent), and average age 32 years. They were more likely to be married (54 per cent) and as likely to have a degree as not. They have been dealing for four years. They spend long hours dealing (47 hours) and travelling to and from work (9.4 hours) each week. By their own admission they take insufficient exercise, and in addition they exhibit the personality characteristics which are typical of highly-stressed individuals and which are considered to result in negative health outcomes.

5

HOW DEALERS RESPOND TO THE JOB OF DEALING

INTRODUCTION

In this chapter we will examine how dealers react to the job of dealing, and whether they are more or less satisfied with their jobs, whether they reflect emotional strain from the job, and how this might affect their health behaviours such as drinking and smoking. We will also determine what dealers report as the major sources of stress in their jobs, and how they attempt to cope with these stressors. We will also look in more detail at certain sub-groups of dealers (e.g. male and female dealers, older and younger dealers). Where there are statistically significant differences between the scores reported by any of the sub-groups (in say, their alcohol consumption), this will be noted in each of the sections following. Statistically significant differences are those differences between groups which are not thought to be due to chance.

JOB SATISFACTION

A fifteen-item inventory was used to assess the job satisfaction of dealers (see Chapter 3). Since each question in the inventory can be scored from 1 to 7, for any individual a job satisfaction score can range from 15 to 105, giving a mid-point score (neither satisfied nor dissatisfied) of 60. It was found that the mean score for the sample was 71.12, with 170 dealers (76 per cent) scoring above the mid-point score. Overall, it appears that dealers are relatively satisfied with their job. In comparison with other groups of employees, these results are less convincing. Figure 5.1 shows that compared with six other groups, dealers are less satisfied than supervisors, managers, and white-collar staff, and more satisfied than blue-collar staff, pilots, and tax officers. Since it would appear to be more sensible to compare dealers with the first three groups named above, dealers do not seem to be particularly satisfied with their jobs.

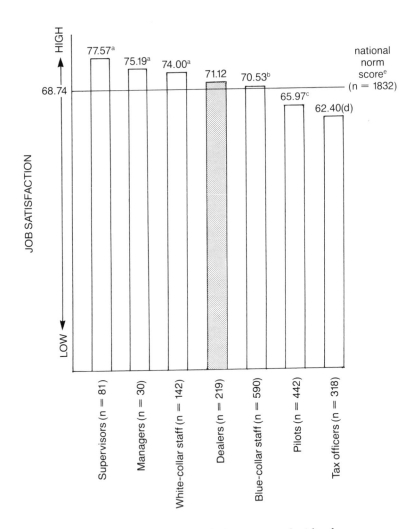

Figure 5.1 Job satisfaction scores of dealers compared with other groups
Sources: [a] Clegg and Wall (1981); [b] Warr *et al.* (1979); [c] Sloan and Cooper (1986); [d] Roden (1985); [e] NFER-Nelson (1992)

Further information about dealers' job satisfaction is shown in Table 5.1. Each of the fifteen questions asked in the inventory concerned one aspect of job satisfaction. Table 5.1 ranks the fifteen dimensions of job satisfaction by the mean scores of the sample, and shows the percentage of the sample which is overall satisfied with each dimension, and the percentage which is overall dissatisfied. Those 'not sure' were eliminated from Table 5.1.

Table 5.1 Job satisfaction scores of dealers in order of importance

Dimension*	Mean	% Satisfied	% Dissatisfied
Your fellow workers	5.46	84.0	10.7
The freedom to choose your own methods of working	5.45	84.4	10.7
The amount of responsibility you are given	5.05	74.2	22.7
The amount of variety in your job	5.03	75.1	16.4
Your immediate boss	5.03	72.4	19.1
Your opportunity to use your abilities	5.02	73.8	20.4
The recognition you get for good work	4.80	69.3	23.6
Your chance of promotion	4.73	65.8	18.0
The attention paid to suggestions you make	4.71	68.0	22.7
Your rate of pay	4.62	64.9	30.2
Your hours of work	4.50	61.3	29.8
Your job security	4.49	57.3	24.0
The physical working conditions	4.36	58.7	38.7
Industrial relations between management and workers in your firm	4.26	47.1	31.4
The way your firm is managed	3.82	40.9	44.0

Note: *Each dimension is scored 1 to 7 – the higher the score the higher the satisfaction.

The highest levels of satisfaction were with 'fellow workers', 'amount of freedom in choosing their own working methods', 'amount of responsibility given', and 'amount of variety in the job'. Perhaps by coincidence, these four dimensions have also been found to be the most satisfying for general practitioners (Cooper, Rout and Faragher 1989). The importance of 'fellow workers' is supported by comments made by dealers when we interviewed them, that dealing is a group or team activity, and the success or otherwise of a dealer is in part determined by the amount and quality of support from colleagues. Those responsible for the selection of Dealing Room staff also emphasised the importance of team work, and this was reflected in their recruitment and selection methods.

Warr, Cook and Wall (1979) suggest that seven of the fifteen items in their job satisfaction questionnaire (freedom, responsibility, variety, opportunity to use one's abilities, recognition, promotion prospects, and attention to suggestions) constitute 'intrinsic' job satisfaction. Table 5.1 shows that these are comparatively highly rated by dealers. The lowest levels of job satisfaction in dealers were derived from what Warr, Cook and Wall (1979) term 'extrinsic' job factors (rate of pay, hours of work, job security, physical working conditions, industrial relations, and the way the firm is managed). Only in their satisfaction with 'the way the firm is managed' do the number of dissatisfied dealers outweigh the number satisfied. But with large minorities of dealers dissatisfied with the 'extrinsic' job factors it is these dimensions which Dealing Room managers and others in the financial sector must concentrate on if they wish to increase the overall job satisfaction of their staff.

Differences Between Various Groups

When various sub-groups of dealers were examined, it was found that the sample is quite homogeneous in terms of job satisfaction. We will draw attention to two differences we did find. Significantly poorer job satisfaction was found in dealers who have no children aged under 18 compared with dealers who do have such responsibilities (see Table 5.2). It may be that the latter group regard their life in general as more satisfying. In addition, these dealers may be able to utilise at work some behaviours similar to those they use at home with their partner and children, i.e. experiences at work and home support each other. This 'spillover' hypothesis (Glowinkowski and Cooper 1985) has been noted in Chapter 3.

Table 5.2 Job satisfaction – comparison of dealers who have/have not children under 18 years of age

Children under 18?	n	Mean score	Significant differences
Yes	71	74.59	
No	147	69.57	(p <0.008)

Staff working for US-owned organisations indicated the poorest job satisfaction of the three groups in the sample (dealers employed in UK-, US-, and European-owned institutions), and the differences, as shown in Table 5.3, are statistically significant. We will look further into differences among these dealers later in this book.

Table 5.3 Job satisfaction – comparison by ownership of bank

Ownership	n	Mean score	Significant differences
European	67	73.57	
British	65	73.00	
US	82	67.88	([a]p <0.008; [b]p <0.019)

Note: [a]compared with European-owned banks; [b] compared with UK-owned banks)

Drinking Habits

According to Baron (1986), nearly 10 million people in the US (more than 5 per cent of the total labour force) can be classified as alcoholic. Harvey and Brown (1988) report the total as nearer 20 million. Whatever the correct figure, alcoholism is a major concern in both the United States and the United Kingdom. There is an increasing trend among organisations to introduce methods of detecting potential and actual alcoholism among its employees.

As we noted in Chapter 1, the safe weekly alcohol limits for men and women are under 21 units and 14 units a week respectively, where a unit of alcohol is equivalent to a ½ pint of beer, or a glass of wine or spirits. Four questions were included in the questionnaires relating to alcohol consumption: first, whether the respondent drank alcohol; second, the units of alcohol consumed per week; third, whether drinkers had felt a recent need to cut down drinking; and fourth, their changes in drinking habits over the previous three months. Results of these four questions are shown in Table 5.4. They indicate that more dealers indulge in heavy drinking per (five day) week, i.e. 3 to 6 units, than the average for professionals. Forty-one per cent of dealers fall into the 'heavy' drinking category compared with the average for professionals of 8 per cent (OPCS, 1986). The average consumption of dealers is 20.81 units per week. In addition, 24 per cent report drinking at least *twice* as much alcohol as the generally-advised *maximum* weekly alcohol intake. A total of 37 per cent of dealers have felt the need to cut down on their drinking, but whether they have been successful or not is uncertain. As Table 5.4 shows, it appears that though 37 per cent have felt the need to cut down their drinking, only 16 per cent have managed to reduce their consumption. To indicate what may be prevalent attitudes to drinking in the Dealing Room, one dealer told us that: 'Maybe some dealers operate better with a few beers at lunch'.

Table 5.4 Drinking habits of dealers

	n	%
Drinkers		
Alcohol drinkers	203	91.4
Non-drinkers	19	8.6
Units of alcohol consumed per week by dealers		
1–14	89	42.8
15–25	86	33.6
30–95	33	23.6
Felt the need to cut down drinking?		
Yes	79	36.7
No	136	63.3
Changes in drinking habits over previous 3 months		
Drink more than usual	26	12.2
Drink the same as usual	152	71.4
Drink less than usual	35	16.4

When the drinking habits of male and female dealers are compared (Table 5.5), it is found that while almost all males drink (95 per cent), only 72 per cent of females are drinkers. A spot dealer told us: 'I notice there are more young women (dealers) drinking now'.

Of those who do drink, both male and female dealers consume, on average, the *maximum* 'sensible' limit. As would be expected, male dealers drink more then female dealers. (Because of the physical differences between the sexes, alcohol affects women more quickly than men. In men, between 55 per cent and 65 per cent of body weight is water, compared with 45 per cent to 55 per cent in women (Health Education Authority 1989). Consequently, similar alcohol intake is made more dilute in men.)

Table 5.5 Alcohol habits by sex of dealer

	Male	Female
Drinkers – number (and percentage)	177 (95.1%)	26 (72.2%)
Drinkers' consumption (average units per week)	21.93	14.00
Felt the need to cut down drinking – number (and percentage)	63 (34.8%)	16 (50.0%)
Changes in drinking habits over previous 3 months – number (and percentage)		
Drink more than usual	19 (10.6%)	7 (22.6%)
Drink the same as usual	130 (72.2%)	20 (64.5%)
Drink less than usual	31 (17.2%)	4 (12.9%)

Alcohol consumption by marital status and job responsibilities

Single dealers were found to drink significantly more alcohol than married dealers (Figure 5.2). Single dealers consist of more males, are younger, are more likely to be graduates, and have fewer responsibilities, all of which we found to be more associated with higher alcohol intake. Perhaps single dealers have a life-style more likely to be associated with opportunities, and the desire, to drink more alcohol.

Figure 5.2 also shows that dealers responsible for no other personnel at work drink significantly more alcohol per week than their colleagues who do have such responsibilities. This may be explained by the fact that those with such responsibilities have less opportunity and desire for alcohol intake. They may feel that they need to maintain a clear head in order to make (management) decisions, and also need to present generally more 'sober' behaviour.

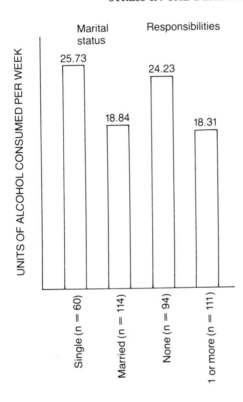

Figure 5.2 Alcohol consumption by marital status and responsibilities

Smoking Habits

Participation in cigarette smoking in the UK within the professional group of employees is approximately 17 per cent. In order to determine the smoking habits of dealers, we asked three questions. First, whether the respondent smoked; second, if so, the number of cigarettes (or equivalent) smoked; and third, changes in smoking habits over the previous three months. Results are shown in Table 5.6, and indicate that the group of dealers under examination consists of more smokers (27.2 per cent) than is typical for professionals. Of smokers, 62 per cent smoke more than 10 per day, and 26 per cent smoke more than 20 per day. The dealer who does smoke smokes on average 17.7 cigarettes per day. About equal numbers have increased and reduced the numbers of cigarettes smoked over the previous three months.

Table 5.6 Smoking habits of dealers

	n	%
Smokers		
Male	53	28.5
Female	8	22.2
Total	61	27.2
Non-smokers		
Male	133	71.5
Female	28	77.8
Total	161	72.8
Number of cigarettes (or equivalent) smoked by dealers per day		
1–5	13	22.4
6–10	9	15.5
11–15	8	13.8
16–20	13	22.4
21–30	9	15.5
31–60	6	10.3
Changes in smoking by dealers over previous 3 months		
Smoke more than usual	11	17.7
Smoke same as usual	41	66.1
Smoke less than usual	10	16.1

Hingley and Cooper (1986) point out that smoking rates had decreased between 1972 and the mid-1980s, leaving smokers in a minority in all social groups, at 38 per cent for men and 33 per cent for women. If dealers are regarded as professionals, then almost twice as many smoke as are found in other professional groups. If compared with the general population, however, the number of smokers is less than the average.

When we compare the smoking habits of male and female dealers, Table 5.6 shows that 29 per cent of men and 22 per cent of women are smokers. There appear to be fewer male dealers who smoke compared with the general population; the number of women dealers is too small for us to make any reliable assertions.

Mental Health

The mental health of dealers was measured by two sections of the questionnaire. Results from the Occupational Stress Indicator show that dealers have significantly poorer overall mental health compared with many other occupational groups. Figure 5.3 shows that dealers' overall mental health is poorer (significantly so) than middle and senior managers, management consultants, and Board Directors of major companies, and is even poorer (again significantly so) than blue-collar factory workers. Compared with the mean score of the 7,526 people who have completed this Indicator, dealers' overall mental health is about average. We can say then, that dealers are as mentally healthy as the general population.

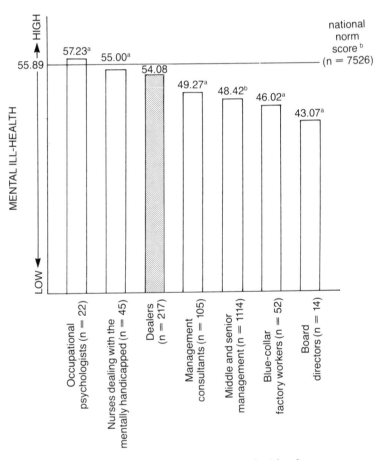

Figure 5.3 Dealers' mental health scores compared with other groups
Sources: [a] Cooper, Sloan and Williams (1989); [b] NFER-Nelson (1992)

While the OSI mental health questionnaire we used gives a general overview of the mental health of an individual, the second measure used to examine the mental health of dealers provides a more detailed analysis. The three measures of the Crown-Crisp Experiential Index (CCEI) used in the present study provide information about the free-floating anxiety (FFA), somatic anxiety (SOM), and depression (DEP) levels of dealers. Crown and Crisp (1979) describe free-floating anxiety as:

> evident in an individual who is afraid, but unlike normal fear, cannot discern the object which is the cause of that fear. It consists of dread, indefinable terror, tension without a cause or panic. The somatic concomitants of anxiety include breathlessness, headaches, and other aches and pains. Depression means sadness of mood, difficulty in thinking clearly, and slowing of actions and activity.

Crisp *et al.* (1978) have examined these three aspects of individual mental health in the general population. It is possible, therefore, to compare dealers with Crisp *et al.*'s (1978) data, which were collected from adults aged 20–69 registered with the sole group general practice in a small English town and its satellite villages. Results have also been provided for both sexes. Our results are shown in Table 5.7 and indicate that both male and female dealers express greater free-floating anxiety and depression, but less somatic anxiety, than the general population.

Table 5.7 Dealers' scores on three scales of the Crown-Crisp Experiential Index

	Males		Females	
Sub-scale	Dealers (n = 184)	General population* (n = 310–15)	Dealers (n = 36)	General population* (n = 339–60)
Free-floating anxiety	3.84	3.01	5.53	4.12
Somatic anxiety	3.20	3.98	4.03	4.86
Depression	2.98	2.63	4.00	3.77

*Source: Crisp et al. (1978)

Though female dealers' scores on the two mental health inventories suggest that they have poorer mental health than their male colleagues, this is not necessarily the case. Previous research (e.g. Crown and Crisp 1979; Taylor and Chave 1964) shows that while in general females completing these types of questionnaires indicate significantly poorer mental health, they do not necessarily exhibit the *objective* outcomes of mental ill-health. In other words, women tend to score higher on questionnaires assessing mental well-being, probably because they are more open to their feelings and symptoms than men.

A comparison of male and female scores on the three CCEI scales with scores presented in other studies is shown in Table 5.8. Male dealers' scores are compared with pilots (Sloan and Cooper 1986) and higher grade tax officers (Roden 1985). Female dealers' scores are compared with nurses (Hingley and Cooper 1986), word process operators (Cox 1984), and higher grade tax officers (Roden 1985). Dealers take up the middle position on all three scales.

Table 5.8 Comparison of male and female dealers' scores on three CCEI scales with other groups

Scale	Mean s.d.		Mean s.d.		Mean s.d.	
a) Male	Dealers		Tax officers[a]		Pilots[b]	
	(n=186)		(n=185)		(n=442)	
Free-floating anxiety	3.84	3.01	5.0	3.6	2.41	4.23
Somatic anxiety	3.20	2.64	3.8	3.3	2.31	1.91
Depression	2.98	2.56	4.0	3.0	2.55	2.24
b) Female	Dealers		Word process operators[c]		Tax officers[a]	
	(n=36)		(n=65)		(n=131)	
Free-floating anxiety	5.53	4.12	5.2	3.5	6.9	3.9
Somatic anxiety	4.03	2.77	3.7	2.3	4.2	3.0
Depression	4.00	2.81	3.3	2.6	4.9	3.0

Sources: [a]Roden (1985), [b]Sloan and Cooper (1986), [c]Cox (1984)

The commonly-held perception of dealers is that they are 'burnt-out' by the age of 35. Indeed, one Dealing Room manager told us:

> Dealers can lose the urge to make money for the company, and for themselves . . . to win, to beat their opponent, their ego, around 35.

Another said:

> I don't believe the 40 plusses have the appetite, are aggressive enough.

In contrast we were told by a forward deposits dealer that:

> It's a complete myth that you're finished at 35. There are many older chaps, but there might be some truth in it. The work has a mystique, barriers of language are built up, people *think* they can't do it.

A spot dealer agreed:

> You're not burnt out at 35, not in this bank. It's an attitude of mind. Fifty is a good retirement age, 35 is too young. It depends on the organisation, the pressure you're under. One dealer at this bank did go 'do-lally' . . . he was pensioned off.

A foreign exchange dealer, asked when dealers' performance might deteriorate said:

> Dealers' performance falls off because you're too clever to learn, or ageing, or conservative, or because skills change, or you've no more hunger or drive.

Older versus younger dealers and mental health.   To determine some of the facts, we compared younger and older dealers on the mental health scales. Since only four women are aged 35 or over, no comparisons were carried out for them on the three CCEI scales. Younger dealers (i.e. less than 35 years old) have *poorer* overall mental health than their older colleagues, as measured by the OSI (Table 5.9). Younger dealers also indicate *more* free-floating anxiety, and *less* somatic anxiety (Table 5.9), both of which are in agreement with data presented for the wider population by Crown and Crisp (1979). Thus, it appears that dealers are no more likely to show poorer mental health as they age than does the general population.

Table 5.9 Mental health scores of younger and older dealers

Age	Free-floating anxiety	Somatic anxiety	Depression	Mental health
	mean	mean	mean	mean
35 years and above	3.54[a]	3.48[a]	2.98[a]	52.74[c]
Less than 35 years	3.99[b]	3.06[b]	2.98[b]	54.54[d]

Note: [a]n = 60/61, [b]n = 124/125, [c]n = 65, [d]n = 151

Managers versus non-managerial dealers and mental health.
Dealers who have responsibilities for others in the Dealing Room
have poorer overall mental health than their colleagues (Table 5.10).
Within the CCEI scales, both male and female dealers with responsibilities indicate poorer free-floating and somatic anxiety scores
than their colleagues with no responsibilities for others. The responsibilities associated with the management and/or supervision of
Dealing Rooms results in more anxiety for the person in charge.
None of the differences in the mental scales was statistically significant, however.

Table 5.10 Mental health scores of dealers with and without
responsibilities for others

Number of people for whom responsible	Male dealers			Female dealers			Mental health
	FFA	SOM	DEP	FFA	SOM	DEP	
None	3.91[a]	3.22[a]	2.94[a]	6.22[b]	4.72[b]	4.00[b]	54.01[c]
1 or more	3.66[d]	3.12[d]	2.98[d]	4.83[e]	3.33[e]	4.00[e]	53.72[f]

Note: [a]n = 99 to 101; [b]n = 18; [c]n = 115; [d]n = 82; [e]n = 18; [f]n = 98

Promotion prospects. Those dealers who expect to wait longer for
promotion (two or more years) show poorer overall mental health
than their colleagues (Table 5.11). For male dealers, those who

expect to wait longer for promotion indicate significantly *more* free-floating anxiety and depression, and more somatic anxiety than their male colleagues. These results support those of Brook (1973), who suggests that under-promotion can result in minor psychological or major psychosomatic symptoms. However, for female dealers, those who expect to have to wait longer for promotion indicate *less* free-floating anxiety and somatic anxiety than their female colleagues, but, as with male dealers, are more depressed.

Table 5.11 Mental health scores of dealers by the length of time awaiting promotion

Expected promotion	Male dealers			Female dealers			Mental health
	FFA	SOM	DEP	FFA	SOM	DEP	
In 2 or more years	4.43[a]	3.53[a]	3.40[a]	4.59[b]	4.06[b]	4.35[b]	55.04[c]
In less than 2 years	3.42[d]	2.87[d]	2.58[d]	6.50[e]	4.17[e]	3.61[e]	52.92[f]

Note: [a]n = 73 to 74; [b]n = 18; [c]n = 90; [d]n = 99 to 100; [e]n = 18; [f]n = 114

Hours of work. The average number of hours spent by dealers at work is 47, and this figure was used to divide our sample of dealers into two groups. The first group (n = 147) consists of those people who spend 47 or more hours per week at work and/or in the office (though many dealers stated during the interviewing sessions that they also work at home, in their car, on the London underground, etc.). The second group (n = 66) is made up of those dealers who spend less than 47 hours per week working. The average hours worked by the two groups were 52.65 and 34.15 hours, respectively.

Those dealers who spend longer hours working indicate poorer mental health than their co-workers (Table 5.12). Male dealers who work longer hours show *poorer* mental health on all three of the mental health sub-scales than their male colleagues; however, female dealers who work longer hours show *better* free-floating and somatic anxiety than their female colleagues. None of the differences between the mental health scores, however, is statistically significant.

117

Table 5.12 Mental health scores of dealers by the number of hours at work

Number of hours at work	Male dealers			Female dealers			Mental health
	FFA	SOM	DEP	FFA	SOM	DEP	
47 or more	4.03[a]	3.31[a]	3.20[a]	5.32[b]	3.82[b]	4.00[b]	54.49[c]
Less than 47	3.48[d]	2.91[d]	2.53[d]	6.25[e]	4.75[e]	4.00[e]	52.66[f]

Note: [a]n = 121 to 123; [b]n = 28; [c]n = 147; [d]n = 58; [e]n = 8; [f]n = 64

Travelling to work. Those dealers who spend two or more hours travelling to and from work show poorer mental health on all the mental health scales, other than depression, than those dealers who spend less than two hours travelling (Table 5.13). The mean number of hours relevant to each group was 2.39 and 1.00, respectively.

Table 5.13 Mental health scores of dealers by the number of hours travelling to and from work

Number of hours travelling	Male dealers			Female dealers			Mental health
	FFA	SOM	DEP	FFA	SOM	DEP	
At least 2 hours	3.98[a]	3.17[a]	2.92[a]	5.89[b]	4.42[b]	3.95[b]	54.68[c]
Under 2 hours	3.48[d]	3.10[d]	3.00[d]	5.12[e]	3.59[e]	4.06[e]	52.49[f]

Note: [a]n = 118 to 120; [b]n = 19; [c]n = 134; [d]n = 62 to 63; [e]n = 17; [f]n = 79

National culture. When the mental health of dealers working in British-, US- and European-owned institutions was examined, those working in US-owned Dealing Rooms showed the poorest mental health on all scales (Table 5.14). Perhaps the reason was given by one spot dealer we interviewed:

> The Americans are a race of actors, everything's hyped up. They keep you on the boil all the time.

Another dealer working in a UK-owned bank told us:

Dealers working for US and Japanese banks get calls in the middle of the night. I don't want that.

Table 5.14 Mental health scores of dealers by ownership of institution

Ownership of institution	FFA	SOM	DEP	Mental health
British[a]	3.61	2.77	2.44	53.39
US[b]	4.44	3.62	3.60	56.16
European[c]	3.30	3.13	2.65	52.03

Note: [a]n = 61 to 66; [b]n = 63 to 80; [c]n = 55 to 66

Since the number of women working in the three types of institution (six in British, sixteen in US, and fourteen in European) was too few to permit valid analysis, examination of scores on the three CCEI scales was carried out for male dealers only. Overall mental health is poorest in US-owned Dealing Rooms, followed by British-owned, with the best scores found in European-owned Dealing Rooms. There are statistically significant differences between those dealers working in US-owned Dealing Rooms and both of the other two groups.

The same pattern (US poorest, British next, European best) is also shown in the CCEI free-floating anxiety sub-score. In the somatic anxiety and depression sub-scales, US dealers again display poorest scores, but European dealers are found in the middle range, with British dealers showing best scores. US dealers express significantly greater depression than their British and European colleagues.

COPING WITH STRESS

The methods used by an individual to cope with the daily pressures and stresses encountered in their work situation are major factors in determining the levels of stress experienced and the outcomes of this stress.

Dealers were asked in the questionnaire to rate thirty items in terms of the extent to which they had actually used them as ways of coping with stress in the previous three months. Scores for each item could range from 1 (never used) to 6 (very extensively used). Table 5.15 shows the mean scores for each of the thirty items in order of their use by dealers.

119

By far the two most popular methods of coping with stress were by 'dealing with the problems immediately as they occur', and 'having stable relationships'. Not only were the average scores of these two methods the highest recorded (at 4.38 and 4.37, respectively), but when we look at the scores of each of the thirty items in a different way, we get the same results. When the percentage of dealers who state that they used the thirty techniques either 'very extensively', 'extensively', or 'on balance' is examined, the same two methods are shown to be the most popular (at 86.6 per cent and 86.1 per cent respectively).

These two coping techniques are quite different. Since dealers are constantly faced with large amounts of information, and must of necessity make quick decisions, it would seem clear that they cannot allow themselves to carry problems around with them. They would soon suffer from what has been termed 'information overload'. The second coping technique most favoured by dealers implies that they recognise the need for co-operation with their colleagues at work.

Four other stress coping strategies scored an average of 4 or above – 'deliberately separate "home" and "work"', 'set priorities and deal with problems as they occur', 'try to deal with the situation objectively in an unemotional way', and 'try to "stand aside" and think through the situation'. The least common methods used by dealers to cope with stress are reported as 'resort to rules and regulations', and 'force one's behaviour and life-style to slow down' (with averages of 2.89 and 2.72 respectively). These two techniques were also used least frequently by dealers as shown by the third column in Table 5.15.

The results shown in Table 5.15 suggest that there may be a number of underlying patterns used by dealers to cope with occupational stress. We will look into these patterns in the next chapter. Here, we will compare the use made by dealers of six major stress coping methods with the use made of them by other occupational groups. These are the six methods (see Chapter 4) which have been isolated by Cooper, Sloan and Williams (1988) who describe them as follows:

Social support measures the degree to which individuals rely on others as a means of coping with stress . . . *task strategies* measures the way the individual copes with stress by reorganisation of work. These range from organisation in the micro-sense of tasks, but may also entail reliance upon organisational processes in the wider sense . . . *logic* involves the adoption of

Table 5.15 Stress coping strategies used by dealers in order of usage

Stress coping strategy	Mean score	% using coping strategy either 'very extensively', 'extensively', or 'on balance'
1 Deal with the problems immediately as they occur	4.38	86.6
2 Have stable relationships	4.37	86.1
3 Deliberately separate 'home' and 'work'	4.21	70.0
4 Set priorities and deal with problems accordingly	4.18	82.6
5 Try to deal with the situation objectively in an unemotional way	4.14	82.5
6 Try to 'stand aside' and think through the situation	4.08	80.3
7 Regular holidays	3.99	69.1
8 Try to recognise my own limitations	3.98	78.6
9 Having a home that is a refuge	3.97	69.6
10 Plan ahead	3.91	67.7
11 Seek support and advice from my superiors	3.90	74.1
12 Use selective attention (concentrating on specific problems)	3.86	70.7
13 Suppress emotions and try not to let the stress show	3.84	64.7
14 Effective time management	3.67	60.7

unemotional and rational approaches to the situation, and may involve the suppression of any feelings that might be expressed but will also involve actively trying to be objective . . . *home and work relationships* as a coping strategy may take various forms, from the existence of certain qualities in home life to what the individual does when at home . . . *time coping* recognises 'time management' as a valuable coping skill . . . and *involvement* involves the process of the individual sub-

Table 5.15 Continued

Stress coping strategy	Mean score	% using coping strategy either 'very extensively', 'extensively', or 'on balance'
15 Accept the situation and learn to live with it	3.65	66.1
16 Look for ways to make the work more interesting	3.63	62.1
17 Resort to hobbies and pastimes	3.60	55.4
18 Reorganise my work	3.59	57.6
18 Not 'bottling things up' and being able to release energy	3.59	57.3
18 Expand interests and activities outside work	3.59	54.9
21 Stay busy	3.56	57.1
22 Talk to understanding friends	3.55	56.5
23 Delegation	3.23	40.2
24 Coffee/smoking/drinking/drugs	3.20	48.2
25 Use distractions (to take my mind off things)	3.19	41.5
26 Seek as much social support as possible	3.14	36.6
27 Try to avoid the situation	3.01	32.6
28 'Buy time' and stall the issue	2.96	29.0
29 Force one's behaviour and life-style to slow down	2.89	27.2
30 Resort to rules and regulations	2.72	21.0

merging or committing themselves to the situation, i.e. coping by forcing themselves to come to terms with 'reality'.

(Cooper, Sloan and Williams 1988)

Table 5.16 shows that dealers make less use of all six coping strategies than does the normative population, as indicated by results from the large national database. This suggests that dealers either feel that they need to make less use of these methods of dealing with stress, or that they are unable to make use of them.

Table 5.16 Comparison of dealers' methods of coping with stress with other groups

Coping method	Dealers n = 225	Middle and senior Managers [a] n = 1114	Board Directors [b] n = 14	National norm score [a] n = 7526
Social support	14.97	14.65	13.57	15.17
Task strategies	23.84	25.72	25.07	25.39
Logic	12.06	12.65	12.71	12.45
Home and work relationships	15.35	14.41	14.64	15.43
Time	13.90	14.28	13.57	14.35
Involvement	22.22	23.03	22.79	23.22

Sources: [a]NFER-Nelson (1992); [b]Cooper, Sloan and Williams (1989)

Dealers also make less use of four of the six coping strategies than middle and senior managers, the exceptions being with social support and in their use of time management. Because of the nature of their job, dealers do not appear to be able to make effective use of time management techniques, nor, as far as we were able to determine, did they receive much, if any, training in utilising this important method of coping with stress. The interesting question is whether the coping methods dealers use are effective, a topic we will explore in the next chapter.

When we look in more detail at how sub-groups of dealers make use of the various coping strategies, we find that there are very few significant differences. Female dealers make more use of 'social support' than male dealers; dealers aged 35 years or above make more use of 'time management' than younger dealers; 'task strategies' are employed more by married dealers than by other marital groups; dealers responsible for others in the Dealing Room utilise more of both 'task strategies' and 'time' than those with no such responsibilities; and dealers in British-owned organisations make less use of 'social support' than their colleagues in European-owned institutions. We will discuss the implications of the differences which do exist in Chapter 7.

Sources of Stress in the Job

Following an analysis of the twenty-six interviews we carried out, and based on what we know about the sources of stress at work *in general*, we asked dealers to complete one inventory in the stress questionnaire which would determine how *dealers* rated the potential major work-related sources of stress in *their* job. We took the sixty-one-item questionnaire which forms part of the Occupational Stress Questionnaire (Cooper, Sloan and Williams 1988), and added to it twenty-six items which are particularly relevant to dealers, making a total of eighty-seven items. The questionnaire was entitled 'Sources of pressure in your job' and contains items related to both job and home.

Table 5.17 shows how dealers responded to this questionnaire. Each of the eighty-seven items is shown as listed in the questionnaire, with the average score each was given on the scale of 1 to 6, where 1 indicates no stress caused by the item and 6 indicates that the item is a very definite source of stress. The table is presented in descending order of the average scores assigned by dealers to each source of stress. The table also shows the percentage of dealers who rated the particular item as either 4, 5, or 6, that is, as 'generally, 'definitely', or 'very definitely' a source of stress.

Dealers report that the item which is most stressful to them is 'misreading the market'. This is by far the source of most stress for dealers, with a mean score of 4.46 compared with the second-most stressful item, 'having far too much work to do', which had a mean score of 3.96. A total of 73.8 per cent of dealers scored 'misreading the market' as at least a '4', while 'having far too much work to do' was rated at least a '4' by 63.6 per cent of dealers.

The effect of misreading the market was highlighted by one of our dealers:

> When you've got the right position and it's going your way there's no need to panic, you sit back and let it happen. When you're caught out it's not a nice feeling, you want to work all the harder to get it back, to cut losses and make a profit.

In examining Table 5.17, we can see that a number of the items seem to be related to each other. For instance, 'misreading the market', 'attaining my own personal levels of performance', 'having a run of financial losses', and 'implications of mistakes I make' all seem to indicate that the very basic work of the dealer, buying and selling, is a source of great stress. Similarly, 'having far too much to

Table 5.17 Sources of stress in the dealers' job

Source of stress in the job	Mean score	% Stressed*
Misreading the market	4.46	73.8
Having far too much work to do	3.96	63.6
Morale and organisational climate	3.86	60.0
Attaining my own personal levels of performance	3.80	61.5
Lack of consultation and communication	3.73	59.2
Pressure to perform at a high level	3.71	59.1
Having a run of financial losses	3.65	54.2
Implications of mistakes I make	3.62	55.5
Coping with office politics	3.60	45.3
Being undervalued	3.58	48.9
Having to work very long hours	3.56	51.1
Achieving my individual or group profit target	3.51	50.9
Coming second-best out of a transaction	3.50	51.1
Having a career path after my present job	3.50	48.9
Having to take risks	3.49	47.1
Making important decisions	3.42	47.5
Staff shortages and unsettling turnover rates	3.41	47.1
Inadequate feedback about my own performance	3.41	43.0
Characteristics of the organisation's structure and design	3.41	40.6
Lack of power and influence	3.39	43.7
Unclear promotion prospects	3.38	43.4
'Personality' clashes with others	3.37	42.1
Inadequate information sources	3.36	41.7
Factors not under my direct control	3.36	44.3
Inadequate guidance and back up from superiors	3.35	42.4
An absence of any potential career advancement	3.35	42.1
Not being able to 'switch off' at home	3.33	44.9
Opportunities for personal development	3.33	39.4
Demands that work makes on my private/social life	3.31	44.3

Table 5.17 Continued

Source of stress in the job	Mean score	% Stressed*
A lack of encouragement from superiors	3.28	39.1
Pursuing a career at the expense of home life	3.28	43.4
Concern about my future physical health	3.27	43.9
Covert discrimination and favouritism	3.26	37.3
Competing with colleagues	3.25	40.9
Keeping up with new techniques, ideas, technology or innovations or new challenges	3.19	39.7
Coping with large amounts and sources of information	3.19	39.1
Misuse of time by other people	3.18	36.2
Inadequate or poor quality of training/management development	3.17	35.1
Mundane administrative tasks or 'paperwork'	3.17	38.7
Demands my work makes on my relationships with my spouse/children	3.17	41.8
Personal beliefs conflicting with those of the organisation	3.16	33.5
Deterioration in my ability to be as effective	3.14	36.2
Dealing with ambiguous or 'delicate' situations	3.12	37.7
Colleagues' smoking	3.12	35.3
Inadequate knowledge of accounting, economics, etc.	3.11	34.4
The accumulative effects of minor tasks	3.09	33.9
Too warm an environment	3.09	34.5
The size of my financial risk	3.08	38.6
Threat of impending redundancy or early retirement	3.08	32.1
Seeing personal wealth fluctuating	3.08	35.2
Underpromotion – working at a level below my level of ability	3.07	37.8
Rate of pay (including perks and fringe benefits)	3.04	29.0
Too much noise	3.04	34.4
Changing jobs to progress with career	3.03	31.8
Conflicting job tasks and demands in the role I play	3.02	31.6

Table 5.17 Continued

Source of stress in the job	Mean score	% Stressed*
Competing with similar employees in other organisations	3.02	31.2
Changes in the way I am asked to do my job	3.02	28.6
Having to adopt a negative role (such as sacking someone)	3.02	34.8
Feeling isolated	2.99	34.2
Not fully understanding the work	2.98	34.4
Simply being 'visible' or 'available'	2.96	24.9
Attending meetings	2.95	28.0
Ambiguity in the nature of job role	2.94	25.4
Too much or too little variety in work	2.93	23.6
Sharing of work and responsibility evenly	2.93	20.5
Concern about the breakdown of the technological equipment	2.92	28.0
Inability to delegate	2.90	28.6
Getting the attention and support of colleagues	2.87	22.3
Ability to cope with current technologies	2.86	26.2
Insufficient finance or resources to work with	2.86	25.3
Absence of emotional support from others outside work	2.85	25.8
Decisions dominated by the technology (e.g. computer screen)	2.83	24.6
Managing or supervising the work of other people	2.74	28.1
Lack of practical support from others outside work	2.69	16.4
Doing work which most people do not understand	2.64	18.2
Not having enough work to do	2.63	25.4
Taking my work home	2.58	24.4
Absence of stability or dependability in home life	2.55	21.8
Lack of social support by people at work	2.52	9.3
Overpromotion – being promoted beyond my level of ability	2.50	21.0

Table 5.17 Continued

Source of stress in the job	Mean score	% Stressed*
My spouse's attitude towards my job and career	2.48	20.6
Business travel and having to live in hotels	2.42	15.8
Concern about my future mental health	2.38	16.4
Working at a job of which many people disapprove	2.34	13.5
Home life with a partner who is also pursuing a career	2.28	15.5
Simply being seen as a 'Boss'	2.27	9.1
Working with those of the opposite sex	2.02	6.3

Note: *This column indicates the percentage of respondents who find the item to be either 'generally', 'definitely', or 'very definitely' a source of stress; n = 218 to 225

do', 'morale and organisational climate', 'lack of consultation and communication', 'pressure to perform at a high level', 'coping with office politics', and 'being undervalued', suggest that the dealer is greatly stressed by the organisational culture and climate found in the Dealing Room, and by the management of their organisation.

As with the coping techniques, there appear to be underlying patterns in what dealers state are the sources of stress they encounter at work, and we will examine these more closely in Chapter 6. However, here we will compare the stress dealers report as caused by each of the six major sources of stress described in Chapter 3, with feedback from three other similar occupational groups (see Figure 5.4). As we noted in Chapter 4, we based our questionnaire measuring the dealer's sources of stress on the six major stress sources isolated by Cooper, Sloan and Williams (1988). These six sources are described as follows:

Factors intrinsic to the job . . . are those that originate in the fundamental nature of the job itself . . . the amount and scope of tasks, hours, variety, and so on. The *managerial role* . . . measures how individuals perceive the expectations that others have of them. *Relationships with other people* [concerns] contact with other people both inside and outside the organisation. Most important, however, are relationships with superiors. *Career and achievement* [notes that] . . . the need to achieve personal and corporate success can be a major source of satisfaction, or in terms of its blockage, a major stress . . . sources of organisational stress originate from *structural design and process features of the organisation,* though *climate* will embrace individual perceptions of both. One of the features that make managerial and professional work different from other jobs, is that there is a hazy *overlap between work and home.* This is a two-way relationship, with sources of stress at work affecting home life and vice-versa.

(Cooper, Sloan and Williams 1988)

At first sight, none of the figures for dealers appears to be particularly exceptional. Compared with the national OSI norms, dealers are less stressed in five of the six categories. When we compare dealers with both middle and senior managers and with Board Directors, we note that dealers are much more stressed in *all* of the categories. Comparing dealers with managers, we can see that dealers are much more stressed by 'relationships with others at work', by 'career and achievement', by the 'organisational structure and climate', and by the 'home/work interface'. Dealers appear to be about as stressed as middle managers in all six categories.

What Figure 5.4 tells us is that dealers report that they are much more stressed than are managers and Board Directors. Thus, it may be fair to suggest that dealers are more stressed than the people who manage them.

When we broke down the dealers into sub-groups, we found a number of significant differences in the way they responded to the questions about the sources of stress at work. Female dealers reported that they have more stress caused by 'relationships with other people', by 'career and achievement', and by the 'organisational structure and climate', than male dealers; dealers aged over 35 years are more stressed by 'career and achievement' than their younger colleagues; non-graduates are more stressed by the 'managerial role' than graduates; those dealers who had responsibility for others in the Dealing Room were more stressed by the 'managerial role', by 'relationships with other people', and by the 'organisational structure and climate'; those dealers who expected to have to wait at least two years for a promotion were more stressed by 'relationships with other people', and by the 'organisational struc-

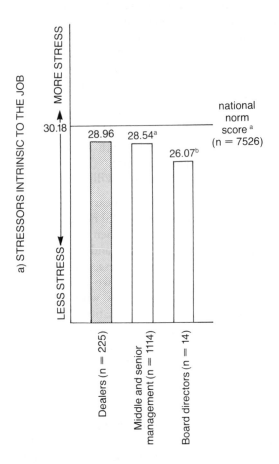

Figure 5.4 Comparison of dealers' reported sources of stress with two other groups
Sources: [a] NFER-Nelson (1992); [b] Cooper, Sloan and Williams (1989)

ture and climate'; dealers who spent at least two hours travelling per day were more stressed by 'factors intrinsic to the job'; and dealers who worked in US-owned institutions reported that they were more stressed by factors 'intrinsic to the job' and by 'career and achievement' than their counterparts in UK-owned Dealing Rooms. In fact, dealers in US-owned Dealing Rooms showed the most stress in four of the six major stress categories we examined.

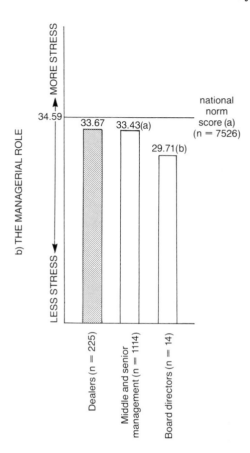

Figure 5.4 Continued

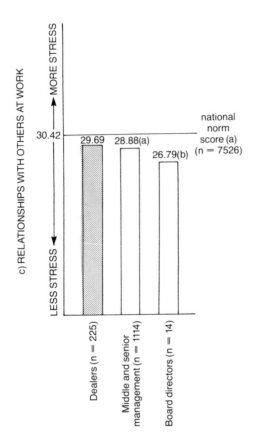

Figure 5.4 Continued

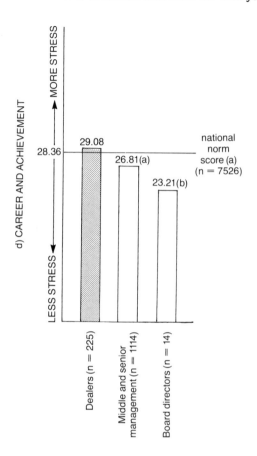

Figure 5.4 Continued

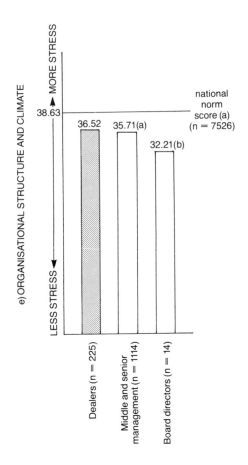

Figure 5.4 Continued

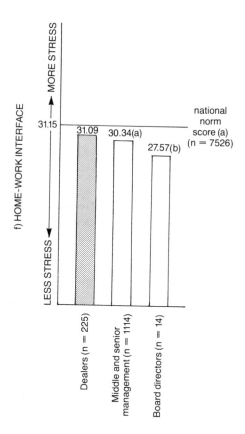

Figure 5.4 Continued

This analysis of the figures suggests that female dealers, dealers with managerial-type responsibilities, and dealers working in US-owned organisations may have major problems with stress. We will determine in the next chapter whether these differences result in health problems for the groups concerned.

6

SOURCES OF STRESS IN THE DEALING ROOM

The previous chapter examined how dealers react to the job of dealing in terms of the stress they report. The stresses in which we are particularly interested are dealers' mental ill-health, job dissatisfaction, and intake of alcohol. The aim of this chapter is to determine how much each of the items we have discussed (in Chapter 3) as *potential* causes of these stresses actually *do* result in stress. For example, it was suggested in Chapter 3 that, overall, people who believe that they are in control of their work life in particular, and their life in general (i.e. those who have internal locus of control), are more satisfied at work than those individuals who believe that other people, and uncontrollable events, determine their lives (i.e. those who have external locus of control). In Chapter 4 we noted that, as a group, dealers have external locus of control, and also that some sub-groups of dealers have particularly internally- or externally-oriented locus of control. The interesting question to be answered now is whether dealers' locus of control *contributes* to their stress (so that later we may suggest if and how their stress may be reduced).

Similarly, we have seen (in Chapter 5) that dealers report that they are very stressed by being required to perform their work at a high level, by having to attain appropriate levels of performance, and by striving to achieve their individual or group profit targets. But how does this stress show itself in dealers? Do they drink more, do they suffer from more job dissatisfaction, do they show poorer mental health? Or do these sources of stress actually reduce the stress outcomes mentioned (i.e. they can be defined as eustress), or have no effects, or other effects of which we are not aware? Was a forward deposits dealer correct in suggesting to us that: 'Hitting the right button can cause stress, and your colleagues overextending themselves'?

In this chapter, therefore, we will attempt to show what the causes of stress in dealers are. To do this, the statistical technique of multiple regression (or regression analysis) is used. Multiple regression is used to determine the relationships between the stress outcomes in which we are interested (that is, mental ill-health, free-floating anxiety, somatic anxiety, depression, job dissatisfaction, and units of alcohol drunk per week), and the potential sources and causes of these stress outcomes (such as locus of control, need to take risks, Type A behaviour, coping techniques used or not used, etc.).

Five of the potential causes of stress in dealers, namely, coronary-prone (Type A) behaviour, locus of control, extroversion, neuroticism, and lie, are represented for each dealer by single scores. So also are all the items of biographical data we obtained about dealers. This is not true, however, of two of the measures, namely Sources of Stress in the Job and Stress Coping Methods. Before carrying out regression analyses it is necessary to reduce the large number of variables (eighty-seven in the former case, and thirty in the latter) to a manageable number. This is done by using another statistical technique known as factor analysis. Factor analysis allows us to reduce large numbers of variables into a few factors. These factors will consist of variables which are strongly related to each other. It gives us a 'feel' for the major stressors experienced by dealers and the methods they use to cope with stress. We will present the factors we found, and then the results of the multiple regressions. In the next chapter, we will discuss our findings in more detail.

FACTOR ANALYSIS OF SOURCES OF STRESS IN THE JOB

Factor analysis of the eighty-seven variables which make up the measure Sources of Stress in the Job produced eleven factors. We have given these eleven factors (subjective) names for convenient reference. Table 6.1 shows the items which constitute each factor. Each item is from the section of the stress questionnaire entitled 'Sources of pressure in your job' (see Appendix 1). An interpretation of each of these factors is now discussed.

Role Conflict and Changes

The three variables which constitute this factor show that Dealing Room staff are stressed by the many changes caused by the rapid

Table 6.1 Factor analysis of sources of stress in the job

FACTOR 1: ROLE CONFLICTS AND CHANGES
   Conflicting job tasks and demands in the role I play
   Staff shortages and unsettling turnover rates
   Changes in the way I am asked to do my job

FACTOR 2: TAKING RISKS AND ACHIEVING HIGH
PERFORMANCE
   Pressure to perform at a high level
   Attaining my own personal levels of performance
   Making important decisions
   Having to take risks
   Implications of mistakes I make
   Achieving my individual or group profit target

FACTOR 3: POOR CAREER AND PROMOTION PROSPECTS
   Opportunities for personal development
   Having a career path after my present job
   An absence of any potential career advancement
   Underpromotion – working at a level below my level of ability
   Too much or too little variety in work
   Unclear promotion prospects
   Not having enough work to do
   Being undervalued

FACTOR 4: THE STRESS OF MANAGEMENT
   Overpromotion – being promoted beyond my level of ability
   Not fully understanding the work
   Inability to delegate
   Managing or supervising the work of other people
   Deterioration in my ability to be effective
   Working at a job of which many people disapprove
   Simply being seen as a 'Boss'

---

expansion of and developments in Dealing Rooms since 'Big Bang',
particularly the continuous recruitment of new staff, the departure
of unsuccessful or inadequate staff, or the loss of staff through
redundancy or quitting. It was noted earlier that Dealing Room staff
usually work in teams, and individual dealers are dependent upon

Table 6.1 Continued

FACTOR 5: SPENDING TIME ON UNPRODUCTIVE ACTIVITIES

The accumulative effects of minor tasks
Sharing of work and responsibility evenly
Mundane administrative tasks or 'paperwork'
Working with those of the opposite sex
Misuse of time by other people
Simply being 'visible' or 'available'

FACTOR 6: THE EFFECT OF WORK ON HOME LIFE

My spouse's attitude towards my job and career
Absence of emotional support from others outside work
Demands my work makes on my relationship with my spouse/children
Lack of practical support from others outside work
Absence of stability or dependability in home life
Demands that work makes on my private/social life
Not being able to 'switch off' at home
Pursuing a career at the expense of home life

FACTOR 7: PERFORMANCE SETBACKS

Having a run of financial losses
Coming second-best out of a transaction
Home life with a partner who is also pursuing a career
Misreading the market
The size of my financial risk
Insufficient finance or resources to work with

FACTOR 8: A POOR OFFICE ENVIRONMENT

Too warm an environment
Too much noise
Colleagues' smoking
Concern about my future physical health

the co-operation and support of their colleagues. Since 47.9 per cent of staff have been in their present job for two years or less (23.5 per cent for one year or less), it may be assumed that many dealing teams or groups have not yet achieved the necessary coherence, trust, skills, or self-confidence which individual dealers rely upon. A sterling

Table 6.1 Continued

FACTOR 9: TECHNOLOGICAL ASPECTS OF THE JOB

Decisions dominated by the technology (e.g. computer screen)

Keeping up with new techniques, ideas, technology or innovations or new challenges

Ability to cope with current technologies

Concern about the breakdown of the technological equipment

FACTOR 10: ORGANISATIONAL CULTURE AND CLIMATE

Characteristics of the organisation's structure and design

Personal beliefs conflicting with those of the organisation

Morale and organisational climate

Coping with office politics

FACTOR 11: LACK OF SUPPORT AND GUIDANCE FROM COLLEAGUES AND SUPERIORS

Competing with colleagues

Inadequate feedback about my own performance

Inadequate or poor quality of training/management development

Inadequate guidance and back up from superiors

A lack of encouragement from superiors

Lack of power and influence

Lack of consultation and communication

---

dealer told us: 'Stability is important. You need good support from employers. That compensates for less money than foreign exchange dealers get'.

Many managers made it clear that new staff are given some six months in which to prove themselves, and a number of organizations were relatively unsympathetic in their attitudes to dealers who have not achieved the required levels of competence. They were quietly 'let go'. The coming and going of staff also implies that dealers may well be asked to take on additional tasks, in the short term at least.

The variable 'changes in the way I am asked to do my job' is not thought to refer to changes in the technology-related aspects of the job (which are noted below) since, after the introduction of new computer-based dealing systems in 1986, the technology of dealing has, at the time of writing, remained relatively unchanged. Since this variable is grouped with 'staff shortages and unsettling turnover rates', it again appears to refer to the effects of staff changes. A total of 28.6 per cent of dealers found this first variable a source of stress, while 47.1 per cent were stressed by staff shortages and turnover, and 28.6 per cent by changes in the way they are asked to do their job.

The three variables in the factor may well be a source of our finding that dealers as a group feel significantly less in control of their work situation than the normative population. Indeed, 95 per cent of dealers examined scored higher (i.e. they show less control), than the average score of the general population.

Taking Risks and Achieving High Performance

This factor is concerned with the continual pressure dealers are under to perform their work at a high level (which 59.1 per cent of dealers report as stressful), and to meet the targets set for them by management or by themselves. Many dealers are required, either individually or within their work group (which could range from a small team to a total Dealing Room), to achieve an appropriate profit target. This appears to be the single most important work performance measure used by management to determine dealers' salaries, and dealers need to sustain a consistently high work performance in order to retain and progress within their job, and to maintain the high incomes to which they have become accustomed. Results show that 61.5 per cent of respondents are stressed by having to attain appropriate levels of performance, and 50.9 per cent by striving to achieve their individual or group profit target.

Three of the variables which make up this factor indicate the stress caused by taking risks and making important decisions (e.g. on the future performance of a currency or commodity), and concern about the potential effects of mistakes. Since these three items are contained within the same factor as the performance variables noted above, it suggests that dealers consider that an incorrect dealing decision may not only lose their employers and customers large sums of money, but also will result in failure to both themselves and their team. A potential bonus or salary increase may be affected, and continually making incorrect decisions may ultimately lead not only to a loss of face, but also to loss of job. A total of 47.5 per cent of dealers found making important decisions stressful, and 55.5 per cent are stressed by the implications of mistakes they may make. The basic activity of taking risks is regarded as a stressor by 47.1 per cent of dealers. The importance of success was underlined by a dealer:

> When you're successful you stand up and let everyone know – 'hurray, I read that one right', and slam the 'phone down. Even more experienced staff do that.

Another dealer was more philosophical:

> When you fail it results in strong language. A run of failure can get to you. It's inevitable, you can't make money all the time. It's a one day job, a new day is a new start.

And a spot dealer, talking about the attraction of dealing, told us:

> On the positive side, there's the thrill, the risk, who can make most money. It's an ego trip. On the negative side, it's things going wrong, not making the money you should. Two or three days of that and you try to find out what went wrong . . . and getting tied up by the computer. It's legalised gambling.

When the six variables in this factor are considered together, it is noticeable that high numbers of dealers find the basic functions and purposes of their job to be stressful. Three of these variables feature in the top ten sources of stress in the job reported by dealers (see Table 5.17). Dealers face these stressors each time they transact a deal (or decide not to) and, therefore, this factor may be regarded as a significant determinant of the stress outcomes (mental ill-health, job dissatisfaction, high alcohol intake) which are considered later.

Poor Career and Promotion Prospects

The eight variables in this factor are quite clearly interrelated. The overall impression given is of a group of dealers who feel that they are working at a level *below* their capabilities, and can see no potential for self-development and career development. This view is supported by comments made by both institutional executives and dealers. They said that most dealers have little opportunity to progress within their present organisations at a time when suitable alternative employment may be contracting. Despite this, 56.4 per cent of dealers expect (hope?) to be promoted within one year. So this conflict may be a major source of stress in dealers. A figure of 39.4 per cent of dealers are stressed by the (inadequate) opportunities available for self-development. Large numbers of dealers are stressed by their career prospects – 48.9 per cent with the (absence of) a career path beyond their present job, 42.1 per cent by an absence of any potential career advancement, 43.4 per cent by unclear promotion prospects, and 48.9 per cent by being undervalued (by their organisation). As we noted in Chapter 4, the chief executive of one organisation was concerned enough to request that some method of determining his staff's attitude to lack of promotion prospects was included in the study.

Two variables in the factor relate to the *amount* and *variety* of work which dealers perform. Since these variables are linked with the factor under review, it indicates that dealers perceive that the work they do does not prepare them for adequate career advancement and progression, that is, they feel that they are 'locked' into the job of dealing and have insufficient skills to offer their own and other employers. A total of 23.6 per cent of dealers are stressed by having too much or too little variety in their work, and 25.4 per cent by not having enough work to do. Dealers are certainly committed to their work. One dealer told us that his aims at work were: 'To make money for the bank, can't when it's quiet, so prefer when it's busy. It's hard work when it's busy'.

The factor may explain the policy of job titles adopted by (particularly US-owned) institutions for staff – Executive, Director, Senior, etc. were titles given to staff at comparatively low levels of seniority in organisations with very flat personnel structures. This may be a method used to motivate staff who feel trapped in jobs.

The Stress of Management

This factor relates to those dealers who are stressed by their inability to carry out their job effectively. A number of dealers expressed their feelings during interviews: many felt that they did not have sufficient background in relevant business operations to enable them to appreciate the wider aspects of the job – 34.4 per cent of dealers are stressed by their 'inadequate knowledge of accounting, economics, etc.'. Similarly, 34.4 per cent of dealers are stressed by 'not fully understanding the work', and 21 per cent by being promoted beyond their level of ability.

Dealers responsible for the work of other people, and who may be in 'promoted' posts, are significantly more stressed by the Managerial Role than dealers who have no such personnel responsibilities (see Chapter 5). So this factor may be especially relevant to those dealers working in a 'promoted' post, and who have the additional task of 'managing or supervising the work of other people'. Dealers working in promoted posts also find 'Relationships with Other People' significantly more stressful than other dealers, and 'inability to delegate' may be one example of the causes of this stress. A figure of 28.6 per cent of dealers found this 'inability' stressful; 28.1 per cent state that managing or supervising the work of other people is stressful; and 9.1 per cent are stressed by their role as 'boss'. One dealer remarked that: 'The industry doesn't produce good managers'.

The stressor 'deterioration in my ability to be effective' is interpreted, not as relating to negative changes in the personality or mental or physical abilities of individual dealers (only 5.8 per cent of dealers believed that their performance at work had deteriorated over the preceding six months), but to the effects of working in a 'management' position, and 'simply being seen as a "Boss"'. A total of 36.2 per cent of dealers found this a stressor.

The item 'working at a job of which many people disapprove' was included in the stress inventory to reflect the moral and ethical attitudes which many of those outside the City have to dealing. However, its inclusion in this factor suggests that few dealers regard it as a questionable activity (only 13.5 per cent are stressed by the item) and 'the job' referred to in the questionnaire item may have been interpreted by dealers as meaning the job of 'Boss'.

In summary, the factor suggests the concerns of dealers who, for various reasons, e.g. lack of resources, inadequate training, poor interpersonal skills, and poor job design, are unable to carry out their job adequately. This group will tend to be dealers in supervisory posts.

Spending Time on Unproductive Activities

This factor encompasses the stress relating to what dealers regard as trivial but necessary tasks in the Dealing Room, and to the fair distribution of these tasks and of work and responsibility in general across the Dealing Room workforce. For instance, dealers are required to spend some time completing the paperwork associated with their job, and it was noted during the period we observed Dealing Room practices that this task is often left until the last part of the daily schedule, when the dealer has ceased to trade. If the day was busy, and the dealer continually trading, paperwork was left to accumulate. A total of 33.9 per cent of dealers found that the accumulative effects of minor tasks were stressful, and 38.7 per cent say the same of the administrative tasks or 'paperwork' they have to do.

As we have pointed out, dealers tend to work in groups and to be dependent upon other members of the group for information and support. During our interviews, many dealers made it clear that they did not believe that the workload was shared fairly across the group in which they were working, and this is reflected by the item 'sharing of work and responsibility evenly', regarded as stressful by 20.5 per cent of dealers. The item 'misuse of time by other people' is stressful to 36.2 per cent of dealers, and is probably associated with the belief in the unfair distribution of work, and/or with the administrative tasks which have to be completed.

The inclusion of the stressor 'working with those of the opposite sex' may be explained within the context of the factor in a number of ways. Members of the opposite sex may be regarded by both male and female dealers as not accepting their fair share of work, as being the cause of additional work, or of 'distracting' dealers from their main job function. This item was the least important source of job-related stress in the eighty-seven-item inventory, with only 6.3 per cent of dealers regarding it as stressful.

The final item within the factor, 'simply being "visible" or "available"', may refer to the requirement that the dealer should be resident at his or her workstation for long periods of time, even when no trading is being carried out, to answer queries from colleagues or from potential customers, or because of management requirements. A figure of 24.9 per cent of dealers found this stressful.

The overall view of this factor is of the stress caused by the amount of time spent in tasks regarded by dealers as only indirectly related to the job of dealing.

The Effect of Work on Home Life

This factor refers to the relationships between work and life outside the Dealing Room. Of dealers questioned, 66.8 per cent are married/co-habiting, but there is no reason to believe that this factor does not apply equally to other dealers. It suggests the inadequacy of emotional support from outside the workplace, whether from a spouse or partner, or from other people. A figure of 25 per cent of dealers are stressed by 'absence of emotional support from others outside work', and 16.4 per cent by 'lack of practical support from others outside work'.

The amount of time dealers spend weekly at work (47.08 hours), and travelling to and from work (9.39 hours), will reduce the amount of time dealers are able to spend with family or friends, and a number of dealers interviewed pointed out that their work leaves them mentally and emotionally, if not also physically, exhausted, and this is reflected in their behaviour at home. One dealer said:

> People can go home tired and that affects relationships. Your attention span is abysmal, and it affects relationships and performance.

A foreign exchange trader suggested:

> Foreign exchange dealers are younger, so there's more marriage breakdown, and they get their money in more quickly – they're burnt out at 45ish. After a bad day you get home late or go out drinking.

A spot dealer was more specific:

> Some dealers treat their families the same way they behave in the Dealing Room. One reason for some divorces is the aggressive attitudes of dealers at home. A few of my colleagues find it difficult to talk to their wives in a civilised manner. Quite a few of them take work home with them, and spend a few hours every evening following the market. That doesn't help family life.

And a Dealing Room manager told us:

> Dealing becomes a part of you, it's carried around with you. Attitudes change to black and white. You behave the same when buying a house or shopping. Dealing becomes an obsession.

These comments may explain our findings about dealers' family lives. A total of 20.6 per cent of dealers are stressed by their spouse's attitude towards their job and career; 41.8 per cent by the demands their work makes on their relationships with their spouse and children; 21.8 per cent by 'the absence of stability or dependability in home life'; 44.3 per cent by the demands that their work makes on their private and social life; and 43.4 per cent by having to pursue a career at the expense of their home life.

In addition, the attitude of many people to those working in Dealing Rooms is reported to be one of distaste, jealousy, and even of overt hostility (Reid 1988). Thus, dealers may gain little support from 'ordinary' members of the public, and find it more suitable to spend what leisure time they have available with other dealers and with colleagues in similar employment. This is reinforced by comments such as that made by one dealer: 'When I get home I've said all I want to'.

On the other hand, many dealers pointed out that they behaved at home in the same way as they did in the Dealing Room. This may explain why 44.9 per cent of dealers are stressed by not being able to 'switch off' at home. One foreign exchange dealer commented to us:

> At home I think about the events of the day . . . next time I'll do this or that and better myself. Foreign exchange *brokers* have problems at home, they're under more pressure. They're expected to entertain. I couldn't handle it. You're expected to be out buying lunch or drinks.

Performance Setbacks

Among the six variables constituting this factor are two of the top ten sources of stress in the job. 'Misreading the market' is regarded as a source of stress at work by 73.8 per cent of dealers, and 'having a run of financial losses' by 54.2 per cent. The former variable is by far the most stressful work-related item noted by dealers, with a mean of 4.46 on a range of 1 (low) to 6 (high), compared with the mean of 3.96 of the second most stressful item.

The factor is concerned with the causes and effects, particularly those which are financially-related, of dealers failing to achieve their targets. 'Misreading the market' refers to dealers misinterpreting the price trend of the commodity in which they are trading, e.g. expecting the £/$ rate to strengthen, and acting upon that belief, when the reverse turns out to be true. As a result of this, financial losses are incurred by the dealer, and 'having a run of financial losses' was noted by many dealers interviewed as the most distressing and negative aspect of their job. The variable 'coming second-best out of a transaction', regarded by 51.1 per cent of dealers as a stressor, appears to be related to the previous two items, and also refers to the competition which dealers are in when seeking to close a transaction. Soon after a trade is made a dealer will often know, through the computer system used, whether a better selling or buying price could have been quoted to a customer. The importance of these three items is shown by the number of dealers stressed by each.

Two items in the factor are concerned with the amount of finance which the dealer has available to trade, or the extent to which these finances may have been committed. The larger the financial risk the dealer is permitted to take by his or her organisation, the more profit (and loss) can be made. One foreign exchange dealer pointed out that: 'Running bigger positions may cause stress, that is, you have a bigger exposure, you can win or lose more, the risk is larger'.

A total of 38.6 per cent of dealers are stressed by the size of the risks they take. A number of institutions promote and progress staff by allowing them to deal in larger amounts. When setbacks occur, as they inevitably do, dealers who are more financially extended will lose more money. Though many dealers told us during interviews that they would welcome more finance to trade with, and 25.3 per cent are stressed by 'insufficient finance or resources to work with', it can be a mixed blessing.

At first sight, it may not be immediately clear how the final item in the factor is related to the others. It suggests that having a 'home life with a partner who is also pursuing a career' is regarded by dealers as a potential source of stress in the same way as the setbacks and financial limitations noted above. It may indicate that having such a partner makes setbacks more stressful. Perhaps having such a partner exacerbates the problems dealers face. Perhaps there is 'competition' at home and elsewhere between the partners.

With large numbers of dealers perceiving the items in this factor as stressful, it is clear that it will feature as a major source of the stress outcomes being examined.

It should be noted that this factor is essentially different to the factor 'Taking Risks and Achieving High Performance', which is concerned with intrinsic aspects of the dealer's job.

A Poor Office Environment

From the observations we made during visits to the participating institutions, it is clear that the environment of modern Dealing Rooms is dominated by the computer screen, by the noise of dealers using the multiple telephones at their workplace and calling across benches to their colleagues, and by the loudspeaker systems which link dealers to brokers. While modern Dealing Rooms tend to be air-conditioned, it was noticeable that most male dealers sat at their desks jacketless and in shirtsleeves, while women were dressed in lightweight clothes. Computer equipment produces an appreciable amount of heat, and 34.5 per cent of dealers find the office 'too warm an environment', while 34.4 per cent find 'too much noise' in the office. This latter concern is not surprising since making oneself heard (by colleagues, clients) is essential to dealers. The large open-plan Dealing Rooms produce an unpleasant cacophony of sound during much of the working day.

Smoking tended to be permitted in all the Dealing Rooms we saw, and 35.3 per cent of respondents state that 'colleagues smoking' is a source of stress. Assuming that few of the 17.7 per cent of active smokers (see Chapter 4) will be included in such a statistic, it suggests that about 47 per cent of the 163 *non-smokers* are distressed by their colleagues' smoking. This is reflected by statements made by many dealers during interviews, and a number of respondents added unsolicited comments to our study questionnaire suggesting that smoking should be prohibited in Dealing Rooms.

Overall, the factor implies that the work environment of dealers is a source of stress. Staw (1984) concludes that there is clear evidence of a positive relationship between stress and physical factors such as noise, extreme temperatures, and pollution, and that this stress is in turn related to reduced performance.

The item 'concern about my future physical health', which is also a constituent of the factor, is regarded as a stressor by 43.9 per cent of dealers (and compares with the 16.4 per cent who regard concern for their future *mental* health as a stressor). The noise, the heat, and colleagues' smoking makes many dealers apprehensive about their future *physical* health. Nevertheless, one forward deposits dealer told us, when we asked him whether he and his colleagues were concerned about their health: 'Look, we're just ordinary chaps. Lots of the time we have fun. It's not like work, you never have to carry a briefcase'.

Technological Aspects of the Job

This factor consists of four variables. A total of 39.7 per cent of dealers consider that 'keeping up with new techniques, ideas, technology or innovations or new challenges' is a work stressor. Since the three other variables within the factor ('ability to cope with current technologies', seen as a source of stress by 26.2 per cent, 'decisions dominated by the technology (e.g. computer screen)', regarded as a stressor by 24.6 per cent of dealers, and 'concern about the breakdown of the technological equipment', noted as a stressor by 28 per cent) also relate to the technology of the Dealing Room, it seems reasonable to suggest that the first variable relates particularly to the computer technology found in the Dealing Room.

When we interviewed dealers we did not find them to be particularly concerned with the technologies used in Dealing Rooms, though they may not have been willing to admit to us that there were difficulties. One dealer did tell us: 'When the computer breaks down and you can't get into the telephones, there's a lot of screaming and shouting'.

Attitudes may have been affected by the quality of job training they received, which was generally regarded by dealers as inadequate, and by the frequent breakdowns in the technology. On the very first day of 'Big Bang' the technology failed. Discussing Dealing Room technology, Willcocks and Mason (1987) note that: 'the best publicised technological blunder of the mid-1980's turned out to be the result of a massive underestimation of the volume and timing of computer usage'.

The decisions dealers make are mostly dependent upon the figures which are displayed on their computer screens. Dealers interviewed noted the frustration caused by any failure of the technology, whether SEAQ, Reuters, Telerate, Quotron, the telephone system, or their own personal computer. A spot dealer said: 'The motivation is to make money. It's like betting on the horses. You see the rewards quicker, there's more satisfaction of seeing results immediately'.

Dealers may also be aware of the changes which will be made to the technology. As early as 1987 it was reported that:

Three quarters of City firms will scrap their dealing room technology within the next two years . . . despite the fact that over half installed their systems within the last 12 months . . . 38 per cent and 36 per cent respectively expect to install artificial intelligence and expert systems.

(*Computer Weekly*, 22 October 1987)

and:

The lifespan of existing (computer) systems is likely to be significantly shorter than in other industries, simply because many City institutions made disastrous acquisitions in the first place.

(*Computing*, 27 October 1988)

The factor implies that dealers are stressed by using the technology, by changes in the technology, by its continual breakdown, and by the increasing way it dominates their work:

The markets are driven by the institutions, and the institutions are moving towards being driven by machines.

(Chapman 1988)

Organisational Culture and Climate

Two of the four items which make up this factor are among the ten most stressful work-related items reported by dealers. 'Morale and organisational climate' is listed as the third most severe stressor, perceived as such by 60 per cent of respondents, while for the item 'coping with office politics', which is tenth in the list, the equivalent figure is 45.3 per cent.

Dealers work within institutions over which they have little control and negligible ability to change, and the factor overall suggests their dissatisfaction with such areas as management structure and control, weak lines of reporting and responsibility, centralisation and decentralisation, etc. This is seen as the interpretation of the item 'characteristics of the organisation's structure and design', a stressor to 40.6 per cent of dealers. This variable will implicitly include the stress caused by dealers' lack of participation in decision-making, little opportunity for advancement, too much formalisation of working practices, too high a degree of specialisation, interdependence of departments, and line and staff conflicts. These have been shown by Brief, Schuler and Van Sell (1981) to be sources of stress in many organisations.

Related to the item above is a second variable found within the factor, namely, 'morale and organisational climate'. By 'morale' we mean: 'a group phenomenon involving extra effort, goal communality, commitment, and feelings of belonging. Groups have some degree of morale, whereas individuals have some degree of motivation (and satisfaction)' (Robbins 1987).

The variable concerning 'office politics' is a well-known potential source of stress, particularly in managers (Cooper and Makin 1984).

These three variables appear to be very similar to one of the major categories isolated in Chapter 3 as a source of stress at work, and variously labelled 'organisational structure and climate' or 'organisational climate and culture'.

Dissatisfaction with organisational culture and climate is clearly evident in the fourth item within the factor – 'personal beliefs conflicting with those of the organisation'. This could be taken to refer to the individual dealer's moral and ethical objections to activities which are carried out in the Dealing Room, but which nevertheless provide the employee with overall job satisfaction. In the context of the factor, however, the item is taken to refer to the dealers' belief that they could do things better than the organisation allows. During interviews we found no evidence that dealers were concerned about ethical or moral conflicts at work.

Overall, the factor alludes to stress resulting from working within a rigid, relatively authoritarian and non-participative organisation. Because of the numbers of dealers reporting stress in three of the variables constituting the factor, it would be expected to feature as a predictor of the manifestations of stress among dealers. For some dealers, however, the organisation was almost irrelevant to the job, as a spot dealer told us: 'I'd say most dealers are committed to dealing, not to the organisation. Once a dealer, always a dealer'.

The logo of the Forex Association London (of foreign exchange dealers) shows a globe, with a telephone within, and the legend 'Once a Dealer, Always a Dealer'.

Lack of Support and Guidance from Colleagues and Superiors

While the variables in Factor 10 are concerned with dealers' attitudes to the organisation as a whole, the items which make up Factor 11 are concerned with interpersonal relationships, and communication and feedback within the organisation.

Two of the seven items within the factor refer directly to relationships with supervisors. A total of 42.4 per cent of dealers are stressed by 'inadequate guidance and back up from superiors' and 39.1 per cent by 'a lack of encouragement from superiors', and it is implied in one other item, 'inadequate feedback about my own performance', a source of stress to 43 per cent of dealers. One dealer pointed out, about the job in general: 'Negative aspects are some people; bosses screaming occasionally'.

It seems reasonable to suggest that dealers have a high need for achievement, since dealers prefer the kind of activities, such as dealing, 'which provide immediate and precise feedback information on how they are progressing towards a goal' (Luthans 1989). (Interestingly, if dealers are high-need achievers, then research (e.g. Luthans

1989) suggests that they tend to be moderate risk takers, which may have implications for their job as dealers.) While dealers can often receive immediate feedback from their screen on whether their judgement concerning a deal was correct or not (which was seen by many dealers interviewed as a major attraction of the job), it appears that dealers do not receive sufficient feedback from their managers on specific performance criteria. Lack of feedback in this sense has been shown to be a work stressor (Brief, Schuler and Van Sell 1981).

Dealers may desire performance feedback from supervisors in order to improve their management skills, and this type of feedback may be seen to be a form of personnel training, which many dealers found to be poor or non-existent within their organisations. Similarly, dealers who are not provided with performance feedback will probably feel that they have little chance or opportunity to influence their managers.

Three other items within the factor are also related to poor practices by dealers' managers and supervisors, namley, 'inadequate or poor quality of training/management development', a stressor to 35.1 per cent of dealers, 'lack of power and influence', a stressor to 43.7 per cent of dealers, and 'lack of consultation and communication', a stressor to 59.2 per cent of dealers. These three items indicate the stress caused by the failure of supervisors to communicate adequately with their subordinates. Dealers interviewed noted few opportunities for participation. Margolis *et al.* (1974) found lack of participation at work to be a significant predictor of job-related stress.

A final item in the factor is 'competing with colleagues', which 40.9 per cent of dealers found a stressor. This item has been shown to fall into the general stress category of interpersonal relationships, along with 'inconsiderate or inequitable supervisors' (Brief, Schuler and Van Sell 1981). Dealers interviewed indicated that they compete hard with each other to achieve the greatest individual success, whether measured on a single transaction basis or on a weekly or monthly scale, to achieve the largest bonus, to obtain the business of a particular customer, or to work in a desirable commodity, e.g. the US dollar or the German mark are regarded as more 'prestigious' currencies to trade in than, for instance, the Mexican peso or Irish punt.

Overall, the factor suggests the stress caused by relationships with others at work. One stocks and bonds dealer told us:

On the negative side you're dealing with people who've got big egos. Stress is caused by continually losing money, and when you can't control events, and when other people let you down.

One Dealing Room manager was adamant that he knew why his staff were attracted to dealing:

There's glamour for new entrants. It's exciting, your adrenalin surges. There's the financial aspects. You get immediate results. There's a good working environment. There's a juvenile sense of fun. It's not a formalised workday. There's flexibility, lack of formality in the job.

A dealer in a comparatively small Dealing Room said:

Dealing is exciting, there's no in-tray or out-tray. It's not 9 to 5. You're responsible for your errors. In London, the Money Markets have the big money. Job satisfaction is reading a Market, and putting one over on jobbers. It's exciting. You get a buzz when clients come back, when you get the upper hand.

However, because of the high percentage of dealers expressing dissatisfaction with all the variables comprising this factor, it would be expected to feature strongly among the determinants of the stress outcomes.

FACTOR ANALYSIS OF STRESS COPING METHODS

Having completed factor analysis of sources of stress in the job, we can turn to the set of variables which indicates the stress coping methods used by dealers. Factor analysis of twenty-eight of the variables constituting the questionnaire inventory 'How you cope with stress you experience' produced five factors. The five factors are shown in Table 6.2. They reflect the general patterns of coping used by dealers in managing the stress in their lives.

Prioritise and Plan Work

We saw earlier that 'Having far too much work to do' is regarded as a major stressor by dealers, and the item is quoted as the second greatest source of work-related stress. This 'coping factor' suggests ways in which the dealer attempts to cope with the problem of having too much work to do. Five of the six items which make up

Table 6.2 Factor analysis of stress coping methods

FACTOR 1: PRIORITISE AND PLAN WORK
   Effective time management
   Plan ahead
   Delegation
   Try to 'stand aside' and think through the situation
   Set priorities and deal with problems accordingly
   Reorganise my work

FACTOR 2: USE ACTIVITIES AND FRIENDS OUTSIDE WORK
   Expand interests and activities outside work
   Resort to hobbies and pastimes
   Use distractions (to take my mind off things)
   Seek as much social support as possible
   Talk to understanding friends

FACTOR 3: KEEP THE SITUATION AT ARM'S LENGTH
   Try to avoid the situation
   Resort to rules and regulations

FACTOR 4: HAVE A SUPPORTIVE HOME LIFE
   Having a home that is a refuge
   Having stable relationships
   Deliberately separate 'home' and 'work'

FACTOR 5: USE OBJECTIVE AND UNEMOTIONAL
BEHAVIOUR
   Suppress emotions and try not to let the stress show
   Try to deal with the situation objectively in an unemotional way

---

the factor suggest an attempt by dealers to achieve efficient management of the time available to carry out their tasks. 'Effective time management' is used as a coping technique by 60.7 per cent of dealers; 'plan ahead' by 67.7 per cent; 'try to "stand aside" and think through the situation' by 27.4 per cent; 'set priorities and deal with problems accordingly' by 82.6 per cent; and 'reorganise my work' by 57.6 per cent of dealers.

The final variable, 'delegation', would appear to be particularly related to supervisors and managers in the Dealing Room. The 'ordinary' dealer's main activity is trading and coping with the related activities as they occur, while managers and supervisors have additional tasks to perform, and have the opportunity to delegate work which is denied to their subordinates. A figure of 40.2 per cent of dealers use this technique as a stress coping method.

Use Activities and Friends Outside Work

The importance to dealers of using activities outside work as a means of coping with job-related stress is reflected in this factor. A total of 54.9 per cent of dealers note that they 'expand interests and activities outside work', and 55.4 per cent 'resort to hobbies and pastimes'. These statistics support the figures noted in Chapter 4, that 90.2 per cent of dealers have an interest or hobby, and that 96.6 per cent of these hobbies are unrelated to work.

'Distractions' may be used in the workplace, but when we visited Dealing Rooms we saw that dealers tended to have little time to relax other than by reading a newspaper, attempting a crossword, or (occasionally) assembling paper aeroplanes. Thus, the use of distractions, by 41.5 per cent of dealers, may be an activity carried on by dealers outside the workplace.

The two items 'seek as much social support as possible', used to cope with stress by 36.6 per cent of dealers, and 'talk to understanding friends', by 56.5 per cent, suggest similar techniques for coping with stress. It confirms the point made earlier in Chapter 3, that social support is both a source of stress and a method of coping with stress. Overall, the factor can be seen in conjunction with Factor 6 of Sources of Stress in the Job ('The Effect of Work on Home Life'), which implies that dealers may not receive the support they need to cope. There is a possibility of conflict between the two factors, which we will explore later.

Keep the Situation at Arm's Length

There are two items within this factor. The main thrust of the factor appears to be the ways in which dealers try to *avoid* having to deal with problems, and this contrasts with 'coping factor 1' above, which suggests that dealers actively seek ways to *solve* the problems they encounter at work. Neither item in coping factor 3 features among the more important stress coping strategies used: 'try to avoid the situation' is used by 32.6 per cent, and 'resort to rules and regulations' by 21 per cent of dealers, and these are among the five least-used coping techniques. The latter item may be taken as more applicable to supervisors and managers in their relations with colleagues, rather than related to the rules and regulations associated with dealing and trading.

Have a Supportive Home Life

In contrast with 'coping factor 2' above, which is concerned with using leisure activities and social support outside the workplace to cope with stress, the three items within this factor suggest the specific use of home life as a coping method. This 'coping factor' is similar to one described by Cooper, Sloan and Williams (1988) as a coping method which 'may take various forms from the existence of certain qualities in home life to what the individual does when they are there'.

'Having a home that is a refuge' is a stress coping mechanism adopted by 69.6 per cent of dealers, which indicates the importance placed upon home life whatever the marital status or way of life of the individual. 'Having stable relationships' (which could be within or outside work) is used by 86.1 per cent of dealers.

The remaining variable within the factor suggests that dealers attempt to keep their lives at work and home quite separate, and not to allow the stresses experienced in one to spill over to the other. Deliberately separating home life from work is used by 70 per cent of dealers.

The potential difficulties faced by dealers in using home life as a method of coping with work stress are illustrated by the fact that the home/work interface (see Factor 6 of Sources of Stress in the Job) is itself a potential stressor.

Use Objective and Unemotional Behaviour

This factor contains two items. A figure of 64.7 per cent of dealers 'suppress emotions and try not to let the stress show', and 82.5 per cent of dealers 'try to deal with the situation objectively in an unemotional way'.

However, the two variables within the factor contrast with some of the behaviours exhibited by dealers within the Dealing Room. We heard much shouting and saw a great deal of gesticulating in the

Dealing Room when matters were going well (e.g. closing a business deal or predicting events correctly), or badly (e.g. sustaining losses, making poor decisions). One dealer told us that:

> Some people release tension on the job – they're very demonstrable, shout at the screen.

A forward deposits dealer commented:

> There's no violence in the Room, but I've seen tears, especially in October 1987 [the Stock Market crash].

Dealers interviewed noted these as common features of a dealer's behaviour, and an individual dealer can swing from one behavioural state to another in a short space of time. It is suspected that these changes in a dealer's behaviour also occur outside of the office environment, which may not be conducive to the maintenance of supportive relationships at home or within the dealer's social circles.

When we asked a forward deposits dealer how he coped with the many information sources, he told us:

> You need to disseminate, to be selective. With experience it's very easy to hear what you need to, to close off what you don't, like an aircraft controller. You may have your own sources of information, and colleagues asking for prices, and calls from brokers, so you establish a pecking order. You can't be trained. You must remain calm, not become frustrated. That's the key, you prioritise and pick off.

A spot dealer said:

> You need to be able to look at the screen, speak on the 'phone, listen to colleagues, and think, all at the same time. You might have snippets of information coming in. You select what you need, maybe only three items, like a computer. You need the mind for it, to want to, to feel comfortable doing it. Better not to think how you do it.

PREDICTING STRESS OUTCOMES: REGRESSION ANALYSES

Having completed factor analysis of the two large scales used in the study, and interpreted the meaning of the factors, it is now possible to use regression analysis. This will indicate the sources and causes of the stress outcomes of mental ill-health, free-floating anxiety, somatic anxiety, depression, job dissatisfaction, and alcohol intake.

Based upon our discussion in Chapter 3, and the results of factor analysis, the variables which are considered to be potential sources of the stress outcomes are the dealer's:

Age
Sex
Marital status
Number of children under 18 years
Academic level reached in full-time education
Number of years in job
Number of hours travel to/from work
Number of hours at work
Coronary-prone (Type A) behaviour
Locus of control
Extraversion
Lie score
11 Stress Factors
5 Coping Factors

For statistical reasons, the dealer's degree of neuroticism was only included in the regression analyses of job dissatisfaction and units of alcohol drunk per week. It is not included as a possible cause of mental ill-health, free-floating anxiety, somatic anxiety, and depression.

Regression Tables

In the figures which follow, we show

(i) those variables which are sources of the stress outcome, shown under the heading 'STRESSORS',
(ii) those features of dealer's personalities which contribute to the stress outcome, shown under the heading 'DEALER'S PER-SONALITY', and
(iii) the stress outcome, shown under the heading 'OUTCOME'.

As an example, look at Figure 6.1. This shows that there are three sources of mental ill-health in dealers. The stress factor 'taking risks and achieving high performance', is a source of mental ill-health in dealers, as is the stress caused by 'the job interfering with home life' and 'performance setbacks'. We found that the *more* risks dealers have to take, the *more* mental ill-health is predicted. Similarly, the

159

more performance setbacks, the *more* mental ill-health. However, we also found that the *less* the job interfered with home, the *more* mental ill-health was predicted.

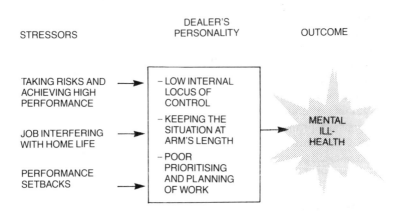

Figure 6.1 Sources of mental ill-health in dealers

We also found that four features of a dealer's personality determine the effect of these three stressors. Where dealers have a *low* internal locus of control, there is *more* mental ill-health predicted. Similarly, where dealers try to cope by 'keeping the situation at arm's length', the *more* mental ill-health is predicted. However, the *less* that dealers try to cope with stress by prioritising and planning work, the *more* mental ill-health is predicted.

It is the particular combination of work stressors and the dealer's personality which results in mental ill-health.

Overall, we were able to account for the sources of 44 per cent of a dealer's mental ill-health by regression analysis.

Two sets of sub-groups of dealers were analysed in further detail. Separate analyses of the causes of mental ill-health, job dis-satisfaction, and alcohol intake were carried out for male and female dealers. Due to the relatively low number of female dealers it was not always possible to obtain valid regression analysis statistics for them. We also carried out separate analyses for dealers working in UK-, US-, and European-owned institutions.

THE SOURCES OF MENTAL ILL-HEALTH IN DEALERS

Figure 6.1 shows the sources of mental ill-health in dealers. 'Taking risks and achieving high performance' (Stress Factor 2) is positively correlated with mental health, indicating that the more that dealers feel required and pressured to maintain a high level of performance, make important decisions, take risks, and achieve targets, the poorer their mental health.

The positive relationship between mental ill-health and 'Keep the situation at arm's length' (Coping Factor 3) suggests that the more that dealers use this coping strategy (i.e. avoid work problems), the more mental ill-health is indicated.

In addition, the *less* the dealer feels in control of the situation at work the more mental ill-health is predicted, as expected (see Chapter 3).

Two further personality variables included in the regression analysis of the sources of mental ill-health in dealers is the coping strategy 'prioritise and plan work', and the stress factor 'performance setbacks'. The former item is negatively related to mental ill-health, which suggests that where a dealer does not or cannot use this coping mechanism, poorer mental health will result. The latter item is positively related to mental ill-health, implying that when dealing activities are perceived as going badly, poorer mental health is an outcome.

Overall, the predictors of mental health are a mix of work stressors, coping methods, and personality and personal factors. Work-related factors ('taking risks and achieving high performance', 'keep the situation at arm's length', 'prioritise and plan work', and 'performance setbacks') constitute 31 per cent of the total mental ill-health explained, or almost three-quarters of the 44 per cent we were able to account for.

THE SOURCES OF FREE-FLOATING ANXIETY IN DEALERS

The sources of free-floating anxiety in dealers are shown in Figure 6.2. Of free-floating anxiety 41 per cent is accounted for by nine variables. Results are similar to that of the sources of mental ill-health. However, while the coping factor 'prioritise and plan work' is shown in both regressions, the sources of free-floating anxiety include three small additional variables.

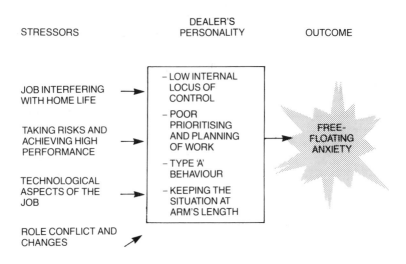

Figure 6.2 Sources of free-floating anxiety in dealers

The stresses relating to the 'technological aspects of the job', Stress Factor 9, are negatively related to free-floating anxiety, indicating that *less* concern by dealers about Dealing Room technology is predictive of *more* free-floating anxiety. Among the regressions carried out, the 'technology' variable was found to be a source only of free-floating anxiety. It may be that those dealers who are more concerned with the technological equipment they use (its potential for breakdown, their ability to cope with it, having to make decisions based on the computer screen, etc.) are less anxious. This may be because they are fully committed to the equipment, recognise and use its potential as an information and decision-making support, and ensure that they keep up-to-date with any changes in the technology. Those dealers who 'avoid' using the equipment, who do not wish to become (too) reliant upon the technology, or who have less confidence in the technology, would appear to be more anxious.

Type A behaviour is positively related to free-floating anxiety. The more Type A personality trait possessed by the dealer, the more free-floating anxiety they show.

THE SOURCES OF SOMATIC ANXIETY IN DEALERS

Figure 6.3 shows the sources of somatic anxiety in dealers. We were able to account for 29 per cent of these sources, and this indicates that there are other factors present which do not form part of our study. The seven variables which predict somatic anxiety include four of those predicting both mental health and free-floating anxiety.

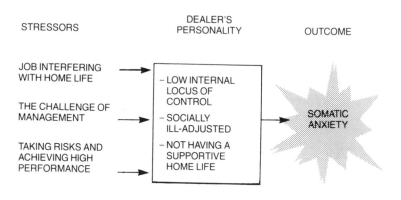

Figure 6.3 Sources of somatic anxiety in dealers

In addition, the stress factor, 'the challenge of management' is *negatively* related to somatic anxiety, indicating that the *less* stressed the dealer feels by 'management'-type tasks, the *more* somatic anxiety will be shown. Dealers, thus, appear to welcome the challenge of 'overpromotion', 'inability to delegate', 'working at a job of which many people disapprove', etc.

The more that dealers use home life to cope with stress at work (Coping Factor 4), the more somatic anxiety is predicted. In addition, a low lie score ('socially ill-adjusted') predicts more somatic anxiety.

THE SOURCES OF DEPRESSION IN DEALERS

Three variables predict depression in dealers (see Figure 6.4). Since they account for 21 per cent of the sources of depression, other variables are present which have not been detected. As with the other mental health scales, Stress Factor 6, indicating the stress effects of work on home life, is the major predictor of depression, and again the relationship is a negative one. Stress Factor 11, 'lack of support and guidance from colleagues and superiors', is also a significant predictor of depression, but not of free-floating or somatic anxiety. The stress caused by the absence of such support is a predictor of more depression in dealers.

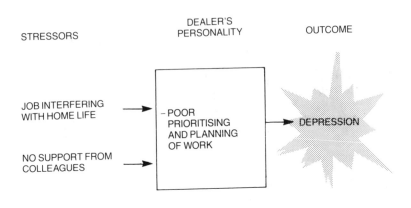

Figure 6.4 Sources of depression in dealers

The final variable significantly predicting depression is Coping Factor 1, 'prioritise and plan work', and the negative relationship indicates that the failure to use such a coping technique results in more depression in dealers.

Since two of three factors predicting depression are concerned with social support – at home and at work – the absence or presence of social support in one form or another appears to be a major predictor of depression in dealers.

THE SOURCES OF JOB DISSATISFACTION IN DEALERS

Eleven items are predictors of job dissatisfaction in dealers (Figure 6.5), and account for 65 per cent of their job dissatisfaction. Six of the stress factors which were produced after factor analysis are predictors of job dissatisfaction; they are, 'lack of support and guidance from colleagues and superiors', 'organisational culture and climate', 'career and promotion prospects', 'taking risks and achieving high performance', 'the office environment', and 'role conflict and changes'. This suggests that the *more* stressed the dealer is with these factors, the *less* job satisfaction is predicted.

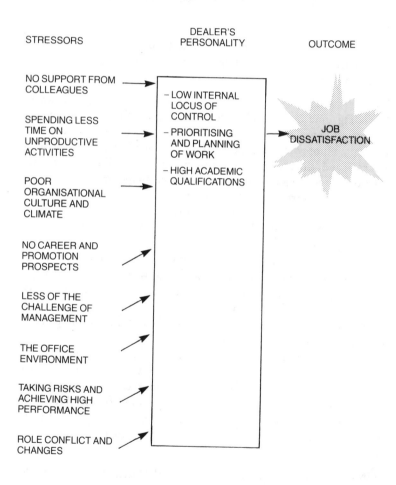

Figure 6.5 Sources of job dissatisfaction in dealers

The importance of successful trading was mentioned by a spot dealer:

> Money is a major inducement and incentive. It's related to the amount of hard work input. Satisfaction comes from making a deal, working in a free environment, not having to conform. Dissatisfaction is the inability to deal, or a failure in the chain, or a dead market for long periods. The job is good when you get it right. It's ego driven, you need freedom and independence.

Another dealer suggested:

> The 'buzz' comes from being able to balance two or three activities at once, or from making a deal, and being seen as the best for that deal.

Two job stressors are *negative* predictors of job dissatisfaction: they are 'spending time on unproductive activities', which would imply that dealers are *more* satisfied if they are able to spend time on activities other than those directly concerned with dealing (e.g. some kind of job variety), and 'the challenge of management', which like this variable's relationship with mental health, is a negative predictor.

Locus of control is positively correlated with job dissatisfaction, so that the less the dealer feels in control of events, the poorer is the job satisfaction (remembering that lower locus of control scores indicate higher perceived control).

One coping factor is included within the list of predictors of job dissatisfaction, namely 'prioritise and plan work', and this is negatively related to job dissatisfaction: the less that dealers prioritise and plan their work, the more job dissatisfaction is felt.

A final item included in Figure 6.5 is 'academic level reached in full-time education'. The positive relationship with job dissatisfaction indicates that, among dealers, the more academically-qualified the staff, the less satisfaction with the job. It may be that less formally educated dealers are more appreciative of the opportunities they have been given by the job (prestige, financial rewards, etc.) and consider *themselves* to be more appropriately qualified to do the job than their colleagues with academic qualifications.

UNITS OF ALCOHOL DRUNK PER WEEK BY DEALERS

It has been noted in Chapter 5 that dealers consume comparatively high amounts of alcohol. Five of the potential reasons why dealers consume large amounts of alcohol are shown in Figure 6.6, though the proportion of drinking explained, at 22 per cent, is rather too low to make any firm assumptions.

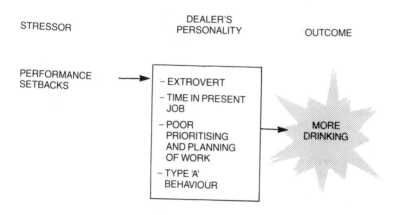

Figure 6.6 Units of alcohol drunk per week by dealers

Extroversion is a positive predictor of drinking (as also noted by Allsopp 1986). Perhaps because extroverts spend more time social-ising (Eysenck and Eysenck 1963), dealers frequently socialise in licensed premises or with the assistance of alcohol.

The number of years the dealer has spent in their present job is also positively related to alcohol intake, i.e. the longer in the job of dealing, the more drinking done. Through time, dealers may adopt the behaviour of their (City) peers, who drink comparatively large amounts of alcohol. Alcohol may also be used as a method of coping with the stress of the job.

Low levels of the stress associated with performance setbacks (Stress Factor 7) is also predictive of higher alcoholic intake, which at first sight appears to be the *reverse* of what might be expected, i.e. it might be reasonable to predict that those dealers who are highly stressed by performance setbacks at work would seek solace in alcohol, and drink more. However, since it has been shown earlier in this chapter that this stress factor predicts mental ill-health, it may be that those who drink more are not concerned about setbacks and the potential implications, and spend more time drinking rather than worrying. Those who are concerned with avoiding setbacks may wish to keep a clear head, avoid drinking, and concentrate on ensuring better performance.

Coping Factor 1, 'prioritise and plan work', is negatively related to alcohol consumption, which seems to support the preceding argument, i.e. the less the dealer is concerned with the work, the more alcohol is drunk. Dealers may drink more as a way of escape from their inability or unwillingness to utilise this method of coping.

The final variable predicting more alcoholic intake is coronary-prone (Type A) behaviour. The group of employees examined exhibit significantly higher coronary-prone behaviour than the norm (see Chapter 4), and so it appears that those exhibiting higher levels of Type A drink even more alcohol (as suggested by Folsom 1985).

STRESS IN FEMALE AND MALE DEALERS

The Sources of Mental Ill-health in Female and Male Dealers

A comparison of the causes of mental ill-health in male and female dealers shows major differences. For women (see Figure 6.7) there are two variables predicting mental ill-health. Firstly, the stress effects of work on home life, Stress Factor 6, and secondly, the coping strategy of 'prioritise and plan work', Coping Factor 1. Both of these are negatively related to mental ill-health.

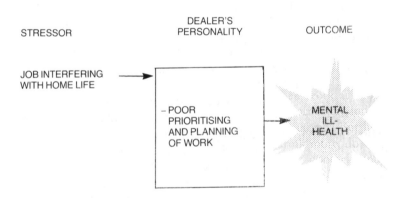

Figure 6.7 Sources of mental ill-health in female dealers

For men (see Figure 6.8), the sources of mental ill-health reflect those of the overall sample of dealers (Figure 6.1), with the stress of taking risks and achieving high performance being the main predictor, and poorly perceived locus of control a second predictor. All variables which were shown to be predictors of mental ill-health in the regression for the whole sample of dealers are included in that for males only, but two further variables are also present as predictors of mental ill-health in male dealers. Firstly, Stress Factor 4, 'the challenge of management', and secondly, coronary-prone (Type A) behaviour, both of which are positive predictors of mental ill-health.

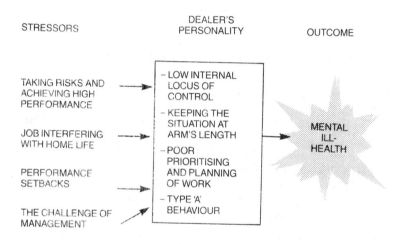

Figure 6.8 Sources of mental ill-health in male dealers

The Sources of Job Dissatisfaction in Female and Male Dealers

Separate regression analyses of job dissatisfaction were carried out for male and female dealers. Three factors predict job dissatisfaction in female dealers (Figure 6.9), and eight in male dealers (Figure 6.10).

For women, more use of Coping Factor 1, 'prioritise and plan work', is a predictor of job *satisfaction*. More concerns with career and promotion prospects (Stress Factor 3), and with the office environment (Stress Factor 8) (i.e. heat, noise, smoking) lower job satisfaction.

For men, the same three variables are also predictors of job dissatisfaction, and have the same relationships. However, whereas

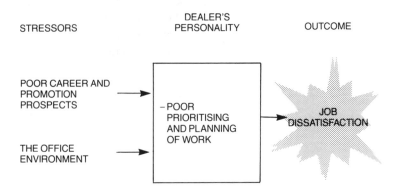

Figure 6.9 Sources of job dissatisfaction in female dealers

for women 64 per cent of job dissatisfaction is explained by these variables, for men they explain only 7 per cent of job dissatisfaction.

The job dissatisfaction of male dealers is primarily determined when they are stressed about receiving support and guidance from colleagues and superiors, and the relationship is *positive*, i.e. *less* concern by the dealer in obtaining such support is indicative of less job dissatisfaction.

Similarly, an external locus of control predicts low job satisfaction in male dealers, and the higher the academic qualification of the dealer, the less the job satisfaction.

A poorly-regarded organisational climate, concern about role conflict and changes, taking risks and achieving high performance, and a stressful office environment, are all stressors which result in job dissatisfaction in male dealers.

Two stress factors are predictors of *increased* job satisfaction in male dealers – 'spending time on unproductive activities' and 'the challenge of management'.

The final variable significantly predicting job dissatisfaction in male dealers is the coping strategy of 'prioritise and plan work', and the less this is utilised the greater the job dissatisfaction.

Alcohol Consumption in Female and Male Dealers

Separate regression analyses of alcohol consumption were carried out for male and female dealers, and there are noticeable differences in what determines alcohol consumption in the sexes.

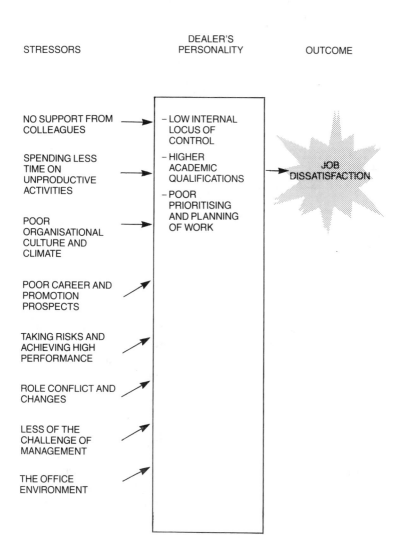

Figure 6.10 Sources of job dissatisfaction in male dealers

Female dealers (Figure 6.11) drink more as they age. In addition, *less* stress caused by lack of support and guidance from colleagues and superiors (Stress Factor 11) predicts *more* drinking. The stress caused by performance setbacks (Stress Factor 7) indicates *higher* drinking in women.

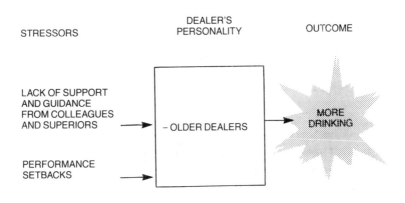

Figure 6.11 Units of alcohol drunk per week by female dealers

This latter variable is also a predictor of alcohol intake in male dealers (Figure 6.12), but it is a *negative* predictor, implying that the stress of performance setbacks results in *less* drinking in men. Thus, men and women appear to treat performance setbacks quite differently in their drinking behaviours.

Four other variables predict the alcohol intake of male dealers. Extraversion is positively related to units of alcohol consumed, i.e. the more extrovert the dealer, the more they drink. The longer the dealer has been in the present job, the more they drink. The less that male dealers use Coping Factor 4, 'Prioritise and plan work', the more drinking is predicted. The final factor significantly predicting alcohol intake in male dealers is coronary-prone (Type A) behaviour, which shows a positive relationship to drinking, i.e. the more Type A the male dealer, the more they drink.

172

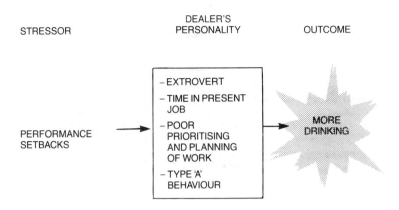

Figure 6.12 Units of alcohol drunk per week by male dealers

STRESS IN DEALERS WORKING IN ORGANISATIONS OF DIFFERENT NATIONAL OWNERSHIP

The Sources of Mental Ill-health in Dealers Working in Organisations of Different National Ownership

UK-owned organisations

The mental ill-health of dealers who work in UK-owned companies (Figure 6.13) is determined by six variables, consisting of two Stress Factors, one Coping Factor, two personality variables, and the sex of the dealer. The more stressed this group of dealers is by taking risks and achieving high performance, and by performance setbacks, the more mental ill-health they express. Being a female dealer predicts poorer mental health, as does being a single dealer. Dealers who exhibit high levels of Type A behaviour also exhibit poorer mental health. Dealers in UK-owned organisations who cope with stress by keeping the situation at arm's length also exhibit poorer mental health.

US-owned organisations

The mental ill-health of dealers who work in US-owned companies is the poorest of the three groups (see Chapter 5), and is predicted by two job stressors, and two Coping Factors (Figure 6.14). The

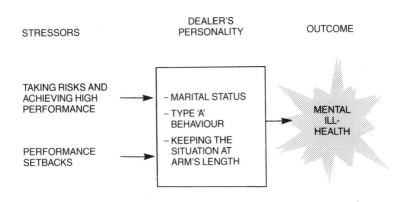

Figure 6.13 Sources of mental ill-health in dealers in UK-owned companies

more that this group of dealers is stressed by role conflict and changes, the more mental ill-health they express. The less that these dealers are stressed by the ways in which work spills over into home life, the more mental ill-health is predicted. The less that these dealers attempt to cope with stress by prioritising and planning their work, the more their mental ill-health. The more that they attempt to cope with stress by keeping the situation at arm's length also results in more mental ill-health. Given the comments made earlier, none of these results is unexpected.

European-owned organisations

The mental ill-health of those dealers who work for European-owned companies, and who exhibited the best scores on the mental ill-health scale (see Chapter 5), is predicted by five variables, that is, three Stress Factors, a Coping Factor, and a family-related variable (Figure 6.15). The more stress caused by taking risks and achieving high performance, and by the office environment, and the less stress caused by the home–work relationship, all predict higher mental ill-health in this group of dealers. Again, given previous results, none of these relationships is unexpected. However, we also found that the more children these 'European' dealers have who are aged under 18, the less mental ill-health, i.e. the fewer children of this age, the poorer the mental health of the dealer. It has been noted in

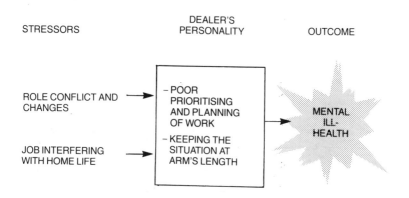

Figure 6.14 Sources of mental ill-health in dealers in US-owned companies

Chapter 5 that dealers with no children under 18 years of age exhibit poorer mental health than dealers who have such children. Therefore, it may be logical to extend this finding and expect that, where a dealer has children aged under 18, those who have more will have the better mental health.

The mental ill-health of dealers in each of the three types of organisations is determined differently. No variable is a common source of mental ill-health in all of the three groups. For dealers in UK-owned organisations mental ill-health is associated with job stressors, personality and demographic variables, and coping techniques. For dealers in US-owned organisations mental ill-health is associated with job stressors and coping techniques. For dealers in European-owned organisations mental ill-health is associated with job stressors, coping techniques, and a demographic variable.

The Sources of Job Dissatisfaction in Dealers Working in Organisations of Different National Ownership

UK-owned organisations

The job dissatisfaction of dealers in UK institutions is similar to that of dealers in European organisations, but is predicted solely by four job-related stressors (Figure 6.16). A stressful organisational culture

175

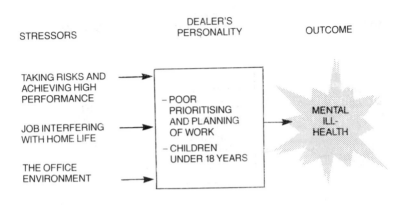

Figure 6.15 Sources of mental ill-health in dealers in European-owned companies

and climate, lack of support and guidance from colleagues and superiors, spending less time on 'unproductive' activities, and more role conflict and changes, all increase the job dissatisfaction of this group of dealers.

US-owned organisations

Dealers in US-owned City organisations have the poorest levels of job satisfaction of the three groups examined. Job dissatisfaction in these dealers is determined by four job-related stressors, a personality disposition, and a biographical variable, and by a coping factor (Figure 6.17). Lack of support and guidance from colleagues and superiors is the most important predictor of job dissatisfaction in this group of dealers. Job dissatisfaction is also increased by a stressful office environment, by poor career and promotion prospects, and by low levels of stress attributable to the technological aspects of the job. An external locus of control and higher academic qualifications also predict more job dissatisfaction in these dealers. The less that US dealers cope with stress by prioritising and planning work is a further predictor of more job dissatisfaction.

European-owned organisations

The job satisfaction of dealers working in European-owned finance houses is better than those working in UK and US equivalents (see

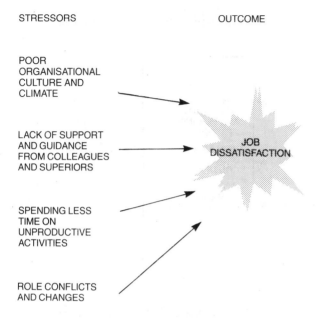

STRESSORS   OUTCOME

POOR
ORGANISATIONAL
CULTURE AND
CLIMATE

LACK OF SUPPORT
AND GUIDANCE
FROM COLLEAGUES
AND SUPERIORS

JOB
DISSATISFACTION

SPENDING LESS
TIME ON
UNPRODUCTIVE
ACTIVITIES

ROLE CONFLICTS
AND CHANGES

Figure 6.16 Sources of job dissatisfaction in dealers in UK-owned companies

Chapter 5). The job dissatisfaction of these dealers is determined by four work stressors, two personality factors, one biographical variable, and one coping method (Figure 6.18). The most significant predictor of job dissatisfaction for these 'European' dealers is lack of support and guidance from colleagues and superiors. Other determinants of job dissatisfaction in this group of dealers include spending less time on unproductive activities, and not taking risks and achieving high performance. The less that these dealers feel in control of the job, and the less use made of the stress coping technique of prioritising and planning work, also result in more job dissatisfaction. These five factors determine most of this group of dealers' job dissatisfaction. Three variables provide small increases in job dissatisfaction. High levels of role conflict and changes, more Type A behaviour, and higher academic qualifications all predict higher job dissatisfaction in dealers in European-owned Dealing Rooms.

Stress Factor 11, 'Lack of support and guidance from colleagues and superiors', is the only source of job dissatisfaction common to

STRESSORS

DEALER'S
PERSONALITY

OUTCOME

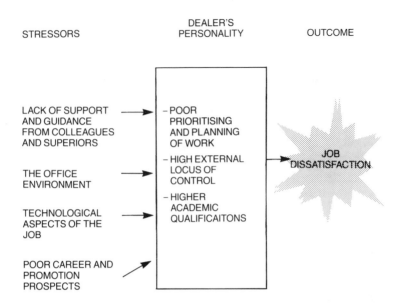

Figure 6.17 Sources of job dissatisfaction in dealers in US-owned companies

dealers in all three types of institution we examined. The least amount of job dissatisfaction we were able to explain was that of UK dealers, and this group's job dissatisfaction does not appear to be affected by their individual personality and demographics, or any of the coping factors, unlike their colleagues in the other organisations.

Alcohol Consumption in Dealers Working in Organisations of Different National Ownership

We found that two different variables are the sources of alcohol consumption in dealers in the three types of institution we examined, and these are summarised in Figure 6.19. Firstly, high extroversion scores (it will be recalled that extroversion is regarded as a personality disposition necessary for dealers) predict higher alcohol consumption in dealers working in UK-owned institutions.

Secondly, the alcohol intake of European dealers is negatively determined by the stress of performance setbacks, i.e. the less they are stressed by performance setbacks the more they drink.

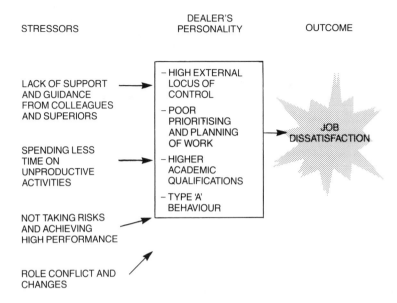

Figure 6.18 Sources of job dissatisfaction in dealers in European-owned companies

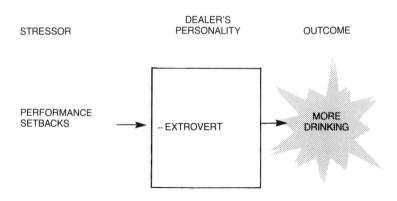

Figure 6.19 Alcohol consumption in dealers working in organisations of different national ownership

Dealers in 'European' institutions appear to react to performance setbacks by drinking less. Dealers in UK organisations drink more because of certain of their personality dispositions.

The amount of the alcohol consumption of the three groups we were able to explain by regression analyses is relatively low, suggesting that other relevant factors are present which we have not detected.

7

DEALERS UNDER STRESS
A Summary

In this chapter we will put together and interpret our findings about dealers as they have been presented in Chapters 4, 5, and 6. We also mention some other interesting results which we have found, and note what our study of dealers working in the City of London adds to our understanding of the phenomenon of stress. In the final chapter we will suggest ways in which we can help reduce the stress problems of dealers and others working in the financial sector.

DEALERS IN THE MONEY MARKETS OF THE CITY OF LONDON

The public perception of dealers as young, single, having had comparatively little advanced education, relatively new to the job, 'burnt out' at 35, and as heavy drinkers and drug takers (e.g. Chapman 1988; Reynolds 1989), is partially substantiated by the results of our study. Dealers work long hours and take insufficient exercise. In addition, they exhibit the personality characteristics which are implicated in many negative health outcomes. They are certainly more stressed than the general population. Dealers indicate poorer mental health and job satisfaction than comparable groups of workers, and drink more than is considered safe for health. Yet despite these findings, they also report that they are able to dissipate work-related stress and that they do have enough time to 'wind down'. These results suggest that dealers may not recognise, or, if they do, are not willing to admit, that they are under stress. Many dealers may face physical and mental problems in the long term.

Sources of Stress in Dealers

We asked dealers to rate 87 potential sources of job-related stress in a questionnaire. Of these 87 potential sources, 13 items scored an average of 3.50 or above on a stress scale of 1 (low stress) to 6 (high stress), i.e. these 13 items are regarded as sources of stress by dealers (see Table 5.17). Looked at from another viewpoint, 11 of the 87 items were considered by dealers to be either 'generally', 'definitely', or 'very definitely' a source of stress. Thus, from either analysis of the 87 questions shown in Table 5.17, dealers do not appear to believe or are willing to admit that they find many of these potential sources as stressful. Yet, in comparison with other white-collar workers, dealers do seem to find the job of dealing stressful. The combination of dealers' personalities, backgrounds, and the job itself, appears to result in these high stress outcomes.

Eleven major groupings of potential sources of stress (i.e. stress factors) were found after factor analysis of the 87 potential stress variables (see Chapter 6). All eleven job-related stress factors contribute to at least one of the negative health outcomes we examined, some more so than others. We will discuss each of these factors in turn.

Role stress. Role conflict and changes (Stress Factor 1) are predictive of free-floating anxiety and lower job satisfaction. These results are supportive of findings reported by French and Caplan (1970), and, expanding the factor to include role ambiguity, that of Bedeian and Armenakis (1981) who also found both of the relationships reported above. Dealers will benefit from a more stable environment than currently appears to exist in Dealing Rooms. A spot dealer told us: 'You never know if the new starters are going to be at their desks the next day. One woman lasted two days. We never saw her again'.

Risk taking. Taking risks and achieving high performance (Stress Factor 2) was found to be the variable most predictive of mental ill-health, and also contributed to free-floating anxiety and to somatic anxiety in dealers. However, the factor is also predictive of increased job satisfaction. These results suggest that this source of stress results in dealers facing conflicting outcomes. They gain additional job satisfaction, but also increased mental ill-health. While it might be expected that this basic task function, for which dealers may have selected or been selected for the job, would provide them with job satisfaction, it may well be that some of the implications of dealing (e.g. making mistakes, letting down their work group), or the lack of support from colleagues and superiors, and the way the task has to be carried out, result in poorer overall mental health and specifically contribute to more free-floating and somatic anxiety. An experienced foreign exchange dealer said:

> The greatest satisfaction in the job comes from getting things right, beating the market. But it's frightening sometimes, especially overnight, waiting to see if you've got it right or wrong. You feel you've let your desk down when that [getting it wrong] happens.

Career blockage. Concern about career and promotion prospects (Stress Factor 3) was found to result in less job satisfaction. This result contrasts with that suggested by Brook (1973) who found such concerns resulted in mental illness rather than job dis-satisfaction, but it is supportive of the findings of Sutherland and Cooper (1986) who have related occupational locking-in to job dissatisfaction as well as to reduced mental well-being.

Managing others. The challenge of management (Stress Factor 4) was found to result in less somatic anxiety and more job satisfaction. Thus, it appears that those dealers in a supervisory or managerial position *gain* job satisfaction from the stresses of the role.

Paperwork. Spending time on unproductive activities (Stress Factor 5) was found to provide more job satisfaction. Dealers gain satisfaction from the stress of the accumulative effects of minor tasks, from the sharing of work and responsibility evenly, from carrying out mundane administrative tasks or 'paperwork', etc. These tasks may be regarded by dealers as providing some relief from the stress associated with the main work of dealing. This was commented upon by a bond salesman: 'I organise my time so that I can clear up my accounts at the end of the day. It's a major achieve-ment not having it waiting on my desk first thing in the morning'.

Home/work stress. The stress effects of work on home life (Stress Factor 6), which includes items such as spouse's attitude towards job and career, and the demands work makes on relationships with spouse and children, was found to result in *better* mental health, and to be the factor which had most effect upon reducing the dealer's free-floating anxiety, somatic anxiety, and depression. A discussion of these unexpected relationships is presented in the section headed 'The Outcomes of Occupational Stress in Dealers' below.

Performance setbacks. Performance setbacks (Stress Factor 7), which represents the stress associated with having a run of financial losses, coming second-best out of a transaction, misreading the market, etc., is a source of poorer mental health, and of less drinking. These relationships show a major concern of dealers.

Office and technology stress. The office environment (Stress Factor 8) – too warm an environment, too much noise, etc. – is a source of lowered job satisfaction. This result supports those of Fine and Kobrick (1978), and Wineman (1982), but our findings disagree with those of Sutton and Rafaeli (1987). Stress caused by the technological aspects of the job (Stress Factor 9), which is concerned with the technology (e.g. computers) used in the Dealing Room, its potential breakdown, etc., results in *less* free-floating anxiety. This finding tends to disagree with those reported elsewhere in the literature, e.g. by Bennett *et al.* (1984), Dainoff *et al.* (1981). Dealers may be among a minority in their attitude to the technology. One dealer told us:

The more information, the better to make judgements,

and the technology which provides the information dealers need does not result in negative outcomes. A Eurobond trader pointed out:

The computer is the only way to do business. Everyone has to use it now. After a while you just take it for granted. It's only a problem when it goes down.

Organisational culture. Concern with the organisational culture and climate of the Dealing Room and of the institution worked for (Stress Factor 10), which includes the dealer's personal beliefs conflicting with those of the organisation, and coping with office politics, results in reduced job satisfaction.

Social support. Lack of support and guidance from colleagues and superiors (Stress Factor 11), which involves competing with colleagues, inadequate feedback about their performance, the inadequate or poor quality of the training and management development they have received, is the strongest source of job dissatisfaction. One foreign exchange dealer showed some anger when he told us: 'Some of my colleagues wouldn't give you the time of day if they thought it would let you get ahead of them'.

In addition, the factor results in increased depression. These results are supported by much of the stress literature.

In summary, the major sources of stress in dealers fall into two categories. Firstly, stress associated with the basic work of dealing, e.g. misreading the market, having a run of financial losses, attaining personal levels of performance. Secondly, stress due to an un-satisfactory organisational culture and poor management, e.g. having too much work to do, poor morale and organisational climate, pressure to perform at a high level, being undervalued. The two categories are related in that organisational management plays a major role in determining the distribution of work, in setting levels of performance, and in determining the personal outcomes which follow from mistakes made by dealers. Overall, the effective man-agement of financial institutions appears to be the single most important influence on the major stressors recognised by dealers.

It is notable that of the three stress factors resulting in increased mental ill-health, two are related to the job of dealing itself, namely Stress Factor 2 (taking risks and achieving high performance), and Stress Factor 7 (performance setbacks). The third stress factor pre-dicts *better* mental health, namely, Stress Factor 6 (the effect of work on home life). Overall, this suggests that aspects basic to the job of dealing result in poorer mental health, but the stress of the home/ work interface results in better mental health.

Only one job-related source of stress, performance setbacks (Stress Factor 7), is related to alcohol consumption, and the relation-ship is negative, i.e. *more* stress results in *less* drinking. The stress which dealers report as associated with the job of dealing appears to have little effect upon drinking habits. High levels of alcohol intake in dealers has its sources outside of the Dealing Room.

Stress in Sub-groups of Dealers

Being a woman dealer. Among the sub-groups of dealers we examined in detail, more stress is perceived by female dealers in factors intrinsic to the job, relationships with others at work, career and achievement, and organisational structure and climate. This indicates that women are stressed by the fundamental nature of the job, by the inadequacies of support from colleagues and superiors at work and by those outside work, by failure to achieve personal and corporate success, and by the basic design of the organisation in which they work and the way in which responsibility is shared. This may be due to discrimination at work, lack of role models for women, the aggressive 'macho' attitudes found in the Dealing Room, and the traditional male domination of professional work in the City. One of the female dealers we interviewed was in charge of a small group of foreign exchange traders. She told us:

185

The men here were not very pleased when I got the job. I have to work twice as hard to show that I can do the job better. I've had trouble with one or two of them in the last few months.

Travelling. More stress is perceived by dealers who travel 2 or more hours per day to and from work (in factors intrinsic to the job). This suggests that the travelling these dealers do adds to basic job stress. They may be more tired on arriving at work. They also indicate having less time to wind down and to manage exercise, and generally appear to be less healthy than their colleagues. The fact that working over 47 hours per week does not result in more stress at work, suggests that travelling (in London) is more debilitating than working additional hours in the Dealing Room.

Being in management. Significantly more stress is noted by dealers who are responsible for one or more persons in the Dealing Room. This shows itself in more stress due to the managerial role, in relationships with other people, and with the organisational structure and climate. Taken together these results suggest that dealers who have a management or supervisory role to carry out find it stressful because they receive inadequate support, both in terms of staff and in back-up from their own superiors. Job roles may be ill-defined, and training and management development of poor quality. Non-graduates express more stress with their role as a manager. Since they have more responsibilities (for others) at work this may also be due to poor training. In addition, the non-graduate may find it difficult to relate to the intake of new graduates of whom they are placed in charge, and to the changing nature of the job of dealing, which requires more analytical, technical, and inter-personal skills.

Career expectations. Dealers expecting to wait at least two years for promotion are significantly more stressed by relationships at work and by the organisational structure and climate. These dealers are already responsible for more colleagues in the Dealing Room and may feel that they have reached a plateau in their career. This may negatively affect their attitudes to their colleagues at work (and vice-versa). However, few dealers commented directly to us that they were concerned about their future career prospects. One admitted:

Most of us realise it's a short life [in dealing]. We'll make as much money as we can while we can. I intend to work here for five years, then set up my own business. I don't know what it is yet.

186

Youth versus experience. Dealers aged under 35 years of age indicate significantly more stress with career and achievement at work. As with dealers who expect to have to wait longer for promotion this group of dealers may recognise that they have achieved as much (or as little) as they are likely to in their present job. This may be exacerbated by redundancies within the City and lack of training and management development which will allow them to undertake a career move.

Working for US-owned firms. Dealers in US-owned institutions are significantly more stressed by factors intrinsic to the job and by career and achievement. It appears that these dealers work in a more stressful environment in terms of workload, pay, variety of work to be completed, etc. In addition, they recognise less opportunity for advancement and development. The demands made of dealers who work for US-owned organisations, and the associated rewards, may be regarded as inequitable by these employees.

Summary. Results from our analysis of sub-groups of dealers suggest a relatively homogeneous group of employees, other than for female dealers, those working in US-owned Dealing Rooms, those responsible for others at work, and those expecting to have to wait at least two years for a promotion. We found no significant differences in the stress relating to the home/work interface within any of the sub-groups of dealers examined. The overlap between home and work as a source of stress is similar whatever the sub-group of dealer we considered.

THE OUTCOMES OF OCCUPATIONAL STRESS IN DEALERS

Mental Ill-health

Dealers indicate significantly poorer mental health than the general population. The causes of this derive from a combination of those elements which are intrinsic to the job of dealing, the methods used by dealers to cope with the job, and the personalities of dealers.

The most significant determinant of mental ill-health in dealers is taking risks and making important decisions, which dealers are required to do every time they make, or do not make a deal. The success or otherwise of this activity is directly related to dealers attaining their personal levels of performance, and achieving their individual or group profit target. The rewards which dealers gain from their job, and their perceived success as a dealer, requires them to maintain a high level of performance both for themselves and for their co-workers. The constant pressure to perform at a high level, and to avoid mistakes, leads to poorer mental health. Thus, tasks basic to dealing appear to result in mental ill-health.

When *performance setbacks* occur, as is inevitable in the job of dealing, this stress adds to the mental ill-health of dealers. These performance setbacks are made worse for dealers who have a partner also pursuing a career, so that the problems of dual-career couples (Lewis and Cooper 1989) appear to be relevant in these cases. Problems at home may be made worse where two partners are working. The interaction between work and home life is itself also a major determinant of mental ill-health in dealers. We found the relationship between work and home life and mental ill-health to be negative. This implies that dealers who perceive *less* stress at home suffer *greater* mental ill-health. Dealers who say that they are *less* stressed by their spouse's attitude towards their (dealer's) job, by the absence of stability and dependability in their home life, and by the demands that work makes on their relationships with their spouse and children, indicate *poorer* mental health than their colleagues who indicate that they are *more* stressed by these and similar problems. These strange relationships may be due to what Kobasa and Puccetti (1983) have described as 'hardiness'. For those low in hardiness, the more support received from their family, the poorer their health. Dealers may find the contrasts between the continual pressures, excitement, and uncertainty at work, etc., and a calm, organised, rational life outside of the Dealing Room to be confusing, unsettling, and, in the long term, perhaps untenable. For the dealer who feels that home life is stressful because of spillover from work (Glowinkowski and Cooper 1985), but who is able to get rid of the tensions at home (for instance, by shouting or otherwise expressing anger) even though this creates more stress at home, mental tension is relieved. Not 'bottling up' the stress at home may be used by many dealers as a coping method. Of course, the effects of this upon the dealer's family may be very negative. We did not look at this aspect of the dealer's life.

Dealers who consider that they have less (locus of) control report poorer mental health. The very nature of the dealer's job gives little control over the work. It is often unpredictable and has peaks and troughs of anxiety and calm, success and failure. Dealers may recognise this by their significantly higher scores on the scale measuring locus of control, i.e. they believe that they are more subject to external control. The locus of control measure is concerned with the way in which dealers perceive the fairness of others' assessment of their performance and appraisal, with relationships with management, and with the control which dealers feel that they have over their work. Again, organisational management appears strongly to affect this personality measure.

Two methods of coping with the stresses of work are associated with poorer mental health in dealers. Those dealers who do not prioritise and plan their work, and those who attempt to cope with stress by keeping the situation at arm's length, suffer more mental ill-health. Both of these relationships appear logical. First, since the work load of a dealer is irregular, with swings from periods of high activity to those of comparative idleness, this may give the dealer little chance to plan work and manage time. The second coping factor, given the nature of the dealer's job, does not appear to be a realistic coping strategy. Dealers work in teams, and must deal with clients and colleagues 'on demand'. Attempting to avoid these situations has negative effects upon mental health.

Of the sub-groups of dealers examined, significantly poorer mental ill-health was found in women, and in dealers with no children under 18 years of age.

Interestingly, one foreign exchange dealer told us:

> Sterling dealers deal with gentlemen. Foreign exchange dealers are more volatile. Go to LIFFE [London International Financial Futures Exchange], they're madmen there,

and a spot dealer said:

> Dealers carry a mystique. The animals now are the brokers, not the dealers.

Free-floating Anxiety

Male dealers report significantly more free-floating anxiety (which is defined as dread, indefinable terror, tension without a cause, or panic, by Crown and Crisp 1979) than the normative male population. Given the unpredictable nature of the job, and the lack of control which dealers report, this is not surprising.

The technological aspects of the job increase free-floating anxiety. Since the dealer depends upon the technology of the

Dealing Room, has little or no control over it, and is stressed by the possibility of its breakdown, it is not surprising that free-floating anxiety, with its unseen and uncontrollable sources, is affected, rather than other aspects of mental health.

The stress of role conflict and changes (conflicting job tasks and demands, staff shortages and turnover), also leads to increased free-floating anxiety (as noted by French and Caplan 1970).

The personality characteristic of coronary-prone (Type A) behaviour also predicts free-floating anxiety. It has been noted earlier that dealers exhibit coronary-prone behaviour similar to other white-collar groups, but significantly more of this action-emotion complex than the average. Dealers might be expected to exhibit such behaviour – they work long hours, are under constant pressure, feel misunderstood by superiors, etc., all of which have been shown to be typical of Type A individuals (Brief *et al.* 1983), and this behaviour shows itself in free-floating anxiety. Significantly poorer free-floating anxiety was found in female dealers, and in male dealers who expected to wait at least two years for promotion.

Somatic Anxiety

Male dealers report significantly less somatic anxiety than the general population, suggesting that these dealers are better able to dissipate and cope with the physical outcomes of stress. They may be the 'peak performers' noted by Boyatzis (1982). Somatic anxiety in dealers is determined in part by both the stress *caused* by having a supportive family/social life and having to *use* this facility as a coping technique. It may be that many dealers feel 'guilty' at causing increased stress at home, and this increases their somatic anxiety. The dealer's work leads to stressful behaviour both at home and socially, and using home as a refuge and 'switching off' at home leads to behaviours that the dealer finds inconsistent, and this results in increased somatic anxiety.

Depression

Lack of the support which dealers need at work results in depression, that is 'slowing of actions and activities' (Crown and Crisp 1979). Dealers who fail to gain sufficient support from their colleagues and superiors, who are not informed about the adequacy of their performance, who feel a lack of power and influence, and who experience a lack of consultation and communication, might be expected to be less psychologically motivated to take risks and conduct business. Again, the support of management is shown as an important factor in dealers' health.

Significantly higher depression was found in female dealers, in male dealers who expect to have to wait at least two years for promotion, and in dealers working in US-owned institutions.

Overall, dealers indicate poor mental health, due to the free-floating but not the somatic aspects of the measure. We found few significant differences between sub-groups on any of the mental health scales. This may reflect the fact that dealers are a relatively homogeneous group.

Job Dissatisfaction

Dealers are as satisfied with their job as blue-collar workers, but less satisfied with their job than many other white-collar professional staff. However, it is important to recognise that dealers report that they are generally satisfied with all aspects of the job we examined other than with the way the firm is managed. This latter finding again indicates the importance of Dealing Room management.

Intrinsic aspects of the dealer's job are regarded as more satisfying than extrinsic aspects such as pay, etc.

The major determinants of job dissatisfaction among dealers are related to the stressors directly associated with the work. Eight of the eleven variables associated with job dissatisfaction are stress factors, indicating the importance of the immediate work environment to dealers' job satisfaction. The eleven variables appear to fall into two types. Firstly, those relating to features and attitudes personal to the individual, and secondly, those determined by factors intrinsic to the job and by the organisational environment in which the dealer works. Once again, organisational management is shown to be a major influence, this time upon dealers' job satisfaction. While the other outcomes we examined are affected by various combinations of stressors, coping methods, personality and demographic variables, it is noticeable that job dissatisfaction is mostly determined by the eight stress factors. We accounted for 65 per cent of dealers' job dissatisfaction, and job stressors account for 80 per cent of this figure.

There is little additional job dissatisfaction added by other variables (locus of control, academic level reached in full-time education, coping by prioritising and planning work). This finding contrasts with Burke (1986) who suggests that the significance of work stress to the quality of the life and health of workers is questionable, and accounts for little job satisfaction. Dealers' job satisfaction is based mainly on the work itself. In support of this, one dealer told us:

> The attraction of being a dealer is that it's not routine, there are sudden changes of tempo. You can see great joy and frustration – joy from having read something right. You regard it as a personal affront if you lose money. If you make money you go home with a smile on your face.

The effect of the job stressors on job satisfaction is negative in five of the eight cases, i.e. more stress = less job satisfaction. However, the relationship between three job stressors and job satisfaction is the reverse of what might be expected.

Dealers who perceive that they are more in control of the work situation (i.e. dealers who have internal locus of control) indicate more job satisfaction (as was predicted by Furnham 1987), as do those dealers who make more use of the coping strategy of prioritising and planning their work.

When we consider sub-groups of dealers, significantly poorer job satisfaction was found in dealers who have no children aged under 18 years of age and in dealers working in US-owned financial institutions. Again, the homogeneity of the group of dealers is indicated.

Alcohol Consumption

Dealers are heavy drinkers, but as only 22 per cent of alcohol consumption in dealers was explained by the regression analysis, important other factors which result in alcohol drinking have not been found. They probably lie outside the scope of this study, in the dealer's social and cultural environment. However, one forward deposits dealer told us that: 'Alcohol *is* a problem here, and is generally'.

Examination of sub-groups of dealers shows that significantly more alcohol is consumed by female dealers, by single dealers, by non-graduates, and by dealers responsible for no others at work.

192

MODERATORS OF THE RELATIONSHIPS BETWEEN STRESS AND STRAIN IN DEALERS

The moderators of the relationships between stress and outcomes in dealers are discussed under three headings, namely stress coping methods, personality, and demographic variables.

Stress Coping Strategies

Thirty potential stress coping strategies were considered by dealers in one of the questionnaires they were asked to complete. Twenty-two items were scored at 3.50 or above on a scale of 1 (low use made of the method) to 6 (high use made of the method), and twenty-one items were 'on balance', 'extensively', or 'very extensively' used by dealers. Both of these analyses indicate that dealers make use of most of the stress coping mechanisms listed. Overall, dealers make more use of stress coping methods than comparable white-collar workers.

Examination of the six major coping methods used by employees (which are derived from Cooper, Sloan and Williams 1988) shows that female dealers make significantly more use of *social support*. They may be more willing, or able, to relate to other people as a support than male dealers.

Significantly more use is made of *time management* by dealers aged over 35 years. With age and experience will come better utilisation of this coping method. In addition, older dealers exhibit less Type A personality, and so will not be under as much self-imposed time pressure as their younger colleagues.

Married dealers make more use of *task strategies* than single dealers. As they have been in the job longer and are older, married dealers, as with older dealers, may have gained more experience in coping with the job by use of this technique. Alternatively, the additional experiences married dealers may have gained of self-organising may be used in the work situation.

Those responsible for managing other people at work make significantly more use of both task and time strategies. Again, the former group is the older, and it may be assumed that they have been given and retained these responsibilities, which may be additional to their job as a dealer, *because* they can successfully utilise these techniques.

Dealers in European-owned organisations make significantly more use of social support than 'UK' (and 'US') dealers, suggesting a more supportive atmosphere in European-owned Dealing Rooms, and indicating that 'European' dealers exhibit personalities more able to utilise the strategy. Perhaps they are selected for these personality traits by their organisations.

Effective coping. Five coping factors were produced after factor analysis of the twenty-eight stress coping methods. Three of the five coping factors were found to be implicated in the outcomes we examined.

Prioritising and planning work (Coping Factor 1), which is concerned with time management, forward planning, prioritising of work, etc., was found to result in improvements in mental health, free-floating anxiety, depression, and job satisfaction, and in less drinking.

Keeping the situation at arm's length (Coping Factor 3), which consists of two items, try to avoid the situation, and resort to rules and regulations, was found to be the second most important source of mental ill-health and also of free-floating anxiety.

A *supportive home life* was found to be used by dealers as a coping method which *increased* somatic anxiety. This method (Coping Factor 4), emphasises having a home that is a refuge from work. The implications of this relationship have been discussed earlier. However, it appears to run counter to much of the literature we examined. The home and social life of dealers would be well worth examining to determine what is actually happening there, in view of the relationships found with mental health. One spot dealer was quite clear in his attitudes: 'There is a limit. You must consider your family and progress to that limit. Some people want to progress beyond that. My wife couldn't tell you what I do, I keep it separate, try not to overlap'.

Noticeably, both coping factors which determine mental health are task-related, rather than concerned with social or home support. Two coping factors did not relate to any of the outcomes, namely, Coping Factor 2, using activities and friends outside work (i.e. hobbies, pastimes, distractions), and Coping Factor 5, using objective and unemotional behaviour. In the former case, this may support the findings of researchers such as Holahan and Moos (1981) who found that for men, only support at *work* was associated with decreases in depression (83.8 per cent of the dealers we examined were male) rather than social support from outside the workplace. In the second case, since dealers have been shown to exhibit high Type A behaviour, it is not surprising that the factor does not feature in dealers' coping methods. Attempts to improve the mental health of dealers should take into account not only the stressors known to produce negative outcomes, but also those coping methods *not* used by dealers.

The Effect of Dealers' Personalities on Stress

All of the personality variables examined had some effect upon the health outcomes of dealers, and two of these, neuroticism and locus of control, are of particular interest.

Dealers were found to be as neurotic as the general population. *Neuroticism*, as noted previously, is found to be the variable most predictive of the outcomes associated with mental health, but it had no effect upon job satisfaction. These results support the findings of Costa and McCrae (1987), who suggest a relationship between neuroticism and *subjective* health complaints (i.e. reporting ill-health), but not *objective* health indicators (e.g. drinking). Our failure to find a relationship between neuroticism and alcohol consumption is supported by the findings of Allsopp (1986).

The dealer's view of their *locus of control* was found to be a predictor of a number of health outcomes. Low perceived control results in poorer mental health, free-floating anxiety, somatic anxiety, and in less job satisfaction. These results support Payne (1988), Spector (1982), Furnham (1987), etc. The relationship between locus of control and 'hardiness' may help to explain why dealers, who are low in control and by extension hardiness, and who receive more social support from their family, have poorer health (Kobasa and Puccetti 1983). Results from the present study do not support the comments of Ganster and Fusilier (1989), however. They noted that researchers have generally not shown that control moderates the relationship between job demands and well-being, though they admit that studies of this type are still relatively scarce.

Type A behaviour resulted in more free-floating anxiety, and in more drinking. Dealers have high Type A personalities, and are heavy consumers of alcohol, and our results suggest that those dealers who are very high Type A drink even more alcohol than their colleagues. The relationships shown in the regression analyses indicate that, overall, Type A behaviour appears to contribute little to the outcomes.

Extroversion was shown to be the major determinant of alcohol intake. Dealers are high extroverts and, as with our discussion above concerning the relationship between Type A behaviour and alcohol intake, it appears that extreme extroverts drink even more alcohol. These results support those of Allsopp (1986) and Eysenck (1965).

Dealers who scored high on the Eysenck and Eysenck (1964) *lie scale* had less somatic anxiety. Extrapolating McCrae and Costa's

195

(1985) interpretation of the lie score to the present study, it appears that those dealers who are less 'well-adjusted, responsible and well-disposed towards others' (McCrae and Costa 1985) suffer poorer mental health, at least in the category of somatic anxiety.

The Effect of Dealers' Demographic Variables on Stress

The *sex* of the dealer determines scores on three of the mental health measures (mental ill-health, free-floating and somatic anxiety). In these three cases results indicate that being a woman predicts higher scores, though this does not necessarily indicate objectively poorer mental health.

The *longer* the dealer has been in their present job, the more alcohol is drunk per week. Our failure to find any relationships between the number of years the dealer has been in their present job and any of the mental health outcomes or with job satisfaction indicates no support for the findings of Wahlund and Nurell (1978).

The inclusion of the *education* variable as a determinant of job dissatisfaction shows that the lower the level of academic qualification reached in full-time education, the greater the job satisfaction. In Dealing Rooms at least, it appears that better qualifications do not equate with better job satisfaction.

Generally, dealer demographics were involved in little of the outcomes, and a number of demographic variables were not involved at all in the health outcomes. Though it has been shown that dealers spend long hours at work and travelling to and from work, neither featured in any of the outcomes, nor did age, marital status, or the number of children under 18 years of age. These results contrast with much of the stress literature we examined.

Summary. Looking at the results together as they affect sub-groups of dealers, they suggest that those dealers aged 35 or over deal with the additional stress they report by their greater use of four of the six major coping strategies and by their advantageous personality profile. The stress of those dealers who travel two or more hours to work per day appears to be dealt with by utilising more of the coping strategies, despite a poorer personality profile. Male dealers drink more because of biological differences with women, and single dealers drink more because of their life-style. However, non-graduates and those responsible for others at work drink more because of job-related stress. Poorer mental health and more job dissatisfaction in 'US' dealers and in dealers with no children aged under 18 years of age, and poorer mental health in women and in those expecting to wait at least two years for promotion, may be due to job-related stress. Those groups of dealers who indicate higher stress at work and higher negative outcomes are the dealers who are most under threat of ill-health in a population which is generally at risk.

FEMALE AND MALE DEALERS

We examined the difference between two sub-groups of dealers in some detail, female and male dealers, and dealers in organisations with owners of differing nationality.

Mental health. On all mental health measures female dealers indicate poorer mental health than male dealers, which may be due to the fact that women generally report higher scores. If differences are real this may be due to two factors. Firstly, for women and men alike, the stress effects of work on home life results in *better* mental health, but for women the stress factor contributes 36 per cent of total mental ill-health, while for men the comparable figure is 6.4 per cent. Female dealers are possibly the 'hardier' (Kobasa and Puccetti 1983), or have recognised and accepted that they have to sacrifice more in order to work as a dealer. This may be reflected in the finding that fewer women are married, and they find less time to relax and wind down.

Secondly, coping by prioritising and planning results in better mental health for both men and women. However, for women the factor contributed to 65 per cent of mental ill-health, but only 4 per cent for men, so that female dealers may be more job-oriented than men. It may be suggested that women show a mental health profile (free-floating and somatic anxiety and depression) which is not significantly different from the normative population because of the combination of these two factors. Men show significantly poorer free-floating anxiety and better somatic anxiety (i.e. they are more 'afraid' but report less physical problems) because of the influence of other variables, particularly taking risks and achieving high performance, and their poorly-perceived locus of control. These and other variables have no effect upon the mental health profile of female dealers. Given our results, it appears that any attempt to improve the mental health (and job satisfaction) of male dealers will require a much wider approach than that for female dealers.

Job dissatisfaction. Female dealers indicate that they are less satisfied with their job than male dealers. It appears that women who can
prioritise and plan their work do increase their job satisfaction, and
as this same coping factor is a predictor of better mental health in
women, its importance is emphasised. Female dealers would benefit
greatly from appropriate training in time management.

Female dealers' job satisfaction can also be enhanced by
improving their career and promotion prospects. Data show that
female dealers have less responsibilities for others at work and they
expect to wait as long as male dealers for promotion. Career prospects, or more likely the lack of them which they see in examining
the current situation in Dealing Rooms, may have major negative
effects upon female dealers.

A third predictor of job dissatisfaction in female dealers shows
that they are more affected by the office environment (heat, noise,
etc.). Fewer women smoke, and those who do smoke less than male
dealers. They may be more aware of the office environment than
their male colleagues because they are more conscious of their health
in general, and how it can be affected by their physical
surroundings.

The job dissatisfaction of male dealers is determined by all of the
factors which affect women, plus some additional items. Failure to
obtain support and guidance from colleagues is the major source of
low job satisfaction in males, indicating that male dealers need this
support more than women. Results suggest that women receive less
of this support but have overcome its absence by other means, while
men require more feedback about their performance. As with the
sources of mental ill-health, lack of control affects the job satisfaction of male dealers more than female dealers.

In general, the job dissatisfaction of male dealers is determined by
a much wider range of job-related stressors than female dealers. Men
appear to be affected by many aspects of the job, while only two
job-related stressors affect women's job satisfaction. As male dealers
seem so concerned with multiple aspects of the job this may also
explain their higher scores (compared with the normative population) on the free-floating anxiety scale. Women appear to be more
single-minded and less affected by the stresses of the job.

Male non-graduates appear to be more satisfied than male
graduates, but this is not a feature of the female trader. It may be that
females, whether graduates or not, have had to work harder, overcome more prejudice, etc. than males, and their consequent

attitudes, strategies, and behaviours may have been carried into the Dealing Room. Male graduates may be encountering major 'real world' problems for the first time in the Dealing Room. However, it is interesting to note that one dealer commented:

> Education is a waste of time for dealers. It's about buying and selling.

Another told us that:

> Being a successful dealer is being in the right place at the right time – it's just buying and selling, any person could do it. The Foreign Exchange, rather than the Stock Exchange, have not gone for highly-educated staff, whereas the Stock Exchange goes for Oxbridge types. There are lots of East Enders, like bookies, quoting two prices. Buy and sell, that's all it is, rather than anything you can learn.

Drinking behaviour. Both male and female dealers' drinking habits are determined in part by performance setbacks, though in opposite directions. Female dealers drink more as they age, which may be a reflection of the lower drinking levels from which they commence. As they spend more time in the City 'culture' they may duplicate the drinking behaviours of their male colleagues. As they fail to achieve advancement in the job and are under continual stress at work they may drink more alcohol. The pressures on women in general to drink alcohol may be greater. Support from colleagues leads to higher alcohol consumption in women, and this suggests that those female dealers who interact with their colleagues in the Dealing Room continue these behaviours outside, at lunch, after work, socially, etc.

For male dealers, two personality dispositions lead to more drinking, namely extraversion and coronary-prone behaviour. This suggests that those dealers who combine both traits drink even more and are at higher risk. Whereas for women age is a predictor of more drinking, for men the number of years in the present job is relevant. Since the two variables have much in common, similar arguments concerning the City culture, lack of advancement, etc. may be applicable to men. However, for both male and female dealers results may be influenced by current attitudes to drinking, i.e. younger dealers may be more responsive to pressures to drink less alcohol, and to substitute low or non-alcoholic drinks, and to be more health conscious in general. Older dealers may be less responsive.

DEALERS IN DEALING ROOMS OF DIFFERING NATIONAL OWNERSHIP

Results show that there are major differences in the sources of mental ill-health, job dissatisfaction, and alcohol intake between dealers working in UK-, US-, and European-owned institutions, indicating that the organisations may be different in many important respects.

Many dealers recognised variations in culture and practices in the various Dealing Rooms. UK-owned Dealing Rooms are seen by many traders as extensions of the traditionally conservative British banks, and one forward deposits dealer in such an institution commented that while his bank was steeped in tradition:

> The Japanese are very aggressive, they work to different rules. The Japanese just hammer, hammer, hammer to get into a customer's business.

A spot dealer from the same bank noted that:

> American dealers go over the top much more often than British dealers. But that's what's expected if you work in a US bank. I don't think it makes you a better dealer.

A dealer in a US-owned bank said during an interview:

> US banks, they pay top dollar and expect top performance. They recruit from Oxbridge, Durham, and the London School of Economics.

Notably, British-owned Dealing Rooms had the lowest percentage of graduates. During visits to the three types of institution it was noted that US-owned Dealing Rooms were the largest, had the most modern equipment, and were the more 'glossy'. Interviews with managers of US-owned Dealing Rooms also showed them to be more aggressive. One described his attitude to staff to us:

> There's no molly-coddling. They need to be able to 'come back'. If there are inherent (personality) problems it breaks out quickly. Some people had to change jobs, they couldn't take the pressure.

He told us that trainees were given six months and then 'let go' if they were unsuccessful. His equivalent in the Dealing Room of a UK-owned Clearing Bank noted that failed dealers go back to bank activities.

These comments reflect differing recruitment methods. Many dealers in UK-owned institutions are recruited internally, while other banks depend more on the graduate 'milk round'. Other relevant comments concerning the different cultures which exist in banks include that of a forward deposits dealer from a UK-owned bank who told us: 'Why stay in this bank? I could earn more elsewhere, but there's job security. The bank has a very good name – some banks I wouldn't touch with a barge pole'.

Results show that female dealers in UK-owned institutions have significantly poorer mental health than their male colleagues, and this may be due to problems specific to these organisations, e.g. fewer promotion prospects, less equable treatment, etc. Being a married dealer in a UK-owned institution indicates better mental health, possibly because these Dealing Rooms have a greater percentage of married dealers, and there was no indication of the stress effects of the home–work interface. The working atmosphere in UK-owned organisations may be more suited to married staff.

Variations in the job dissatisfaction of dealers in the three types of Dealing Rooms examined may also be due to differing work practices. Dealers in UK-owned organisations appear to be more affected by other people, by demands upon their time, and by the organisational culture, while dealers in US-owned Dealing Rooms are additionally concerned by their lack of control (the lowest of the three groups), the office environment (including the technology), and by their promotion prospects. Dealers in European-owned Dealing Rooms are similar to their counterparts in UK-owned Dealing Rooms but are also affected by many of the variables noted by dealers in US-owned Dealing Rooms. It is not clear why lower coronary-prone behaviour is a source of job dissatisfaction only in dealers in European-owned Dealing Rooms, but it again suggests differing staff selection methods and working practices.

In summary, examination of the personalities of dealers shows that dealers in US-owned Dealing Rooms report more of the variables which are taken to result in the stress outcomes we have been examining. Dealers in US-owned Dealing Rooms show more coronary-prone behaviour, poorer (locus of) control, and more extraversion. In addition, they appear to utilise fewer of the coping techniques available. Whereas dealers in European-owned Dealing Rooms react to performance setbacks by drinking less, dealers in the other two institutions drink more because of their personality dispositions. These differences may be due to the staff selection methods used, or to differing organisational cultures and working methods. The effects of recent organisational change and takeovers may be relevant.

A NOTE ON THE LIMITATIONS OF THE STUDY

The findings of our study must be considered both in the context of potential improvements to it, and what we would like to do in the future. Though our sample of dealers is considered to be a representative one, it is representative only of the organisations which agreed to take part in the study. These organisations may themselves not be representative of the financial institutions operating Dealing Rooms in the City of London. There may be significant differences between these organisations and those which did not take part in the project. Those institutions which did not participate in the study may be less concerned with the health of their Dealing Room workforce, and the importance of management attitudes and of organisational culture and climate has been shown by many of the results of the study. Dealers in non-participating organisations may have poorer job satisfaction and greater mental ill-health than the study sample. Results of the present study may be regarded therefore as relatively conservative, i.e. dealers in general may, therefore, have *poorer* mental health, *lower* job satisfaction, and drink *more* than is indicated by our results.

As with post-traumatic stress disorder (PTSD), which can occur long after the stress of a traumatic event (e.g. on the military after combat, on the police after a civil disturbance), there is probably a time-lag in operation between a traumatic Dealing Room event and the disorder (mental ill-health, job dissatisfaction, more drinking). It would be very valuable to go back into the Dealing Rooms to look at the long-term effects upon dealers of their work.

There is also the problem that many dealers may not have admitted to us that they are suffering from stress problems, are unable to cope, etc. Of course, the opposite argument may also apply. Dealers may exaggerate their difficulties in the hope that they may obtain support and help. Objective data about dealers would have been useful in this context. Examination of absence, illness, and staff turnover records might have improved the study results and our interpretation. However, regular medical checks for dealers do not appear to be carried out within most institutions except at the higher organisational levels, and the relevant information will probably not exist. Such data might indicate that dealers who have higher neurotic scores (but who are not necessarily 'neurotic') obtain better results in the Dealing Rooms, so that while a certain amount of 'neuroticism' within dealers is regarded as a desirable trait by Dealing Room management, too much may result in mental ill-health. We would also have liked to collect some information in 'real-time' about the moment-to-moment physiological changes in dealers. This can be done by using hormonal methods (Benton 1987), the electro-encephalogram (Gale 1987), etc.

Finally, we would like to carry out a long-term study of dealers, using a more clinically-oriented approach. Comparisons of dealers working in Dealing Rooms subject to different cultural backgrounds (especially Japanese and East Asian), would provide valuable data, particularly if it were possible to examine dealers working in Dealing Rooms owned by the same organisation in different countries.

8

MANAGING STRESS IN DEALING ROOMS AND THE FINANCIAL SECTOR GENERALLY

INTRODUCTION

The purpose of this chapter is to indicate what actions might be taken by Dealing Room management and their staff to reduce the negative outcomes found by this study to be associated with the job of dealing. As a group, dealers in the City of London are generally satisfied with their jobs but show some indication of the stress by enhanced anxiety levels (e.g. the job interfering with their domestic life), excessive drinking, and other potential problems. These results suggest, at the organisational level, sub-optimum performance and higher staff turnover and absences, in addition to health and family costs for considerable numbers of individual dealers. We will suggest a number of methods by which controlling and preventing the stress of dealing might be approached.

The attitude of many Dealing Room managers and supervisors interviewed suggests that dealers are regarded as a replaceable commodity, earning high salaries in return for doing a potentially stressful job. Few managers appeared to have much regard for the negative long-term effects of the work upon the health of dealers.

However, these attitudes should be challenged. Current demographic changes in the UK and the USA mean that a smaller pool of younger people will be available from which to select Dealing Room staff, replacing staff will be more difficult, and more women, who have particular needs, may be encouraged to join the financial institutions.

There is also more public awareness of stress as a health problem, particularly in the City of London. The moral and ethical questions associated with occupational stress in the Dealing Room, as well as the potential legal penalties, must be addressed by management. In addition to stress resulting in potential loss of financial profits, the effects of any 'uncaring' attitude by management upon other areas of an institution's operations should not be overlooked. Many dealers are recruited from a bank's internal staff, and return to banking duties should they 'fail' in the Dealing Room. Most dealers will have colleagues elsewhere in the organisation as well as close contacts in other companies and rival institutions. Management attitudes to staff are quickly made known in the small world in which financial organisations operate. As one foreign exchange dealer told us: 'In this bank, failed dealers go back to bank activities'.

Recruitment, training, and redundancy methods should also be examined by organisations to determine the cost of poor Dealing Room management. Good dealers who find the work stressful or unsatisfactory may leave to join competitors, and whole teams of dealers may quit one organisation to join a rival, or to set up their own operation (as occurred at, for example, Citicorp Scrimgeour Vickers, see Bevan 1988).

Margins in dealing transactions are very low, 'a tiny fraction of 1 per cent' (Golzen 1990), so that for all the reasons noted above, it is to the advantage of institutional management to recruit and retain quality dealing staff.

STRESS PREVENTION AND STRESS MANAGEMENT

In attempting to improve or maintain the health of dealers, organisations are faced with conflicting aims. Results from our study suggest that the job of dealing appears to attract, and management purposefully to recruit, those individuals who exhibit personality dispositions such as extraversion and neuroticism. These personality traits, together with the demands of the job and the environment in which the work is done, contribute to the unfavourable outcomes noted in the previous chapters. Certain stressors appear to be unavoidable, but management can take appropriate measures to alleviate the associated stress. Institutions can also reduce environmental and organisational stressors.

There are two ways in which management can tackle the problems of stress in the organisation. First, through preventative strategies, and second through curative strategies (Matteson and Ivancevich 1987). Preventative strategies are aimed at eliminating or neutralising a stressor *before* it becomes a stressor. Curative strategies attempt to dissipate or relieve the stress once it has been experienced. Many preventative strategies are included in Stress Management Programmes (SMPs), and curative strategies are often incorporated within stress counselling techniques. The two strategies are often interrelated in practice, so that curative strategies are also found in SMPs.

In addition to these two strategies which might be adopted, there are various levels at which Dealing Room management might attempt to intervene in work-place health promotion. These are at the individual level, at the interface of the individual and organization, and at the organisation level (DeFrank and Cooper 1987). Table 8.1 indicates the interventions (targets) for a comprehensive Dealing Room Stress Management Programme, and the stress outcomes (impacts) which such a programme is intended to modify.

In the case of the individual, the aim is to concentrate on the way in which the dealer responds to and copes with stress, whatever its source. At the second level, the individual/organisational interface, the aim is to concentrate on the outcomes rather than the interventions since these 'are not well developed for this kind of interaction' (DeFrank and Cooper 1987). At the third, organisational level, concentration is upon the organisational environment, and on the structure and policies of financial organisations, all of which can produce stress in employees.

STRESS MANAGEMENT AT THE DEALER LEVEL

At the level of the individual dealer, institutions can help staff to recognise and identify the sources and results of occupational stress by introducing educational and counselling support. Dealers should be provided with a basic understanding of stress and of its potential harmful effects, and also informed of the major stressors related to the job of dealing and the effects of these particular stressors. Dealers should also be given information about methods of coping with job-related stress, and the effects of each of these strategies (Romano 1988).

For instance, the stress we found to be associated with 'taking risks and achieving high performance' (Stress Factor 2) may at first sight appear to derive from within the individual dealer, but management can still help by ensuring organisational support for the trader. Given the intrinsic nature of the items comprising the factor (see Chapter 5), this source of stress seems to require individual stress counselling. Methods of reducing the somatic symptoms of stress need to be addressed, using cognitive coping techniques, for

Table 8.1 Levels of stress management interventions and outcomes

INTERVENTION	OUTCOMES
1 INDIVIDUAL LEVEL	
Relaxation techniques	Mood states (depression, anxiety)
Cognitive coping strategies	Psychosomatic complaints
Biofeedback	Subjectively-experienced stress
Meditation	Physiological parameters
Exercise	(blood pressure, cathecholamines,
Employee assistance programmes	muscle tension)
Time management	Sleep disturbances
	Life satisfaction
2 INDIVIDUAL/ ORGANISATIONAL LEVEL	
Relationships at work	Job stress
Person–environment fit	Job satisfaction
Role issues	Burnout
Participation and autonomy	Productivity and performance
	Absenteeism
	Turnover
	Health care utilisation and claims
3 ORGANISATIONAL LEVEL	
Organisational structure	Productivity
Selection and placement	Turnover
Training	Absenteeism
Physical and environmental	Health care claims
characteristics of job	Recruitment/retention
Health concerns and resources	Success
Job rotation	

Source: DeFrank and Cooper (1987)

example. However, since the stressor is also associated with job satisfaction, management need to ensure that the stress of the factor is not reduced to too low a level. One broker commented that:

> Satisfaction is when you read the market right. You don't feel very good about losing money, but you don't end up in a black cloud. You try again tomorrow.

Another told us that:

> Stress is caused by continually losing money, and when you can't control events, and when other people let you down,

and another that:

> You need to handle defeat sensibly, to understand risks.

One dealer commented:

> On the positive side, there's the thrill, the risk, who can make most money. It's an ego trip. On the negative side, it's things going wrong, not making the money you should. Two or three days of that and you try to find out why it went wrong.

Similarly, the stress of performance setbacks (Stress Factor 7) also appears to be intrinsic to the job, and was recognised as so by many dealers interviewed. For instance, one dealer commented that:

> When you fail it results in strong language. A run of failure can get to you – it's inevitable, you can't make money all the time.

Another told us:

> When you've got the right [financial] position and it's going your way there's no need to panic, you sit back and let it happen. When you're caught it's not a nice feeling, you want to work all the harder to get it back, to cut losses and make a profit.

While organisations may welcome this latter attitude, dealers should be encouraged to develop methods to cope with the effects of taking risks and of performance setbacks, and organisations should make it clear that they accept that dealers are not expected to 'win' from every transaction carried out.

'Keeping the situation at arm's length' (Coping Factor 3) results in many negative health outcomes. Dealers should be told of these relationships and encouraged to use personal techniques (described following) to modify the negative effects.

Curative/Counselling Strategies

Appropriate curative or counselling strategies for individual dealers can be implemented relatively quickly in Dealing Rooms. For example, Matteson and Ivancevich (1987) and Romano (1988) have reviewed the *major individual stress management techniques*, and a number of these can be applied to dealers.

(i) *Relaxation training* can be demonstrated to dealers. This includes breathing exercises, muscle relaxation, meditation, autogenic training (a combination of muscle relaxation and meditation), and mental relaxation strategies. Relaxation training has been found to reduce levels of anxiety and alcohol intake, and to reduce the levels of the perceived symptoms of stress.

(ii) Dealers can use *biofeedback*. In biofeedback, certain bodily functions can be brought under voluntary control, and these include brain waves, heart rate, muscle tension, stomach acidity, and blood pressure. Biofeedback is reported as reducing anxiety, controlling both tension and migraine headaches, reducing stress-related hypertension, and modifying Type A behaviour.

(iii) The application of *cognitive techniques* would be valuable to dealers. The purpose here is to allow the individual dealer to reappraise or restructure situations so that they are no longer considered to be stressful. This is done by removing cognitive distortions, such as overgeneralising, magnifying, and personalising events, and by introducing assertiveness training. The aim is to give individuals more control over their reactions to stressors. Cognitive techniques have been successful in reducing at least one aspect of Type A behaviour, and in reducing blood pressure.

(iv) Dealers should be encouraged to take *exercise*. DeVries (1981) has concluded that moderate rhythmic exercise of as little as 5 to 30 minutes' duration can produce significant tranquillising effects. Routine vigorous exercise can reduce the intensity and duration of anxiety. Exercise may be seen as the contemporary alternative to the 'fight or flight' phase of the response to stress (which we discussed in Chapter 1).

(v) Dealing Room staff could be taught *time management* skills. Poor use of time management has been shown to be a source of most of the negative health outcomes in dealers. Time management should include both work and extra-employment activities. For instance, dealers should be shown how to identify the key areas in their life, develop priorities, and recognise 'time robbers' (Mulligan 1989). While dealers are required to spend much of their time with colleagues, clients, and supervisors at work, any discretionary time they have at work might be better managed. This may result in resistance from an individual dealer's colleagues, who may expect them to spend much of their 'free' time exclusively interacting with them, because it will necessitate changes in the ways dealers interact with each other (Adams 1980). Dealers need to be provided with ways of coping with these negative 'knock-on' effects from their colleagues.

Given the results of our study, all of these techniques would benefit Dealing Room staff, though the actual *form* of stress counselling may be unimportant. For example, Firth and Shapiro (1986) used two forms of stress therapy with forty managerial and professional workers seeking help for job-related distress which had become clinically severe. One form of therapy was designed to include anxiety control training, self-management, and cognitive re-structuring. A second form of therapy was concerned with individuals' relationships with their colleagues. These forms of treatment were chosen to represent the two principal theoretical areas used in psychological treatment. They found that both methods were successful, and there was little difference between them in terms of the outcomes. This supports the findings of Stiles *et al.* (1986) who found that demonstrably different therapies have very similar rates of effectiveness.

STRESS MANAGEMENT PROGRAMMES

Though dealers would undoubtedly benefit from the techniques described in the previous section, they can only be of limited, short-term value. The onus is upon the dealer to utilise the methods outlined, and the organisation itself would not be seen as demonstrating more than a minimum concern for dealers' health. More comprehensive health management programmes should be introduced by financial organisations, which envelop more of the dealer's life-style. This will benefit the organisation, and indicate to dealers the organisation's interest in their general welfare.

Financial organisations should consider adopting and adapting the successful stress management strategies used by other institutions. Most examples of SMPs derive from the United States. While employers in the UK have traditionally been concerned with the health of *prospective* employees, and dealing with job-related accident and illness once a worker is hired, few have attempted to prevent illness in the workforce. In the United States, where there are different attitudes to work-related stress, and where the costs of health care are high, numerous health promotion and Stress Management Programmes have been developed and many of these have proved successful. We will discuss a number of these as good examples of what can be done.

The Employee Assistance Program at Chase Manhattan Bank has a 24-hour telephone line, and the Bank publishes a brochure aimed at acquainting employees with problems such as drug and alcohol abuse, child care, elder care, marital or family relationship concerns, emotional distress, anxiety, depression, and financial difficulties (Kirrane 1990).

The Wellness Works Program of Massachusetts General Hospital offers staff both risk factor assessment and medical evaluation, development of appropriate individual exercise, and nutrition and life-style prescriptions. The programme promotes information sessions on nutrition, coronary-prone behaviour, smoking control, and exercise classes. The programme also assesses employees over a five-year period.

Control Data Corporation's (CDC) Staywell programme is provided free to all its 22,000 employees and their spouses. The programme consists of stress orientation for employees and management, a confidential health screening and health hazard appraisal, and courses designed to promote healthy behaviour in a variety of areas. Employees rate the programme highly in beneficially changing their behaviour. Those employees who were encouraged to give up smoking had 20 per cent less healthcare costs, and those who went on exercise courses had 30 per cent fewer claims and spent less than half the amount of days in hospital. Staff who went on a cardiovascular fitness programme had half the healthcare costs of those who did not (Phillips 1989).

Kimberley-Clark's health care programme for staff includes health screening and health risk appraisal, health education, supervised exercise programmes, employee assistance programmes, occupational health nursing services, and professional and career education. The programme has been very successful in significantly reducing participating employees' weight, body fat, and blood pressure, in rehabilitating employees with drug problems, and in reducing absenteeism and accidents.

New York Telephone's Stress Management Program includes fitness, smoking cessation, blood pressure control, cholesterol reduction, alcohol programmes, and colorectal and breast cancer screening. Hypertension control and the alcohol rehabilitation programme have been very successful.

In the UK, schemes similar to CDC's have been introduced by Johnson and Johnson, North Thames Gas, and the Post Office. CDC in the UK has set up a 24-hour counselling service where employees and their families can talk about any topic they wish. Prime and Tandem use CDC's service on a commercial basis. Rank Xerox and IBM have counselling schemes designed to help employees recognise the symptoms of stress, while some divisions of ICI give their entire workforce stress management training (Davison 1990).

One UK example appears particularly relevant to Dealing Rooms. Post Office staff have been under growing pressure due to restructuring, the need for greater competitiveness, and an increase in the volume of work. These pressures are similar to the situation in many London financial institutions. In the North-West region of the UK Post Office, a programme has been designed to help employees cope with stress and to detect and treat the early signs of stress (Fewster 1989). Blood clotting and cholesterol levels of employees were measured and those with high levels taught simple meditation and relaxation techniques, with monthly individual and group sessions on coping with work-related stress. Improvements recorded include a reduction in blood clotting factors and cholesterol levels in staff, and improvements have been claimed by staff in both quality of home life and enjoyment of work. In another UK Post Office programme involving stress counselling (Cooper and Sadri 1991), there have been significant reductions in sickness absence, somatic and free-floating anxiety, and reductions in depression and improvements in mental well-being (though the job satisfaction of staff did not change significantly).

Financial institutions might also employ the techniques used by alcohol and psychiatric units in National Health Service hospitals, which attempt to help clients understand and control anxiety. Patients are provided with relaxation tapes and literature, and meet regularly in discussion groups (Whitmore *et al.* undated).

Alcohol

Given the results of our study, management of Dealing Rooms must take appropriate action to assist employees with alcohol problems. At Illinois Bell Telephone Company, sickness and disability declined 52 per cent among those who participated in an alcoholism control programme; at Kennecott Copper, absenteeism decreased by 52 per cent and hospital costs decreased by 48 per cent among problem drinkers who participated in a similar programme (Herzingler and Calkins 1986).

Since dealers are heavy drinkers, and a large minority of dealers feel that they need to cut down on their drinking, the introduction of an alcohol policy in the workplace may help employers to: 'identify, intervene, recover and rehabilitate an employee whose drink is affecting his/her work performance' (Allen and Arthur 1990). It would be most appropriate to take action to help employees *before* a deterioration in performance is noted.

A UK survey notes that a number of managers have admitted that the underperformance of staff who only *occasionally* drink at lunchtime costs their organisations: 'far more than the rare cases of alcoholism which they uncovered' (Geake 1990).

The introduction of Employee Assistance Programmes (EAPs) into UK Dealing Rooms should be a priority. In comparison, in the USA over 75 per cent of the Fortune 500 companies have some kind of corporate health programme, and 15,000 EAPs were in use in 1989 (Geake 1990). As a number of dealers take drugs of various sorts on a regular basis, the alcohol assistance programme could be extended to include help for potential drug abusers.

Smoking

Another area of concern to many Dealing Room staff which was indicated by the study was the prevalence of smoking in Dealing Rooms. This can be tackled by a Stress Management Programme which includes assisting smoking reduction in staff. The introduction of no-smoking environments in the Dealing Room should also be considered, given the negative comments of staff. One dealer said:

They should ban smoking, only a minority smoke.

A spot dealer, a non-smoker, told us:

Colleagues worried about health? Some smoke thirty a day – there is some stress involved. I'd be a liar if I said I was discounting health problems, there is stress there, no doubt about that. Passive smoking's a problem. He [pointing to a colleague] smokes thirty a day, and *I* smoke ten! Some dealers need a smoke when they've got a position.

As an alternative to a no-smoking regime, setting aside smoking areas may be a possibility. The possibility that illness shown to be caused by passive smoking in the workplace may be subject to legal penalties should be noted by employers.

Food, Exercise, and Holidays

The provision of accessible and available healthy food, on site, should be considered by management, since many dealers spend long hours at work, and were found to take their lunch in a local public house – sandwiches and beer at lunch were common. However, we did find that a number of US-owned institutions did provide 'health conscious' restaurant food, at low prices (or free). One dealer recognised a problem: 'You're invited out by brokers. Some people become "broker junkies", getting big meals and drinking'.

Organisations should also examine the possibility of introducing a physical exercise facility, to ensure that dealers have the opportunity to exercise adequately. As an alternative, group membership of health clubs, of which many exist in the City of London, should be considered. A 'quiet room' in the Dealing Room facility should certainly be set aside for staff relaxation.

Dealers, particularly those at senior levels, should be encouraged to take adequate time off for holidays. One manager of a Dealing Room told us that:

Hours are 7.15 or 7.30 to 5.30 or 6.15. Weekend is working on the 'phone, the seniors anyway, for half an hour or so: 26 days holiday. I try to get the Senior Dealers away for a 'conference'. After a six months run a break is needed.

Organisations should ensure that lower level staff also take appropriate time off.

In summary, a health care programme similar to that operated by, for instance, Kimberley Clark, or the Wellness Works Program, should be introduced by financial institutions, and staff encouraged to participate on a voluntary and confidential basis. Where organisations have little history of employee health care concern, it will be necessary to introduce schemes piecemeal and slowly. We suggest that these schemes commence with a stress education pro- gramme for staff.

STRESS MANAGEMENT AT THE ORGANISATIONAL LEVEL

The problems of the individual dealer in identifying and coping with the stress of their job can certainly be addressed with the help of their employer. Wide health-care policies can also be introduced into Dealing Rooms. However, organisational management must also examine those of its *own* practices which we have found to result in stress for their employees.

There are various aspects of the job design of dealers which should be examined with a view to improving their job satisfaction and motivation, and reducing stress. For instance, the principles suggested by Hackman *et al.* (1975) for redesigning jobs should be applied in the Dealing Room. This involves improving the skill variety, task identity, task significance, autonomy, and feedback associated with the job. However, it must be recognised that the implications of job redesign are major.

We suggest that the management of Dealing Rooms in particular, and financial institutions in general, consider the following ways in which they might reduce the stress of their employees.

Role Conflict and Changes

Role conflict and changes (Stress Factor 1) can be tackled by determining where the sources of role conflict lie in the Dealing Room. Role conflict may be due to interpersonal conflict, or to rivalry and conflict between groups within the Dealing Room, both of which we found during our inspection of the Dealing Rooms, and which we noted during our interviews with dealers. For instance, one dealer told us: 'Stress – two causes – management attitudes and the competence of colleagues in other departments. The only way to get attention is to be aggressive'. The result of this aggression can include role conflict.

Role conflict in Dealing Room team supervisors can be overcome through better support for supervisors, and leadership and management training would be valuable. The application of individual stress management techniques may also be appropriate in these cases. Nevertheless, the recognition that some minimal level of conflict within organisations is inevitable means that it is not desirable to attempt to remove all conflict (Luthans 1989).

High Staff Turnover

Management should recognise the effects of high staff turnover on those dealers who remain *in situ*, and should employ improved staff selection methods which will result in the maintenance and retention of dealing teams. Williams (1985) suggests that staff selection may be enhanced by using 'experiential realistic job previews' and assessment centres to facilitate the process of staff selection.

Discussing staff selection, the manager of a US-owned Dealing Room told us:

It's difficult, the milk round gives three or four. People wander into this profession. Some people had to change their jobs, they couldn't take the pressure. I find out how trainees are taking it, reacting to success and failure, by how they look in the morning. You can see people's confidence in their physical reactions.

Another Dealing Room manager said:

We select staff for their personality, good academic qualifications, the ability to bounce back, their enthusiasm. They have to be hungry for success, ambitious. They have to have the will to succeed . . . speed of thought – if there's a gap in the market you go for it . . . be intuitive, that's 80 per cent of the job. It's not essential to have a higher-level education. It's like a sport, you want to win. You need self-confidence in decisions, team work and no conflict, and be goal-oriented. It attracts the personalities who can cope.

The personnel manager of one institution commented:

You need to want to take responsibility, to be thick-skinned, to be individual. You need to recognise trends . . . to want autonomy and buck the trend. You need instinct. You get a buzz and excitement from running a position.

Staff shortages at any point in time may also be due to staff absences or illnesses, and the reasons for these should be investigated. We found little evidence of interest in determining why some staff are regularly ill or absent.

On occasion it will be necessary to ask dealers to change the way they carry out their job, to undertake additional tasks, and to change instructions, policies, or procedures in the Dealing Room. However, the stress effects of these changes can be reduced by improved communications, and by explaining to dealers why these changes are necessary. The reduction of staff numbers in Dealing Rooms due to wider economic pressure may add to this source of stress. Organisations should cope with these changes by appropriate forward planning.

Job Rotation

The fact that the stress associated by dealers with spending time on 'unproductive' tasks (Stress Factor 5) leads to *increased* job satisfaction suggests that dealers welcome the chance to get away from the constant activity of dealing. Some form of job rotation for dealers might be valuable, or, if it is possible, job enrichment or job enlargement. Regular breaks from the dealing desk might not be possible, but alternative tasks might be welcomed by Dealing Room staff. Job enlargement or job enrichment should also be considered as a possible alternative to balance the few promotion prospects available to dealers, since these would give those dealers who so wish the chance to utilise and extend their skills and abilities.

Control

Financial institutions, as with most organisations, require stability and predictability in the behaviour of their employees (Buchanan and Huczynski 1985), but dealers, because of their personalities and jobs, may tend to behave in comparatively unstable, variable, spontaneous, random, and altogether 'individual' ways, though one Dealing Room manager did tell us that: 'The market is too big and too fast to go on a joyride. Dealing is like chess. Dealers are driven by fear and greed'.

It may be that to overcome the apparent misfit between dealers' personalities and the need to impose some form of control, financial organisations have installed very rigid social and work control systems, and these should be 'loosened' as far as is possible. Organisations should attempt to increase the control which dealers feel they have over their work, since dealers' current low levels of control are associated with reduced mental health. Improving information flows within the organisation will help improve locus of control, and Dealing Room managers should be encouraged to listen to the suggestions and comments of dealers and to take appropriate action.

Social Support

For most people social support is essential to the maintenance of mental health. We found that dealers do not use social support and activities, or a supportive home life, as effective methods of coping with stress. Organisations should encourage staff to develop interests and pastimes, and these can be organised with the help of the employer, for instance via clubs, social and professional groups, etc.

Support and guidance from colleagues. Lack of support and guidance from colleagues and superiors (Stress Factor 11) was expressed by a number of dealers. In describing the training he had received, one junior foreign exchange dealer commented that he 'sat between two blokes'. Better training of staff and improved management development programmes are also needed to improve job satisfaction and reduce depression. Stress was caused for one dealer: 'When other people let you down . . . and not getting the merit you deserve leads to stress'.

Organisations need to provide dealers with more information about their performance, via regular performance appraisal reviews, and managers in particular need to find ways to encourage staff. This can be done by using any of the well-known motivational and training techniques.

Many studies, including the present one, have found that one of the primary complaints of employees is about their managers' lack of caring and praise-giving skills. To counteract this, financial organisations should consider schemes such as that used by Xerox. They are reported as running workshops for all managers to get them to improve their praise-giving skills (Cooper 1988). In addition, the same organisation has introduced a system where staff can give a 'recognition' certificate to colleagues for excellence in support, attendance, co-operation, or for extra work.

Organisational Culture and Climate

Dealers have told us that the culture and climate they find in their organisations (Stress Factor 10) results in reducing their job

218

satisfaction. A number of dealers emphasised to us the importance of institutional policy. Organisations should examine the structure and design of their institutions. Organisations may be seen by Dealing Room staff as particularly over-bureaucratic, and this results in negative health and performance outcomes. Indeed, it might appear incongruous to find the type of person who is attracted to dealing working in traditional, conservative, financial institutions. If organisations are unwilling or unable to change their structure and climate, improved staff selection methods which will find employees who are able to cope with these problems should be used.

Career and Promotion

Lack of career and promotion prospects (Stress Factor 3) reduces dealers' job satisfaction, and was certainly seen as a problem by many of the dealers we interviewed. Organisational management appear to believe that dealers know very well that there are few opportunities for advancement in the Dealing Room or elsewhere in the institution. The financial rewards of the job are regarded as compensation for this. Younger dealers may indeed accept this view. One dealer considered that: 'The steady trader moves into administration, into policies and so on, then into management. The high return dealer trades in currency longer, or goes into corporate trading or merchant banking'.

However, the reduction in City employment has severely reduced these and other job possibilities. Organisations can help their staff by providing outplacement planning and assistance for staff who are made redundant or who voluntarily leave, or offer training which will allow dealers to move into other employment areas. Many financial institutions are large conglomerates, with diverse operations, and it should certainly be possible to provide some form of career path for appropriate personnel.

While new recruits and younger members of staff may be content to accept the possible short-term nature of their job and the limited employment prospects, older, more experienced members of staff may find that these same concerns affect their health and performance. As Sutherland (1988) suggests: 'If person–environment is poor, mental health deteriorates. Personnel stay because they feel trapped into the way of life (e.g. financially, or because no alternative is available)'.

Other changes that organisations can make to assist longer-established staff include career revisioning. This involves regular, perhaps annual discussions with staff about their career plans, their training needs, and so on.

Managers' and Supervisors' Problems

The problems faced by Dealing Room management, supervisors, and team leaders (Stress Factor 4) are quite typical of managerial stress, but we have found in the present study that the outcomes of this stress are *positive*, leading to better mental health and improved job satisfaction in managers and supervisors. However, organisations need to appreciate that managers who are over-promoted, or who do not fully understand the work, or cannot or will not delegate, may be grossly overworking to keep down the job, and hiding their insecurity (Robertson and Cooper 1983). There will be negative consequences for their own work performance and for other dealers in the Dealing Room.

This problem can be tackled by improving training and clarifying roles for managers. There may also be inadequate resources available to support managers. The problems faced by Dealing Room managers may be reflected in the comments of one spot dealer interviewed:

> The higher you go in the Room, the less dealing you do. Some people don't want to get away from Dealing – they've got to be there, got to sit there with a couple of 'phones. Some dealers like to be big – 'I do this, I do that'. They might make a small loss, but there's the prestige of putting a price in. There are some here who just like quoting prices, without thinking of the consequences. That's a part of dealing.

Thus, many managers may be unable to concentrate solely on managing, and they continue to trade as before, in addition to carrying out their managerial tasks. The selection of candidates for potential promotion needs to be considered more carefully, and job analysis methods used to produce appropriate job specifications.

Home Life

The negative relationship between the effects of work on home life (Stress Factor 6), and the mental health outcomes, indicates that dealers' families and home and social life may be suffering because of 'spillover' effects. Many comments were made to us by dealers about this aspect of the job:

> 'After a hard day's work you go out for a drink with your colleagues. There are dozens of pubs within a few minutes walk of here. So you get home late two or three nights a week. Wives don't like that'.
>
> 'Social life in the week is non-existent – its glamour is money'.
>
> 'The long hours kill social life'.
>
> 'There are times when I hardly see my kids'.
>
> 'Some people talk to their wives the way they talk in the Dealing Room. Brokers have to entertain, to go out four nights a week. That won't go down well with wives. Some (dealers) go out drinking five nights a week. I want good prices and services, but not through entertaining'.

The problem for organisations is that they have, and may prefer to have, little control of dealers outside the Dealing Room. However, if organisations want to assist dealers in this aspect of stress management they might adopt the strategies employed by Phillips and Drew (see Chapter 1), who have recognised the importance of family life and support to their employees' health and performance at work.

A reduction in dealers' working hours might be helpful to family and social life, but dealers themselves also need to recognise the effects of their behaviour upon their families. This study has found that dealers may be using home relationships to dissipate their work-induced stress and this may have undesirable effects upon their spouse or partner and family. Many dealers appear to be part of a dual-career couple, and Jordan *et al.* (1989) have suggested *a five-step intervention plan* that can be adapted by organisations to assist dealers and their families. This requires dealers and their partners to concentrate on carrying out common strategies together, and to examine the following areas of their relationship:

(a) Goals and values.

This concentrates on assessing role expectations in terms of career, marital, parental, and personal activities, for both the dealer and for their partner. Couples can be helped to establish mutual and individual goals, and explore the long-term consequences of their plans.

(b) Communication training.

This may be needed because even the most articulate dual-career couple may not have good marital communications. It can include non-verbal communication training.

(c) Negotiation and concentrating skills training.

This is based on quid pro quo or good-faith contracts. In the former case, one partner's target behaviour is contingent upon the partner's performance of another target behaviour. In the second case one partner's behaviour is rewarded or punished according to the terms of the 'contract'.

(d) Time management techniques.

This involves both partners setting priorities and scheduling tasks.

(e) Stress management techniques.

This includes those methods noted earlier in this chapter.

One dealer's comments seem very relevant: 'It helps to have a partner outside the business, and to get away from colleagues'.

Neuroticism

Since neuroticism was found to be a significant predictor of mental ill-health in dealers (see Chapter 6), organisations should introduce staff recruitment methods which will include personality testing, attempting to ensure that individuals selected are not overly neurotic. Though some neuroticism is undoubtedly a requirement for successful dealing, it has been noted by Buchanan and Huczynski (1985) that: 'neurotics are not self-reliant and tend to submit to institutional power without question. They feel they are controlled by events, by others and by fate'.

Thus, individuals who have high neuroticism will tend to have low locus of control, as we found in dealers. A certain combination of extraversion and neuroticism is a necessary requirement in the Dealing Room, but it is important to manage the environment that minimises neurotic behaviour.

Female Dealers

The problems apparently faced by female dealers, especially poor job satisfaction, can be dealt with by ensuring that there is a policy of equal opportunity and equal treatment within the Dealing Room.

Despite better academic qualifications female dealers report fewer responsibilities within the Dealing Room, suggesting fewer promotion opportunities.

One male dealer's attitude to his female co-workers was that: 'women [dealers] are seen as more "catty", they take things personally, they bear a grudge', presumably, in his view, unlike male dealers.

Interviews with a number of the small proportion (16.2 per cent) of women dealers found in Dealing Rooms indicate that they do indeed believe that they are discriminated against, and that males make no allowances for them, particularly in their language and physical behaviour. However, another male dealer admitted that while women can be as capable as men, they are also just as 'blue' (with language).

Many women felt that they were expected to fail in the job, and this may become a self-fulfilling prophecy. While women dealers were, on average, slightly younger, only just over one half as many were married as males, suggesting that there are problems faced by female dealers who wish to start and raise a family. Organisations can assist female dealers by allowing them to return to work after maternity leave with no penalty in terms of lost status, as has been widely introduced in the UK Clearing Bank sector. These 'career break' schemes are necessary to help women pursue their careers in dealing and in the financial sector generally.

Encouraging more women to join and remain in the workforce may have beneficial effects for men in that female dealers appear to cope better with job-related stress than their male counterparts. These behaviours may be taken up by male dealers to their benefit.

The Office Environment

The job satisfaction of dealers was reduced by the stress of the office environment (Stress Factor 8). Management should examine the modern, open-plan, technology-dominated offices in which Dealing Rooms tend to operate. There seems little that can be done about the noise prevalent in such offices other than by dividing the floor-space into smaller offices, and this may not be realistic given that dealers need to gain immediate access to their colleagues. The noise associated with equipment can certainly be reduced. For instance, noisy computer printers can be replaced by laser printers, but noise may be an inevitable aspect of the job.

Other Forms of Working
The long-term potential of homeworking, teleworking, or flexible working should be considered by organisations:

> Thanks to a development in dealing-room technology, stock-brokers will find that their office furniture – a bank of screens, two telephone sets (one for each ear), and loudspeakers shouting out a cacophony of prices – can now be shifted miles away from their City offices.
>
> (Connor 1989)

Equipment costs for such working methods are considered to be comparatively inexpensive, £5,000 per desk (Connor 1989), and these alternative methods of working may be attractive to many dealers. It will allow them to spend more time at home with their families, reduce travelling time, and may offer staff more control over their work patterns as well as reduced housing costs outside the London area. These changes will, however, affect organisational control of staff, and there are the problems of potentially reduced employee visibility, and of a reduction in the shared work experiences and social intercourse of employees. Staff would also need to be assured that the changes would not result in replacing one set of problems with another.

THE MANAGEMENT OF STRESS MANAGEMENT PROGRAMMES

There is a potential problem in determining the best location in the organisation structure of financial institutions of Stress Management Programmes and policies. Those within the organisational personnel or human resources function might seem to be appropriate. However, as we pointed out in Chapter 4, there are many factors which put the personnel function in a poor position to formulate stress management policies. If those responsible for stress management within an organisation are not able to recognise and deal with the problem, there is little chance that those with less authority will be able to do so. The recruitment of in-house specialist stress counsellors, rather than using external specialists, is recommended by Sadri *et al.* (1989). Dealers would probably find it easier to approach and work with counsellors not seen as part of the formal organisational structure but who nevertheless understand the working of the organisation in general and dealing in particular. Total confidentiality within any Stress Management or Employee Assistance Programme is essential.

Length of Stress Management Programmes

Stress Management Programmes for dealers need not be overlong. Jenner (1986) considers that very brief training events of around an hour or so can be useful if they go over well and lead to longer workshops. In an hour, sources of stress, coping strategies, and design of a regime that incorporates positive habits without adding new pressures, can be covered.

Higgins (1986) found that two 7-session stress reduction programmes both significantly decreased the emotional exhaustion and personal strain of fifty-three female, mainly white-collar workers. One programme consisted of progressive relaxation and systematic desensitisation, and the other involved instruction in time management, rational-emotive therapy, and assertiveness training. Higgins (1986) also suggests that relatively brief programmes of stress management (approximately six hours long) can produce significant reductions in self-reported stress. (This contrasts with the conclusions reached by Ganster et al. (1982) who believe that much longer programmes are needed for effectiveness, suggesting a minimum of sixteen hours. Dealing Room management should err on the side of longer programmes.)

Failure of Programmes

Dealing Rooms which attempt to introduce full Stress Management Programmes need to be aware of the reasons for the failure of many of these programmes. Niven and Johnson (1989) have suggested that SMPs might fail due to a number of reasons and Dealing Room management must take these points into consideration:

(i) relaxation training cannot change in an afternoon the behaviour of thirty or forty years. Dealers need to be encouraged to practise constantly. Time and facilities for this must be made available to dealers.

(ii) the measurement of the success of SMPs, and the selection of staff to participate, are often based on questionnaires, which may be an unreliable method. Alternative methods of selecting staff at potential risk need to be considered. Organisations may need to tighten up their personnel records system to detect those who have regularly taken days off sick, etc. These people should be interviewed with a view to determine what the causes are. Personnel records could also be used to determine the personalities, training backgrounds, and so on, of successful dealers, of those who leave, become ill, etc., information which could help reduce turnover, and improve selection methods.

(iii) providing staff with the general principles of stress management is no guarantee that staff can apply them to their own specific work and home contexts. Continual group discussion meetings early on in the programmes will be more beneficial. Again, time and facilities to hold such meetings should be provided by Dealing Room management.

(iv) staff need to be encouraged that small changes in behaviour can be achieved easily.

(v) staff need to be given the skills to deal with responses at the emotional, behavioural, and cognitive levels, not just one or the other.

(vi) a successful, comprehensive, Stress Management Programme will require input from different psychological and managerial disciplines. Appropriate stress counselling and management staff and teams will require to be organised by the employing institutions.

SUMMARY

This study has shown that all the job-related stress factors which were thrown up by our analyses contributed in some degree to the health outcomes of dealers. We also found that the personality of the dealer, their methods of coping with stress, and demographic factors were also related to some or all of the outcomes. These results suggest that a comprehensive Stress Management Programme should be implemented in Dealing Rooms, since the causes and moderators of stress are so widespread and numerous.

The study has also shown that certain sources of stress appear to be associated intrinsically with the job of dealing, and dealers should be helped to recognise and cope with these stressors. Other sources of stress are related to Dealing Room management and environment, and to organisational structure, and it is appropriate for management, rather than the individual worker, to tackle these aspects of stress.

Institutions should begin by undertaking a stress audit of their Dealing Rooms and implementing appropriate actions to remedy the problems found. US-owned Dealing Rooms, and those which have recently been the subject of a takeover (Cartwright and Cooper 1990) appear to have particular difficulties. The problems faced by women, by dealers who have been in the job for some years, and by non-graduates, need particular attention.

Organisations which invest in stress management and stress prevention can justify their strategy by a simple cost/benefit analysis. A place on a typical stress management course costs £200–£600 (Landale 1989), or at the executive level, £3,000 (Fewster 1989). These figures compare with suggestions that stress is estimated to cost a company of 1,000 employees £200,000 per annum (Phillips 1989), and at the higher management level Xerox estimate that the cost of losing a senior executive through stress exceeds £300,000 (Ostell 1988).

Though it may be due to omission rather than commission, management attitudes to Dealing Room staff should never equate with that typified by Gray (1983), which we stated at the beginning of this report.

APPENDIX

STRESS QUESTIONNAIRE

MANCHESTER POLYTECHNIC

▎Manchester
▎**School of Management**

A JOINT RESEARCH PROJECT – STRESS IN THE FINANCIAL MARKETS

Introduction

These questionnaires are designed to measure both the sources and effects of occupational stress; a topic which has been much researched and for which there are many definitions. Generally speaking, occupational stress is regarded as a response to situations and circumstances that place special demands on an individual.

The sources of stress are multiple, as are the effects. It is not just a function of being 'under pressure'. The sources may be work-related, but home life will also be implicated. The effects in terms of health may not just concern how you feel physically but how you react and behave; again both in your job and your home.

These questionnaires are **strictly anonymous and confidential**: no names are requested, and there is no way in which any individual can be identified. They have been designed to gather information on groups of individuals. There are seven questionnaires entitled: How you assess your current state of health; The way you behave generally; How you interpret events around you; Your job satisfaction; Sources of pressure in your job; Your habits; and, How you cope with the stress you experience. There is also a questionnaire to collect significant biographical data.

As the questionnaires are being completed in a work context, the results will naturally be used in a work application. The explicit intention of the research project is to indicate the potential sources and effects of stress in those who work in the financial markets, to the mutual benefit of the individuals and organisations concerned.

What we would like you to do:

Answer all the questions – remember all data is anonymous
- Give your first and natural answer

228

STRESS QUESTIONNAIRE

- Work quickly and efficiently through the questionnaires
- Base your answers on how you have felt **during the last three months**
- If you make a mistake, cross it out and make your new answer
- Check each questionnaire to ensure that you have answered all the items
- Place the completed set of questionnaires in the envelope provided and return to us
- Let us know if you would like details of the research results, or have any comments

Completion of the questionnaires will take approximately 45 minutes–1 hour.

Thank you for your co-operation in this research project and for completing the questionnaires.

Cary L. Cooper
Manchester School of Management
University of Manchester
Institute of Science and Technology

Howard Kahn
Department of Business
Information Technology
Manchester Polytechnic

APPENDIX

1. Biographical data

Your answers to these questions will provide useful background information – facts about yourself rather than your opinions.

Please answer by circling the appropriate items, or write in the boxes provided

You and your family

Sex: male/female
Age:
Nationality:
Marital status: *Married/single/divorced/separated/widowed/cohabiting*
If not married now, have you ever been in the past?   *Yes/No*
If married now, does your partner work? *Yes/No/Full-time/Part-time/occasionally*
Your partner's job:
Number of children: *Under 18*
                         Over 18

Your education

Age on leaving full-time education:
Academic level reached in full-time education:
–   No formal qualifications
–   O-level or equivalent
–   A-level or equivalent
–   Degree level or equivalent
–   Higher degree level

Your employment history

How many years with present company?
How many years in present job?
How many years in previous job?
Job title:
For how many people are you responsible?
Brief job description:
When do you expect your next promotion?   *Within 1 year/5years/over 5 years/never*
Where do you work (region)?
What are your financial commitments as an approximate percentage of monthly income?
Number of hours travel daily to/from the office:
Number of hours spent at work/in office per week:
How is your work performance assessed?   *Company results/group performance/individual results*

Your habits

Do you maintain a desired body weight?   *Almost all the time/sometimes/ almost never*

Do you take any planned exercise?   *Always/usually/when possible/ occasionally/not usually/rarely*

Do you manage an 'ideal' exercise program (for example 15–30 minutes exercise, 3 times a week)?   *Always/usually/sometimes/not usually/never*

Do you smoke cigarettes?   *Yes/No*

If you smoke cigarettes, how many per day?

Have you noticed changes in how much you smoked over the last three months?   *More than usual/same as usual/less than usual*

Do you drink alcohol?   *Yes/No*

If yes, how many units per week on average (where 1 unit = half pint of beer, or glass of wine or one measure of spirits)?

Have you ever felt the need to cut down your drinking?   *Yes/No*

Over the last three months have you noticed any changes in your need for pills, drugs, tranquillisers, etc?   *More than usual/same as usual/less than usual*

If you do need pills, drugs, etc., what is the main one used?

Your interests

Do you find time to 'relax and wind down'?   *Always/usually/when possible/not usually*

Do you have an interest or hobby?   *Yes/No*

If yes, is it in some way related to work?   *Yes/No*

In general do you mix socially with work colleagues?   *Yes/No*

Recent life history

At what age do you expect to change to a less demanding job?

Over the last six months has your own performance at work   *Improved/ remained steady/deteriorated?*

2. How you assess your current state of health

Part A of this questionnaire focuses on feelings and behaviour and how these are affected by the pressure you perceive in your job. Part B is concerned more specifically with the frequency of occurrence of manifestly physical problems.

The questions assume that you can assess your health with a fair degree of accuracy and also that you will be honest in your responses.

Part A: How you feel or behave

Please answer by circling your position on the six-point answering scale.

Consider the questions with reference to how you have felt over the last three months.

Very strongly agree   6

Strongly agree   5

Agree	**4**
Disagree	**3**
Strongly disagree	**2**
Very strongly disagree	**1**

1 Would you say that you tended to be a rather overconscientious person who worries about mistakes or actions that you may have taken in the past, such as decisions? 6 5 4 3 2 1

2 During an ordinary working day are there times when you feel unsettled and upset though the reasons for this might not always be clearly obvious? 6 5 4 3 2 1

3 When you consider your level and quality of job performance recently, do you think that your contribution has been significantly useful? 6 5 4 3 2 1

4 As difficult problems occur at work that require your attention, do you find that you can think as clearly and as concisely as you used to? 6 5 4 3 2 1

5 When the pressure starts to mount at work, can you find a sufficient store or reserve of energy which you can call upon at times when you need it that spurs you on into action? 6 5 4 3 2 1

6 Are there times at work when you feel so exasperated that you sit back and think to yourself that 'life is all really just too much effort'? 6 5 4 3 2 1

7 As you do your job have you noticed yourself questioning your own ability and judgement and a decrease in the overall confidence you have in yourself? 6 5 4 3 2 1

8 Generally and at work, do you usually feel relaxed and at ease? 6 5 4 3 2 1

9 If colleagues and friends behave in an aloof way towards you, do you tend to worry about what you may have done to offend them as opposed to just dismissing it? 6 5 4 3 2 1

10 If the tasks you have implemented, or jobs you are doing, start to go wrong do you sometimes feel a lack of confidence, and panicky, as though events were getting out of control? 6 5 4 3 2 1

11 Do you feel confident that you have properly identified and efficiently tackled your work or domestic problems recently? 6 5 4 3 2 1

12 Concerning work and life in general, would you describe yourself as someone who is bothered by their troubles or a 'worrier'? 6 5 4 3 2 1

13 When trying to work do you find yourself disproportionately irritated by relatively minor distractions such as answering the telephone or being interrupted? 6 5 4 3 2 1

14 As time goes by, do you find yourself experiencing fairly   654321
    long periods in which you feel rather miserable or
    melancholy for reasons that you simply cannot 'put your
    finger on'?

15 Would you say that you had a positive frame of mind in   654321
    which you feel capable of overcoming your present or any
    future difficulties and problems you might face such as
    resolving dilemmas or making difficult decisions?

16 When you think about your past events do you feel   654321
    regretful about what has happened, the way you have
    acted, decisions you have taken, etc.?

17 Would you describe yourself as being a rather 'moody' sort   654321
    of person who can become unreasonable and bad
    tempered quickly?

18 Are there times at work when the things you have got to   654321
    deal with simply become too much and you feel so
    overtaxed that you think you are 'cracking-up'?

Part B: Your physical health

Please **tick** the answer that applies to you.

1 Do you often feel upset for no obvious reason? *Yes. . . . . . No. . . . . .*

2 Are you troubled by dizziness or shortness of breath? *Never. . . . . .*
   Often. . . . . . **Sometimes.** *. . . . . .*

3 Can you think as quickly as you used to? *Yes. . . . . . No. . . . . .*

4 Have you felt as though you might faint? *Frequently. . . . . .*
   Occasionally. . . . . . Never. . . . . .

5 Do you often feel sick or have indigestion? *Yes. . . . . . No. . . . . .*

6 Do you feel that life is too much effort? *At times. . . . . . Often. . . . . .*
   Never. . . . . .

7 Do you feel uneasy and restless? *Frequently. . . . . . Sometimes. . . . . .*
   Never. . . . . .

8 Do you sometimes feel tingling or pricking sensations in your body, arms or
   legs? *Rarely. . . . . . Frequently. . . . . . Never. . . . . .*

9 Do you regret much of your past behaviour? *Yes. . . . . . No. . . . . .*

10 Do you sometimes feel panicky? *No. . . . . . Yes. . . . . .*

11 Has your appetite got less recently? *No. . . . . . Yes. . . . . .*

12 Do you wake unusually early in the morning? *Yes. . . . . . No. . . . . .*

13 Would you say you were a worrying person? *Very. . . . . . Fairly. . . . . . Not
    at all. . . . . .*

14 Do you feel unduly tired and exhausted? *Often. . . . . . Sometimes. . . . . .*
    Never. . . . . .

15 Do you experience long periods of sadness? *Never.*...... *Often.*......
Sometimes.......

16 Do you often feel 'strung-up' inside? *Yes.*...... *No.*......

17 Can you get off to sleep all right at the moment? *No.*...... *Yes.*......

18 Do you have to make a special effort to face up to a crisis or difficulty?
Very much so....... *Sometimes.*...... *Not more than anyone else.*......

19 Have you ever had the feeling you were 'going to pieces'? *Yes.*......
No.......

20 Do you often suffer from excessive sweating or fluttering of the heart?
No....... *Yes.*......

21 Do you find yourself needing to cry? *Frequently.*...... *Sometimes.*......
Never.......

22 Do you have bad dreams which upset you when you wake up?
Never....... *Sometimes.*...... *Frequently.*......

23 Has your sexual interest altered? *Less.*...... *The same or greater.*......

24 Have you lost your ability to feel sympathy for other people? *No.*......
Yes.......

3. The way you behave generally

Quite apart from feelings and reactions, the way you approach things and your
overall style of behaviour are important. In this questionnaire you are required
to record the extent to which you agree or disagree with statements about
yourself and your behaviour.

Please answer by **circling** the number which indicates the extent of your
agreement/disagreement.

Very strongly agree	6
Strongly agree	5
Agree	4
Disagree	3
Strongly disagree	2
Very strongly disagree	1

1 Because I am satisfied with life I am not an especially   6 5 4 3 2 1
ambitious person who has a need to succeed or progress
in their career.

2 My impatience with slowness means for example that when   6 5 4 3 2 1
talking with other people my mind tends to race ahead and
I anticipate what the person is going to say.

3 I am a fairly confident and forceful individual who has no   6 5 4 3 2 1
qualms about expressing feelings or opinions in an
authoritative and assertive manner.

4 I am not an especially achievement-oriented person who   6 5 4 3 2 1
continually behaves in a competitive way or who has a
need to win or excel in whatever I do.

5　When I am doing something, I concentrate on only one　　654321
　activity at a time and am fully committed in giving it 100 per
　cent of my effort.

6　I would describe the manner of my behaviour as being　　654321
　quite challenging and vigorous.

7　When I compare myself with others I know, I would say that　654321
　I was more responsible, serious, conscientious, and
　competitive than they are.

8　I am usually quite concerned to learn about other people's　654321
　opinions of me, particularly recognition others give me.

9　Even though I take my job seriously, I could not be　　654321
　described as being completely and absolutely dedicated to it.

10　I have a heightened pace of living in that I do things quickly　654321
　such as eating, talking, walking, and so on.

11　When I am establishing priorities, work does not always　654321
　come first because although it is important, I have other
　outside interests which I also regard as important.

12　I am a fairly easy going individual, who takes life as it　654321
　comes and who is not especially 'action-oriented'.

13　I am a very impatient sort of person who finds waiting　654321
　around difficult, especially for other people.

14　I am time conscious and lead my life on a 'time is money　654321
　and can't be wasted' principle.

4. How you interpret events around you

The object of this questionnaire is to record how much you feel you can or
cannot influence the things that go on around you. You are asked to indicate
your level of agreement to the following statements.

Please answer by **circling** the number which best represents your answer on
the following scale.

Very strongly agree　　　6
Strongly agree　　　　　5
Agree　　　　　　　　　4
Disagree　　　　　　　3
Strongly disagree　　　2
Very strongly disagree　1

1　The trouble with workers nowadays is that they are subject　654321
　to too many constraints and punishments.

2　Assessments of performance do not reflect the way, and　654321
　how hard, individuals work.

3　With enough effort it is possible for employees generally, to　654321
　have some influence over top management and the way
　they behave.

4 It is not possible to draw up plans too far ahead because so many things can occur that make the plans unworkable. 6 5 4 3 2 1

5 Socialising is an excellent way to develop oneself and an emphasis on such things in organisations is important. 6 5 4 3 2 1

6 Even though some people try to control company events by taking part in social affairs or office politics, most of us are subject to influences we can neither comprehend nor control. 6 5 4 3 2 1

7 Being successful and getting to be 'boss' depends on ability – being in the right place at the right time or luck have little to do with it. 6 5 4 3 2 1

8 Management can be unfair when appraising subordinates since their performance is often influenced by accidental events. 6 5 4 3 2 1

9 Being an effective leader is more often a function of personal skills than it is of taking advantage of every available opportunity. 6 5 4 3 2 1

10 It is upper management rather than ordinary employees who are responsible for poor company performance at an overall level. 6 5 4 3 2 1

11 The things that happen to people are more under their control than a function of luck or chance. 6 5 4 3 2 1

12 In organisations that are run by a few people who hold the power, the average individual can have little influence over organisational decisions. 6 5 4 3 2 1

5. Your job satisfaction

This set of items deals with various aspects of your job. Please tell us how satisfied or dissatisfied you feel with each of these features of your present job. Use the scale below to indicate your feelings.

Please answer by **circling** the number of your answer against the scale shown. Remember – there are no right or wrong answers. Give your first and natural answer by working quickly, but be accurate, and answer all questions.

I'm extremely dissatisfied 1
I'm very dissatisfied 2
I'm moderately dissatisfied 3
I'm not sure 4
I'm moderately satisfied 5
I'm satisfied 6
I'm extremely satisfied 7

1 The physical working conditions. 1 2 3 4 5 6 7

2 The freedom to choose your own method of working. 1 2 3 4 5 6 7

3 Your fellow workers. 1 2 3 4 5 6 7

4 The recognition you get for good work. 1 2 3 4 5 6 7

5	Your immediate boss.	1 2 3 4 5 6 7
6	The amount of responsibility you are given.	1 2 3 4 5 6 7
7	Your rate of pay.	1 2 3 4 5 6 7
8	Your opportunity to use your abilities.	1 2 3 4 5 6 7
9	Industrial relations between management and workers in your firm.	1 2 3 4 5 6 7
10	Your chance of promotion.	1 2 3 4 5 6 7
11	The way your firm is managed.	1 2 3 4 5 6 7
12	The attention paid to suggestions you make.	1 2 3 4 5 6 7
13	Your hours of work.	1 2 3 4 5 6 7
14	The amount of variety in your job.	1 2 3 4 5 6 7
15	Your job security.	1 2 3 4 5 6 7

6. Sources of pressure in your job

Almost anything can be a source of pressure (to someone) at a given time, and individuals perceive potential sources of pressure differently. The person who says they are 'under a tremendous amount of pressure at work at the moment' usually means that they have too much work to do. But that is only half the picture. The items below are all potential sources of pressure. You are required to rate them in terms of the degree of pressure you perceive each may place on you.

Please answer by **circling** the number of your answer against the scale shown.

Very definitely is a source 6
Definitely is a source 5
Generally is a source 4
Generally is not a source 3
Definitely is not a source 2
Very definitely is not a source 1

1	Having far too much work to do.	6 5 4 3 2 1
2	Misreading the market.	6 5 4 3 2 1
3	Lack of power and influence.	6 5 4 3 2 1
4	Not fully understanding the work.	6 5 4 3 2 1
5	Overpromotion – being promoted beyond my level of ability.	6 5 4 3 2 1
6	Not having enough work to do.	6 5 4 3 2 1
7	The size of my financial risk.	6 5 4 3 2 1
8	Managing or supervising the work of other people.	6 5 4 3 2 1
9	Coping with office politics.	6 5 4 3 2 1

10	Taking my work home.	6 5 4 3 2 1
11	Having a run of financial losses.	6 5 4 3 2 1
12	Rate of pay (including perks and fringe benefits).	6 5 4 3 2 1
13	Personal beliefs conflicting with those of the organisation.	6 5 4 3 2 1
14	Underpromotion – working at a level below my level of ability.	6 5 4 3 2 1
15	Working at a job of which many people disapprove.	6 5 4 3 2 1
16	Inadequate guidance and back up from superiors.	6 5 4 3 2 1
17	Lack of consultation and communication.	6 5 4 3 2 1
18	Not being able to 'switch off' at home.	6 5 4 3 2 1
19	Doing work which most people do not understand.	6 5 4 3 2 1
20	Keeping up with new techniques, ideas, technology or innovations or new challenges.	6 5 4 3 2 1
21	Ambiguity in the nature of job role.	6 5 4 3 2 1
22	Inadequate or poor quality of training/management development.	6 5 4 3 2 1
23	Competing with colleagues.	6 5 4 3 2 1
24	Attending meetings.	6 5 4 3 2 1
25	Lack of social support by people at work.	6 5 4 3 2 1
26	My spouse's attitude towards my job and career.	6 5 4 3 2 1
27	Getting the attention and support of colleagues.	6 5 4 3 2 1
28	Having to work very long hours.	6 5 4 3 2 1
29	Decisions dominated by the technology (e.g. computer screen).	6 5 4 3 2 1
30	Conflicting job tasks and demands in the role I play.	6 5 4 3 2 1
31	Covert discrimination and favouritism.	6 5 4 3 2 1
32	Inadequate information sources.	6 5 4 3 2 1
33	Mundane administrative tasks or 'paperwork'.	6 5 4 3 2 1
34	Inability to delegate.	6 5 4 3 2 1
35	Threat of impending redundancy or early retirement.	6 5 4 3 2 1
36	Coping with large amounts and sources of information.	6 5 4 3 2 1
37	Feeling isolated.	6 5 4 3 2 1
38	A lack of encouragement from superiors.	6 5 4 3 2 1
39	Staff shortages and unsettling turnover rates.	6 5 4 3 2 1
40	Concern about the breakdown of the technological equipment.	6 5 4 3 2 1

STRESS QUESTIONNAIRE

41	Demands my work makes on my relationship with my spouse/children.	6 5 4 3 2 1
42	Being undervalued.	6 5 4 3 2 1
43	Inadequate knowledge of accounting, economics, etc.	6 5 4 3 2 1
44	Having to take risks.	6 5 4 3 2 1
45	Ability to cope with current technologies.	6 5 4 3 2 1
46	Changing jobs to progress with career.	6 5 4 3 2 1
47	Too much or too little variety in work.	6 5 4 3 2 1
48	Working with those of the opposite sex.	6 5 4 3 2 1
49	Achieving my individual or group profit target.	6 5 4 3 2 1
50	Inadequate feedback about my own performance.	6 5 4 3 2 1
51	Business travel and having to live in hotels.	6 5 4 3 2 1
52	Misuse of time by other people.	6 5 4 3 2 1
53	Coming second-best out of a transaction.	6 5 4 3 2 1
54	Simply being seen as a 'Boss'.	6 5 4 3 2 1
55	Unclear promotion prospects.	6 5 4 3 2 1
56	The accumulative effects of minor tasks.	6 5 4 3 2 1
57	Deterioration in my ability to be as effective.	6 5 4 3 2 1
58	Absence of emotional support from others outside work.	6 5 4 3 2 1
59	Insufficient finance or resources to work with.	6 5 4 3 2 1
60	Demands that work makes on my private/social life.	6 5 4 3 2 1
61	Competing with similar employees in other organisations.	6 5 4 3 2 1
62	Changes in the way I am asked to do my job.	6 5 4 3 2 1
63	Simply being 'visible' or 'available'.	6 5 4 3 2 1
64	Lack of practical support from others outside work.	6 5 4 3 2 1
65	Concern about my future physical health.	6 5 4 3 2 1
66	Factors not under my direct control.	6 5 4 3 2 1
67	Sharing of work and responsibility evenly.	6 5 4 3 2 1
68	Home life with a partner who is also pursuing a career.	6 5 4 3 2 1
69	Concern about my future mental health.	6 5 4 3 2 1
70	Dealing with ambiguous or 'delicate' situations.	6 5 4 3 2 1
71	Seeing personal wealth fluctuating.	6 5 4 3 2 1
72	Having to adopt a negative role (such as sacking someone).	6 5 4 3 2 1

73 An absence of any potential career advancement. 6 5 4 3 2 1

74 Pressure to perform at a high level. 6 5 4 3 2 1

75 Morale and organisational climate. 6 5 4 3 2 1

76 Attaining my own personal levels of performance. 6 5 4 3 2 1

77 Making important decisions. 6 5 4 3 2 1

78 Having a career path after my present job. 6 5 4 3 2 1

79 'Personality' clashes with others. 6 5 4 3 2 1

80 Implications of mistakes I make. 6 5 4 3 2 1

81 Opportunities for personal development. 6 5 4 3 2 1

82 Too much noise. 6 5 4 3 2 1

83 Absence of stability or dependability in home life. 6 5 4 3 2 1

84 Pursuing a career at the expense of home life. 6 5 4 3 2 1

85 Characteristics of the organisation's structure and design. 6 5 4 3 2 1

86 Too warm an environment. 6 5 4 3 2 1

87 Colleagues' smoking. 6 5 4 3 2 1

7. Your habits

Here are some questions regarding the way you behave, feel, and act. After each question is a space for answering 'YES' or 'NO'. Try to decide whether 'YES' or 'NO' represents your **usual way** of acting or feeling. Then put a **cross in the circle** under the column headed 'YES' or 'NO'. Work quickly and don't spend too much time over any question.

1 Do you often long for excitement? YES NO

2 Do you often need understanding friends to cheer you up? YES NO

3 Are you usually carefree? YES NO

4 Do you find it very hard to take no for an answer? YES NO

5 Do you stop and think things over before doing anything? YES NO

6 If you say you will do something do you always keep your promise, no matter how inconvenient it might be to do so? YES NO

7 Does your mood often go up and down? YES NO

8 Do you generally do and say things quickly without stopping to think? YES NO

9 Do you ever feel 'just miserable' for no good reason? YES NO

10 Would you do almost anything for a dare? YES NO

11 Do you suddenly feel shy when you want to talk to an attractive stranger? YES NO

12	Once in a while do you lose your temper and get angry?	YES	NO
13	Do you often do things on the spur of the moment?	YES	NO
14	Do you often worry about things you should not have done or said?	YES	NO
15	Generally, do you prefer reading to meeting people?	YES	NO
16	Are your feelings easily hurt?	YES	NO
17	Do you like going out a lot?	YES	NO
18	Do you occasionally have thoughts and ideas that you would not like other people to know about?	YES	NO
19	Are you sometimes bubbling over with energy and sometimes very sluggish?	YES	NO
20	Do you prefer to have a few but special friends?	YES	NO
21	Do you daydream a lot?	YES	NO
22	When people shout at you, do you shout back?	YES	NO
23	Are you often troubled about feelings of guilt?	YES	NO
24	Are all your habits good and desirable ones?	YES	NO
25	Can you usually let yourself go and enjoy yourself a lot at a lively party?	YES	NO
26	Would you call yourself tense or 'highly strung'?	YES	NO
27	Do other people think of you as being very lively?	YES	NO
28	After you have done something important, do you often come away feeling you could have done better?	YES	NO
29	Are you mostly quiet when you are with other people?	YES	NO
30	Do you sometimes gossip?	YES	NO
31	Do ideas run through your head so that you cannot sleep?	YES	NO
32	If there is something you want to know about, would you rather look it up in a book than talk to someone about it?	YES	NO
33	Do you get palpitations or thumping in your heart?	YES	NO
34	Do you like the kind of work that you need to pay close attention to?	YES	NO
35	Do you get attacks of shaking or trembling?	YES	NO
36	Would you always declare everything at the customs, even if you knew that you could never be found out?	YES	NO
37	Do you hate being with a crowd who play jokes on one another?	YES	NO
38	Are you an irritable person?	YES	NO
39	Do you like doing things in which you have to act quickly?	YES	NO

241

40	Do you worry about awful things that might happen?	YES	NO
41	Are you slow and unhurried in the way you move?	YES	NO
42	Have you ever been late for an appointment or work?	YES	NO
43	Do you have many nightmares?	YES	NO
44	Do you like talking to people so much that you never miss a chance of talking to a stranger?	YES	NO
45	Are you troubled by aches and pains?	YES	NO
46	Would you be very unhappy if you could not see lots of people most of the time?	YES	NO
47	Would you call yourself a nervous person?	YES	NO
48	Of all the people you know, are there some whom you definitely do not like?	YES	NO
49	Would you say that you were fairly self-confident?	YES	NO
50	Are you easily hurt when people find fault with you or your work?	YES	NO
51	Do you find it hard to really enjoy yourself at a lively party?	YES	NO
52	Are you troubled with feelings of inferiority?	YES	NO
53	Can you easily get some life into a rather dull party?	YES	NO
54	Do you sometimes talk about things you know nothing about?	YES	NO
55	Do you worry about your health?	YES	NO
56	Do you like playing pranks on others?	YES	NO
57	Do you suffer from sleeplessness?	YES	NO

8. How you cope with stress you experience

Whilst there are variations in the ways individuals react to sources of pressure and the effects of stress, generally speaking we all make some attempt at coping with these difficulties – consciously or subconsciously.

This final questionnaire lists a number of potential coping strategies which you are required to rate in terms of the extent to which you actually use them as ways of coping with stress.

Please answer by **circling** the number of your answer against the scale shown.

Very extensively used by me 6
Extensively used by me 5
On balance used by me 4
On balance not used by me 3
Seldom used by me 2
Never used by me 1

1 Deal with the problems immediately as they occur.   6 5 4 3 2 1

2	Try to recognise my own limitations.	6 5 4 3 2 1
3	'Buy time' and stall the issue.	6 5 4 3 2 1
4	Look for ways to make the work more interesting.	6 5 4 3 2 1
5	Reorganise my work.	6 5 4 3 2 1
6	Seek support and advice from my superiors.	6 5 4 3 2 1
7	Resort to hobbies and pastimes.	6 5 4 3 2 1
8	Try to deal with the situation objectively in an unemotional way.	6 5 4 3 2 1
9	Effective time management.	6 5 4 3 2 1
10	Suppress emotions and try not to let the stress show.	6 5 4 3 2 1
11	Having a home that is a refuge.	6 5 4 3 2 1
12	Talk to understanding friends.	6 5 4 3 2 1
13	Deliberately separate 'home' and 'work'.	6 5 4 3 2 1
14	'Stay busy'.	6 5 4 3 2 1
15	Plan ahead.	6 5 4 3 2 1
16	Not 'bottling things up' and being able to release energy.	6 5 4 3 2 1
17	Expand interests and activities outside work.	6 5 4 3 2 1
18	Have stable relationships.	6 5 4 3 2 1
19	Use selective attention (concentrating on specific problems).	6 5 4 3 2 1
20	Use distractions (to take my mind off things).	6 5 4 3 2 1
21	Set priorities and deal with problems accordingly.	6 5 4 3 2 1
22	Try to 'stand aside' and think through the situation.	6 5 4 3 2 1
23	Resort to rules and regulations.	6 5 4 3 2 1
24	Delegation.	6 5 4 3 2 1
25	Force one's behaviour and life-style to slow down.	6 5 4 3 2 1
26	Accept the situation and learn to live with it.	6 5 4 3 2 1
27	Try to avoid the situation.	6 5 4 3 2 1
28	Seek as much social support as possible.	6 5 4 3 2 1
29	Regular holidays.	6 5 4 3 2 1
30	Coffee/smoking/drink/drugs.	6 5 4 3 2 1

Please check that you have completed all sections, then return the questionnaire as indicated.

Thank you very much for your time and co-operation.

BIBLIOGRAPHY

Abdel-Halim, A.A. (1981) 'Effects of role stress – job design – technology interaction on employee work satisfaction', *Academy of Management Journal*, 24(2): 260–73.

Adams, J.D. (1980) *Understanding and Managing Stress*, San Diego: University Associates, Inc.

Alcohol Concern (1987) *The Drinking Revolution*, London: Alcohol Concern.

Allen, L. and Arthur, E. (1990) *Drink*, Channel 4 Television.

Allsopp, J.F. (1986) 'The distribution of on-licence beer and cider consumption and its personality determinants among young men', *European Journal of Marketing*, 20: 44–62.

Amick, B.C., III, and Ostberg, O. (1987) 'Office automation, occupational stress and health: A literature analysis with specific attention to expert systems', *Office: Technology and People*, 3(3): 191–209.

Arndt, S., Feltes, J. and Hanak, J. (1983) 'Secretarial attitudes towards word processors as a function of familiarity and locus of control', *Behaviour and Information Technology*, 2: 17–22.

Arthur, R.J. and Gunderson, E.K. (1965) 'Promotion and mental illness in the Navy', *Journal of Occupational Medicine*, 7: 452–6.

Auletta, K. (1986) *Greed and Glory on Wall Street*, Harmondsworth: Penguin.

Baaker, C.D. (1967) 'Psychological factors in angina pectoris', *Psychomatic Medicine*, 8: 43–9.

Baron, R.A. (1986) *Behavior in Organisations*, Newton, Massachusetts: Allyn and Bacon, second edition.

Bedeian, A.G. and Armenakis, A.A. (1981) 'A path-analytic study of the consequences of role conflict and ambiguity', *Academy of Management Journal*, 24(2): 417–24.

Beehr, R.A. (1985) 'Organisational stress and employee effectiveness: a job characteristics approach', in T.A. Beehr and R.S. Bhagat (eds) *Human Stress and Cognition in Organisations*, New York: Wiley.

Beehr, T.A. and Franz, T.M. (1986) 'The current debate about the meaning of job stress', *Journal of Organisational Behavior Management*, 8(2): 5–18.

Benight, C.C. and Kinicki, A.J. (1988) 'Interaction of Type A behavior and controllability of stressors on stress outcomes', *Journal of Vocational Behavior*, 33: 50–62.

Bennett, J., Case, D., Sandelin, J. and Smith, M. (eds) (1984) *Visual Display Terminals: Usability Issues and Health Concerns*, Englewood Cliffs: Prentice-Hall.

Benton, D. (1987) 'Adrenal hormone production as indices of occupational stress', in A. Gale and B. Christie (eds) *Psychophysiology and the Electronic Workplace*, Chichester: Wiley.

Berglas, S. (1986) *The Success Syndrome*, New York: Plenum Press.

Bevan, J. (1988) 'Citicorp hones operations in market-making', *The Sunday Times*, 18 December.

Blumenthal, J.A., McKee, D.C., Haney, T. and Williams, R.B. (1980) 'Task incentives, Type A behavior pattern, and verbal problem solving performance', *Journal of Applied Social Psychology*, 10(2): 101–14.

Booth-Kewley, S. and Friedman, H.S. (1987) 'Psychological predictors of heart disease: A quantitative review', *Psychological Bulletin*, 101: 343–62.

Bootzin, R.R. and Max, D. (1980) 'Learning and behavioral theories', in I.L. Kutash, L.B. Schlesinger and Associates (eds) *Handbook on Stress and Anxiety*, San Francisco: Jossey-Bass.

Bosworth-Davies, R. (1988) *Fraud in the City: Too good to be true*, London: Penguin.

Boyatzis, R.E. (1982) *The Competent Manager*, New York: John Wiley and Sons.

Bradford, M. (1988) 'New awareness cited for insurance in stress claims', *Business Insurance*, 22(2): 12–14.

Breslow, L. and Buell, P. (1960) 'Mortality from coronary heart disease & physical activity of work in California', *Journal of Chronic Diseases*, 11: 615–26.

Brief, A.P., Rude, D.E. and Rabinowitz, S. (1983) 'The impact of Type A behaviour pattern on subjective workload and depression', *Journal of Occupational Behaviour*, 4: 157–64.

Brief, A.P., Schuler, R.S. and Van Sell, M. (1981) *Managing Job Stress* Boston: Little, Brown.

Briner, R. (1986) *The Relationship Between Stress and Illness: A Historical and Theoretical Review of Some Conceptual and Methodological Problems in Research* (unpublished M.Sc. Thesis) University of Durham.

Bromet, E.J., Dew, M.A., Parkinson, D.K. and Schulberg, H.C. (1988) 'Predictive effects of occupational and marital stress on the mental health of a male workforce', *Journal of Organisational Behavior*, 9(1): 1–13.

Brook, A. (1973) 'Mental stress at work', *The Practitioner*, 210: 500–6.

Brooks, G.W. and Mueller, E.F. (1966) 'Serum urate concentrations among university professors', *Journal of the American Medical Association*, 195: 415–18.

Brummet, R.L., Pyle, W.C. and Flamholtz, E.G. (1968) 'Accounting for human resources', *Michigan Business Review*, 20: 20–5.

Brunson, B.I. and Matthews, K.A. (1981) 'The Type A coronary-prone behavior pattern and reactions to uncontrollable stress: an analysis of performance strategies, affect, and attribution during failure', *Journal of Personality and Social Psychology*, 40: 906–18.

Buchanan, D.A. and Huczynski, A.A. (1985) *Organisational Behaviour*, Hemel Hempstead: Prentice-Hall.

Buck, V. (1972) *Working Under Pressure*, London: Staples.

Bulmer, M. (1988) 'Some reflections upon research in organisations', in A. Bryman (ed.) *Doing Research in Organisations*, London: Routledge.

Burke, R.J. (1982) 'Occupational locking-in: some empirical findings', *Journal of Social Psychology*, 118: 177–85.

—— (1986) 'The present and future status of stress research', *Journal of Organisational Behavior Management*, 8(2): 249–67.

—— (1988) 'Sources of managerial and professional stress in large organizations', in C.L. Cooper and R. Payne (eds) *Causes, Coping and Consequences of Stress*, Chichester: Wiley.

Burke, R.J. and Greenglass, E.R. (1987) 'Work and family', in C.L. Cooper and I.T. Robertson (eds) *International Review of Industrial and Organisational Psychology 1987*, Chichester: Wiley.

Buzan, T. (1982) *Use Your Head*, London: BBC.

Cain, C.M. (1987) 'Job stress cases mounting', *Business Insurance*, 21(9): 1 and 28.

Cakir, A. (1981) 'Belastung und Beanspruchung bei Bildschirmtatigkeiten', in M. Frese (ed.) *Stress im Buro*, Bern: Huber.

Campion, M.A. and Mitchell, M.M. (1986) 'Management turnover: Experiential differences between former and current managers', *Personnel Psychology*, 39(1): 57–69.

Cannon, W.B. (1932) *The Wisdom of the Body*, New York: Norton, second edition.

—— (1935) 'Stresses and strains of homeostasisi', *American Journal of Medical Science*, 189(1).

Cantacuzino, M. (1989) 'A crying shame', *New Woman*, August.

Caplan, R.D., Cobb, S., French, J.R.P., Van Harrison, R. and Pinneau, S.R. (1975) *Job Demands and Worker Health: Main Effects and Occupational Differences*, Washington, D.C.: Government Printing Office.

Caplan, R.D. and Jones, K.W. (1975) 'Effects of workload, role ambiguity, and Type A personality on anxiety, depression, and heartrate', *Journal of Applied Psychology*, 60: 713–19.

Cartwright, S. and Cooper, C.L. (1989) *The Stressful Cost of Careless Mergers*, London: *The Sunday Times*, 22 January.

—— (1990) 'The Impact of mergers and acquisitions on people at work: Existing research and issues', *British Journal of Management*, 1(2): 65–76.

—— (1992) *Mergers and Acquisitions: the Human Factor*, Oxford: Butterworth-Heinemann.

Castro, J. (1986) 'Battling the enemy within', *Time*, 17 March, 52–61.

Cavanagh, M.E. (1988) 'What you don't know about stress', *Personnel Journal*, 67(7): 53–9.

Chapman, C. (1988) *How the Stock Exchange Works*, London: Hutchinson.

Chesney, M.A. and Rosenman, R.H. (1983) 'Specificity in stress models: examples drawn from Type A behaviour', in C.L. Cooper (ed.) *Stress Research: Issues for the Eighties*, Chichester: Wiley.

Chusmir, L.H. and Franks, F.V. (1988) 'Stress and the woman manager', *Training and Development Journal*, 42(10): 66–70.

Clegg, C.W. and Wall, T.D. (1981) 'A note on some new scales for measuring aspects of psychological well-being at work', *Journal of Occupational Psychology*, 54: 221–5.

Cobb, S. (1976) 'Social support as a moderator of life stress', *Psychosomatic Medicine*, 38: 300–14.

Cobb, S. and Kasl, S.V. (1977) *Termination – The Consequences of Job Loss*, USA: H.E.W. Publications, 77–224, NIOSH.

Cohen, S. (1986) 'Cognitive processes as determinants of environmental stress', in C.D. Spielberger and I.G. Sarason (eds) *Stress and Anxiety*, Vol. 10, Washington, D.C.: Hemisphere.

Connor, S. (1989) '£5,000 for hi-tech homework', *Daily Telegraph*, 13 September.

Cooke, R.A. and Rosseau, D.M. (1984) 'Stress and strain from family roles and work–role expectations', *Journal of Applied Psychology*, 69: 252–60.

Cooper, C.L. (1981) 'Social support at work and stress management', *Small Group Behavior*, 12(3): 285–97.

—— (1983) 'Problem areas for future stress research: Cancer and working women', in C.L. Cooper (ed.) *Stress Research: Issues for the Eighties*, Chichester: Wiley.

—— (1984) 'Alcoholism at work', *Leadership and Organisational Development Journal*, 5(5): 15–16.

—— (1985) 'The stress of work: An overview', *Aviation, Space & Environmental Medicine*, July, 627–32.

—— (1986) 'Job distress: Recent research and the emerging role of the clinical occupational psychologist', *Bulletin of the British Psychological Society*, 39: 325–31.

—— (1988) 'Good managers learn how to Praise', *The Sunday Times*, 4 December E18.

Cooper, C.L. and Davidson, M.J. (1982) 'The high cost of stress on women managers', *Organisational Dynamics*, 10(4): 44–53.

Cooper, C.L. and Ferguson, A. (1990) 'Top executives pay a heavy price for success', *Independent on Sunday*, 25 March, p. 27.

Cooper, C.L. and Makin, P. (1984) *Psychology for Managers*, London: British Psychological Society and Macmillan.

Cooper, C.L. and Marshall, J. (1976) 'Occupational sources of stress: A review of the literature relating to coronary heart disease and mental ill-health', *Journal of Occupational Psychology*, 49: 11–28.

—— (eds) (1980) *White Collar and Professional Stress*, Chichester: Wiley.

Cooper, C.L. and Melhuish, A. (1980) 'Occupational stress and managers', *Journal of Occupational Medicine*, 22(9): 588–92.

Cooper, C.L. and Payne, R. (1967) 'Extroversion and some aspects of work behaviour', *Personal Psychology*, 20: 45–7.

—— (eds) (1978) *Stress at Work*, Chichester: Wiley.

—— (1988) *Causes, Coping and Consequences of Stress at Work*, Chichester: Wiley.

Cooper, C.L. and Sadri, G. (1991) 'The impact of stress counselling at work', Journal of Social Behavior & Personality, 6: 411–23.

Cooper, C.L. and Smith, M.J. (eds) (1985) *Job Stress and Blue Collar Work*, Chichester: Wiley.

Cooper, C.L., Cooper, R. and Eaker, L. (1988) *Living with Stress*, London: Penguin.

Cooper, C.L., Rout, U. and Faragher, B. (1989) 'Mental health, job satisfaction and job stress among General Practitioners', *British Medical Journal*, 298: 366–70.

Cooper, C.L., Sloan, S.J. and Williams, S. (1988) *Occupational Stress Indicator Management Guide*, UK: NFER-Nelson.

—— (1989) *Occupational Stress Indicator. Data Supplement 1989*, UK: NFER-Nelson.

Coppen, A. and Metcalfe, M. (1963) 'Cancer and extroversion', *British Medical Journal*, 6 July: 18–19.

Costa, P.T. and McCrae, R.R. (1987) 'Neuroticism, somatic complaints and disease: Is the bark worse than the bite?', *Journal of Personality*, 55: 299–316.

Cottington, E.M., Matthews, K.A., Talbott, E. and Kuller, L.H. (1986) 'Occupational stress, suppressed anger, and hypertension', *Psychosomatic Medicine*, 48(3–4): 249–60.

Cox, A.C. (1984) *An Investigation into the Social and Psychological effects of Word-processors* (unpublished Ph.D. Thesis) University of Manchester.

Cox, T. (1978) *Stress*, London: Macmillan.

—— (1985) *Stress*, London: Macmillan.

—— (1988) *Stress – The Price to be Paid*, BUPA Symposium, 'The Management of Health'.

Crisp, A.H., Ralph, P.C., McGuiness, B. and Harris, G. (1978) 'Psychoneurotic profiles in the adult population', *British Medical Journal*, 51: 293–301.

Crown, S. and Crisp, A.H. (1979) *Manual of the Crown-Crisp Experiential Index*, UK: Hodder and Stoughton.

Cummings, T.G. and Cooper, C.L. (1979) 'A cybernetic framework for studying occupational stress', *Human Relations*, 32(5): 395–418.

Dailey, R.C., Ickinger, W. and Coote, E. (1986) 'Personality and role variables as predictors of tension discharge rate in three samples', *Human Relations*, 39(11): 991–1003.

Dainoff, M.J., Happ, A. and Crane, P. (1981) 'Visual fatigue and occupational stress in VDT operators', *Human Factors*, 23: 421–4.

Dalton, A. (1989) *Dangerous Lives*, London: Channel 4 Television.

Davidson, M.J. and Cooper, C.L. (1983) *Stress and the Woman Manager*, Oxford: Martin Robertson.

Davison, J. (1990) 'Bosses call time on the workaholic ethic', *The Sunday Times*, 19 May, A5.

DeFrank, R.S. and Cooper, C.L. (1987) 'Worksite stress management

Interventions: their effectiveness and conceptualisation', *Journal of Managerial Psychology*, 2(1): 4–10.

Derevenco, P., Baban, A. and Anghel, I. (1988) 'Psychophysiological and behavioral characteristic related to risks for cardiovascular diseases and to occupational stress', 2nd European International Association for Interdisciplinary Study of Higher Nervous Functions Conference (1987 Magdeburg, Germany), *Activitas Nervosa Superior*, 30(2): 99–100.

Derr, C.B. (1986) 'Five definitions of career success: Implications for relationships', *International Review of Applied Psychology*, 35: 415–35, London: Sage.

DeVries, H.A. (1981) 'Tranquilizer effects of exercise: A critical review', *The Physician and Sports Medicine*, 9: 47–55.

Dickenson, F. (1988) *Drink and Drugs at Work*, London: Institute of Personnel Management.

Edwards, J.R. (1988) 'The determinants and consequences of coping with stress', in C.L. Cooper and R. Payne (eds) *Causes, Coping and Consequences of Stress at Work*, Chichester: Wiley.

Elliott, G.R. and Eisdorfer, C. (eds) (1982) *Stress and Human Health*, New York: Springer.

Epstein, S. (1986) 'Anxiety, Arousal, and the Self-Concept', in C.D. Spielberger and I.G. Sarason (eds) *Stress and Anxiety*, Vol. 10, Washington, D.C.: Hemisphere.

Evison, R.J. (1988) 'Effective stress management: Management of inappropriate negative emotions', *The Occupational Psychologist*, 6: 11–21.

Eysenck, H.J. (1965) *Smoking, Health and Personality*, UK: Weidenfeld & Nicolson.

—— (1967) *Biological Basis of Personality*, Springfield, Illinois: Charles C. Thomas.

—— (1980) *The Causes and Effects of Smoking*, London: Maurice Temple Smith.

—— (1981) *A Model for Personality*, Berlin: Springer.

—— (1985) 'Personality, cancer and cardiovascular disease: A causal analysis', *Personality and Individual Differences*, 6(5): 535–56.

Eysenck, H.J. and Eysenck, S.B.G. (1964) *Manual of the Eysenck Personality Index*, UK: Hodder & Stoughton.

Eysenck, S.B.G. and Eysenck, H.J. (1963) 'The validity of questionnaires and rating assessments of extroversion and neuroticism and their factorial validity', *British Journal of Psychology*, 54: 51–62.

Fewster, C. (1989) 'Stress', *Industrial Society Magazine*, September, 29–31.

Fine, B.J. and Kobrick, J.L. (1978) 'Effects of altitude and heat on complex cognitive tasks', *Human Factors*, 20: 115–22.

Finn, F.N., Hickey, N. and O'Docherty, E.F. (1969) 'The psychological profiles of male and female patients with CHD', *Irish Journal of Medical Science*, 2: 339–41.

Firth, J. and Shapiro, D.A. (1986) 'An evaluation of psychotherapy for job-related distress', *Journal of Occupational Psychology*, 59: 111–19.

Folkman, S. (1982) 'An approach to the measurement of coping', *Journal of Organisational Behaviour*, 13: 95–107.

249

Folkman, S., Schaefer, C. and Lazarus, R.S. (1979) 'Cognitive processes and mediators of stress and coping', in V. Hamilton and D.M. Warbuton (eds) *Human Stress and Cognition*, Chichester: Wiley.

Folsom, A.R. (1985) 'Do Type A men drink more frequently than Type B men?', Findings in the multiple risk factor intervention trial (MRFIT), *Journal of Behavioural Medicine*, 8(3): 227–35.

Frankenhaeuser, M. and Gardell, B. (1976) 'Underload and overload in working life: Outline of a multidisciplinary approach', *Journal of Human Stress*, 2: 35–46.

Frankenhaeuser, M. and Johansson, G. (1986) 'Stress at work: psycho-biological and psychosocial aspects', *International Review of Applied Psychology*, 35(3): 287–99.

French, J.R.P. and Caplan, R.D. (1970) 'Psychosocial factors in coronary heart disease', *Industrial Medicine*, 39: 383–97.

—— (1972) 'Organisational stress and individual strain', in A.J. Marrow (ed.) *The Failure of Success*, New York: AMACON.

Frese, M. (1985) 'Stress at work and psychosomatic complaints: A causal interpretation', *Journal of Applied Psychology*, 70: 314–28.

—— (1987) 'Human-computer interaction in the office', in C.L. Cooper and I.T. Robertson (eds) *International Review of Industrial and Organizational Psychology 1987*, Chichester: Wiley.

Friedman, M. and Rosenman, R.H. (1974) 'Type A behavior and your heart', New York: Knopf.

Friedman, M., Rosenman, R.H. and Carroll, V. (1958) 'Changes in the serum cholesterol and blood clotting time in men subjected to cyclic variation of occupational stress', *Circulation*, 17: 852–61.

Froggatt, K.L. and Cotton, J.L. (1987) 'The impact of Type A behavior pattern on role overload-induced stress and performance attributions', *Journal of Management*, 13(1): 87–98.

Frost, T.F. (1985) 'The sick organisation', *Personnel*, 62(5): 40–4 and (6): 44–9.

Furnham, A. (1981) 'Personality and activity preference', *British Journal of Social Psychology*, 20: 57–68.

—— (1987) 'The social psychology of working situations', in A. Gale and B. Christie (eds) *Psychophysiology and the Electronic Work- place*, Chichester: Wiley.

Fusilier, M.R., Ganster, D.C. and Mayes, B.T. (1986) 'The social support and health relationship: Is there a gender difference?', *Journal of Occupational Psychology*, 59(2): 145–53.

Gale, A. (1987) 'The electroencephalogram', in A. Gale and B. Christie (eds) *Psychophysiology and the Electronic Workplace*, Chichester: Wiley.

Gale, A. and Christie, B. (eds) (1987) *Psychophysiology and the Electronic Workplace*, Chichester: Wiley.

Ganellen, R.J. and Blaney, P.H. (1984) 'Stress, externality, and depression', *Journal of Personality*, 52(4): 326–37.

Ganster, D.C. and Fusilier, M.R. (1989) 'Control in the workplace', in C.L. Cooper and I.T. Robertson (eds) *International Review of Industrial and Organisational Psychology 1989*, Chichester: Wiley.

Ganster, D.C., Fusilier, M.R. and Mayes, B.T. (1986) 'Role of social support in the experience of stress at work', *Journal of Applied Psychology*, 71(1): 102–10.

Ganster, D.C., Mayes, B.T., Sime, W.E. and Tharp, G.D. (1982) 'Managing organisational stress: A field experiment', *Journal of Applied Psychology*, 67: 533–42.

Garfield, C. (1986) *Peak Performers. The New Heroes in Business*, London: Hutchinson.

Geake, E. (1990) 'It's well worth keeping the workforce happy', *Computer Weekly*, 26 May.

Giles, E. (1987) 'Stress in your own backyard', *Personnel Management*, 19(4): 26–9.

Gillespie, D.F. (1983) *Understanding and Combating Burnout*, Monticello, Ill: Vance Bibliographies.

Glowinkowski, S.P. (1985) *Managerial Stress: A Longitudinal Study* (unpublished Doctoral Thesis) University of Manchester.

Glowinkowski, S.P. and Cooper, C.L. (1985) 'Current issues in organizational stress research', *Bulletin of the British Psychological Society*, 38: 212–16.

—— (1986) 'Managers and professionals in business/industrial settings: the research evidence', *Journal of Behavioural Medicine*, 8(2): 177–93.

Golzen, G. (1989) 'Into the age of the "knowledge worker"', *The Sunday Times*, 12 November, E1.

—— (1990) 'Experts oust City barrow boys', *The Sunday Times*, 18 February, F11.

Gray, J. (1983) 'What's behind the fastest money game of all', *Medical Economics*, 60(24): 118–32.

Greene, C.N. and Schriesheim, C.A. (1980) 'Leader-group interactions: A longitudinal field investigation', *Journal of Applied Psychology*, 65: 50–9.

Greenhaus, J.H. and Beutell, N.J. (1985) 'Sources of conflict between work and family roles', *Academy of Management Review*, 10(1): 76–88.

Greenhaus, J.H. and Kopelman, R.E. (1981) 'Conflict between work and non-work roles: Implications for the career planning process', *Human Resource Planning*, 4: 1–10.

Gutek, B.A., Repetti, R.L. and Silver, D.L. (1988) 'Nonwork roles and stress at work', in C.L. Cooper and R. Payne (eds) *Causes, Coping and Consequences of Stress at Work*, Chichester: Wiley.

Hacker, W. (1985) 'Activity: A fruitful concept in industrial psychology', in M. Frese and J. Sabini (eds) *Goal Directed Behavior*, Hillsdale: Erlbaum.

Hackman, J.R. Oldham, G.R., Janson, R. and Purdy, K.A. (1975) 'A new strategy for job enrichment', *California Management Review*, 17(4): 57–71.

Hamilton, A. (1986) *The Financial Revolution*, Harmondsworth: Penguin.

Hamilton, V. (1979) '"Personality" and stress', in V. Hamilton and D.M. Warburton (eds) *Human Stress and Cognition*, Chichester: Wiley.

Hartman, H. (1939) *Ego Psychology and the Problem of Adaptation*, New York: International Universities Press.

Harvey, D.F. and Brown, D.R. (1988) 'OD interpersonal interventions', in D.F. Harvey and D.R. Brown (eds) *An Experiential Approach to Organisational Development*, Englewood Cliffs, New Jersey: Prentice-Hall International, third edition.

Haynes, S.G. and Feinleib, M. (1980) 'Women, work and coronary heart disease: Prospective findings from the Framingham Heart Study', *American Journal of Public Health*, 70: 133–41.

Health Education Authority (1989) *That's the Limit*, London: Health Education Authority.

Herd, J.A. (1988) 'Physiological indices of job stress', in J.J. Hurrell, Jnr., L.R. Murphy, S.L. Sauter and C.L. Cooper (eds) *Occupational Stress: Issues and Developments in Research*, London: Taylor & Francis.

Herried, C., Peterson, M.F. and Chang, D. (1985) 'Type A, occupational stress and salesperson performance', *Journal of Small Business Management*, 23(3): 59–65.

Herzlinger, R.E. and Calkins, D. (1986) 'How companies tackle health care costs: Part III', *Harvard Business Review*, 86(1): 70–80.

Higgins, N.C. (1986) 'Occupational stress and working women: The effectiveness of two stress reduction programs', *Journal of Vocational Behaviour*, 29(1): 66–78.

Hingley, P. and Cooper, C.L. (1986) *Stress and the Nurse Manager*, Chichester: Wiley.

Hobfoll, S.E. (1989) 'Conservation of resources: A new attempt at conceptualising stress', *American Psychologist*, 44(3): 513–24.

Hockey, G. (1972) 'Effects of noise on human efficiency and some individual differences', *Journal of Sound and Vibration*, 20: 299–304.

Holahan, C.J. and Moos, R.H. (1981) 'Social support and psychological distress: A longitudinal analysis', *Journal of Abnormal Psychology*, 90: 365–70.

Holland, J.L. (1973) *Making Vocational Choices: A Theory of Careers*, Englewood Cliffs: Prentice-Hall.

Hollinger, R.C. and Clark, J.P. (1983) *Theft by Employees*, Lexington, Massachusetts: Lexington Books.

Holmes, D.S., McGilley, B.M. and Houston, B.K. (1984) 'Task-related arousal of Type A and Type B persons: Level of challenge and response specificity', *Journal of Personality and Social Psychology*, 46: 1322–7.

Holmes, D.S. and Will, M.J. (1985) 'Expression of interpersonal aggression by angered and nonangered persons with the Type A and Type B behavior patterns', *Journal of Personality and Social Psychology*, 33: 460–6.

Holmes, T.H. and Rahe, R.H. (1967) 'The social readjustment rating scale', *Journal of Psychosomatic Research*, 11: 213–18.

Horowitz, M.J. (1979) 'Psychological responses to serious life events', in V. Hamilton and D.M. Warburton (eds) *Human Stress and Cognition*, Chichester: Wiley.

House, J.S. (1972) *The Relationship of Intrinsic and Extrinsic Work Motivations to Occupational Stress and Coronary Heart Disease Risk* (unpublished Ph.D. Thesis) University of Michigan.

—— (1981) *Work Stress and Social Support*, Reading, Mass: Addison-Wesley.

Howard, J.H., Cunningham, D.A. and Rechnitzer, P.A. (1976) 'Health patterns associated with Type 'A' behaviors; A managerial population', *Journal of Human Stress*, 2: 24–31.

Hunsaker, P.L. and Pavett, C.M. (1988) 'Drug abuse in the brokerage industry', *Personnel*, July, 65: 54–8.

Hurrell, J., Jnr., Murphy, L.R., Sauter, S.L. and Cooper, C.L. (1988) *Occupational Stress: Issues and Development in Research*, London: Taylor & Francis.

Irving, R.H., Higgins, C.A. and Safayeni, F. (1986) 'Computerised performance monitoring systems: use and abuse', *Communications of the ACM*, 29: 794–801.

Ivancevich, J.M. and Matteson, M.T. (1980) *Stress and Work*, Glenview, Illinois: Scott, Foresman.

—— (1987) *Organisational Behavior and Management*, PLANO, Texas: Business Publications.

Ivancevich, J.M., Matteson, M.T. and Preston, C. (1982) 'Occupational stress, Type A behaviour, and physical well being', *Academy of Management Journal*, 25: 373–91.

Jackson, S.E. (1983) 'Participation in decision making as a strategy for reducing job-related strain', *Journal of Applied Psychology*, 68: 3–19.

Jamal, M. (1984) 'Job stress and job performance controversy: An empirical assessment', *Organisational Behaviour and Human Performance*, 33: 1–21.

Janman, K., Jones, J.G., Payne, R.L. and Rick, J.T. (1988) 'Clustering individuals as a way of dealing with multiple predictors in occupational stress research', *Journal of Human Stress*, 14(1): 17–29 (now *Behavioral Medicine*).

Jenkins, C.D. (1971) 'Psychologic and social precursors of coronary disease', *New England Journal of Medicine*, 284(5): 244–55.

Jenner, J.R. (1986) 'On the way to stress resistance', *Training and Development Journal*, 40(5): 111–15.

Jick, T.D. (1983) 'The stressful effects of budget cutbacks in organisations', in L.A. Rosen (ed.) *Topics in Managerial Accounting*, New York: McGraw-Hill.

Jick, T.D. and Mitz, L.F. (1985) 'Sex differences in work stress', *Academy of Management Review*, 10(3): 408–20.

Johansson, G. and Aronsson, G. (1984) 'Stress reactions in computerised administrative work', *Journal of Occupational Behaviour*, 5: 159–81.

Johnson, J.H. and Sarason, I.G. (1979) 'Recent developments in research on life events', in V. Hamilton and D.M. Warburton (eds) *Human Stress and Cognition*, Chichester: Wiley.

Jordan, C., Cobb, N. and McCully, R. (1989) 'Clinical issues of the dual-career couple', *Social Work*, 34(1): 29–38.

Kahn, H. and Cooper, C.L. (1986) 'Computing stress', *Current Psychological Research and Reviews*, 5(2): 148–62.

—— (1990) 'Mental health, job satisfaction, alcohol intake and occupational stress among dealers in financial markets', *Stress Medicine*, 6: 285–98.

Kahn, R.L. (1989) 'Role Conflict and Ambiguity in Organisations', in M.T. Matteson and J.M. Ivancevich (eds) *Management and Organisational Behavior Classics*, Homewood, Illinois: Irwin.

Kahn, R.L., Wolfe, D.M., Quinn, R.P., Snoek, J.D. and Rosenthal, R.A. (1964) *Organisational Stress: Studies in Role Conflict and Ambiguity*, New York: Wiley.

Kasl, S.V. (1978) 'Epidemiological contributions to the study of work stress', in C.L. Cooper and R. Payne (eds) *Stress at Work*, Chichester: Wiley.

—— (1983) 'Pursuing the link between stressful life experiences and disease: a time for reappraisal', in C.L. Cooper (ed.) *Stress Research: Issues for the Eighties*, Chichester: Wiley.

Katz, D. and Kahn, R. (1978) *The Social Psychology of Organisations*, New York: John Wiley, second edition.

Kaufmann, G.M. and Beehr, J.A. (1986) 'Interactions between job stressors and social support: Some counter-intuitive results', *Journal of Applied Psychology*, 71: 522–6.

Kessler, R.C., Price, R.H. and Wortman, C.B. (1985) 'Social factors in psychopathology. Stress, social support and coping processes', *Annual Review of Psychology*, 36: 531–72.

Kets De Vries, M. and Miller, D. (1984) *The Neurotic Organisation*, London: Jossey-Bass.

Kirrane, D. (1990) 'EAPs: Dawning of a new age', *HR Magazine*, 35(1): 30–4.

Kobasa, S.C.O. (1988) 'Conceptualization and measurement of personality in job stress research', in J.J. Hurrell, Jnr., L.R. Murphy, S.L. Sauter and C.L. Cooper (eds) *Occupational Stress: Issues and Developments in Research*, London: Taylor & Francis.

Kobasa, S.C.O. and Puccetti, M.C. (1983) 'Personality and social resources in stress resistance', *Journal of Personality and Social Psychology*, 45: 839–50.

Kornhauser, A. (1965) *Mental Health of the Industrial Worker*, New York: Wiley.

Kreitner, R., Sova, M.A., Wood, S.D., Friedman, G.M. and Reif, W.E. (1985) 'A search for the U-shaped relationship between occupational stressors and the risk of coronary heart disease', *Journal of Police Science and Administration*, 13(2): 122–31.

Kutash, I.L., Schlesinger, L.B. and Associates (1980) *Handbook on Stress and Anxiety*, San Francisco: Jossey-Bass.

Landale, T. (1989) 'Addressing stress', *Personnel Today*, 13 June, 34–5.

LaRocco, J.M., House, J.S. and French, J.R.P., Jnr. (1980) 'Social support, occupational stress and health', *Journal of Health and Social Behaviour*, 21: 202–18.

Lazarus, R.S. (1966) *Psychological Stress and the Coping Process*, New York: McGraw-Hill.

Leavy, R.L. (1983) 'Social support and psychological disorder: a review', *Journal of Community Psychology*, 11: 3–21.

Lebovits, B.Z., Shekelle, R.B. and Ostfeld, A.M. (1967) 'Prospective and retrospective studies of CHD', *Psychosomatic Medicine*, 19: 265–72.

Levinson, H. (1964) *Executive Stress*, New York: Harper and Row.

Lewis, M. (1989) *Liar's Poker*, London: Hodder & Stoughton.

Lewis, S.N.C. and Cooper, C.L. (1987) 'Stress in two-earner couples and stage in the life cycle', *Journal of Occupational Psychology*, 60(4): 289–303.

Lewis, S. and Cooper, C.L. (1989) *Career Couples*, London: Unwin.

Liebman, M. (1970) 'The effects of sex and race norms on personal space', *Environmental Behaviour*, 2: 208–46.

Likert, R. (1961) *New Patterns of Management*, New York: McGraw-Hill.

Lin, N., Ensel, W.M., Simeone, R.S. and Kuo, W. (1979) 'Social support, stressful life events, and illness: A model and an empirical test', *Journal of Health and Social Behaviour*, 20: 108–19.

Lourie, R.H. (1981) 'Pressure in a grey flannel suit', *Direct Marketing*, December, 46–9.

Luthans, F. (1989) *Organisational Behavior*, New York: McGraw-Hill Book Company, fifth edition.

McClelland, D.C. (1975) *Power: The Inner Experience*, New York: Irvington.

McClelland, D.C. and Jemmott, J.B. (1980) 'Power motivation, stress and physical illness', *Journal of Human Stress*, December, 6–15.

McCrae, R.R. and Costa, P.T., Jnr. (1985) 'Comparison of EPI and psychoticism scales with measures of the five-factor model of personality', *Personality and Individual Differences*, 6(5): 587–97.

McDonnell, R. and Maynard, A. (1985) 'The cost of alcohol misuse', *British Journal of Addiction*, 80: 27–35.

McGrath, J.E. (1976) 'Stress and behavior in organisations', in M.D. Dunnette (ed.) *Handbook of Industrial and Organisational Psychology*, Chicago: Rand McNally.

MacKay, C.J. and Cooper, C.L. (1987) 'Occupational stress and health: some current issues', in C.L. Cooper and I.T. Robertson (eds) *International Review of Industrial and Organisational Psychology 1987* Chichester: Wiley

McLean, A.A. (1980) *Work Stress*, Reading, Massachusetts: Addison-Wesley.

Marcelissen, F.H., Winnubst, J.A., Buunk, B. and De Wolff, C.J. (1988) 'Social support and occupational stress: A causal analysis', *Social Science and Medicine*, 26(3): 365–73.

Margolis, B.L., Kroes, W.H. and Quinn, R.P. (1974) 'Job stress: An unlisted occupational hazard', *Journal of Occupational Medicine*, 16: 654–61.

Marino, K.E. and White, S.E. (1985) 'Departmental structure, locus of control and job stress: The effect of a moderator', *Journal of Applied Psychology*, 70(4): 782–4.

Marks, M.L. and Mirvin, P.H. (1986) 'The merger syndrome', *Psychology Today*, 20(10): 36–42.

Martin, R. and Wall, T.D. (1989) 'Attentional demand and cost responsibility as stressors in shopfloor jobs', *Academy of Management Journal*, 32(1): 69–86.

Matteson, M.T. and Ivancevich, J.M. (1983) 'Note on tension discharge rate as an employee health status predictor', *Academy of Management Journal*, 26: 540–5.

—— (1987) 'Individual stress management interventions: evaluation of techniques', *Journal of Managerial Psychology*, 2(1): 24–30.

Menninger, K. (1938) *Man Against Himself*, New York: Harcourt Brace Jovanovich.

Miller, K.I. and Monge, P.R. (1986) 'Participation, satisfaction and productivity: a meta-analytic review', *Academy of Management Journal*, 29(4): 727–53.

MIND (1992) *The MIND Survey: Stress at Work*, London: MIND.

Miner, J.B. and Brewer, J.F. (1976) 'Management of ineffective performance', in M.D. Dunette (ed.) *Handbook of Industrial and Organisational Psychology*, Chicago: Rand McNally.

Minkler, M. and Biller, R.P. (1979) 'Role shock: A tool for conceptualising stresses accompanying disruptive role transitions', *Human Relations*, 29(2): 125–40.

Mintzberg, H. (1973) *The Nature of Managerial Work*, New York: Harper and Row.

Moss, L. (1981) *Management Stress*, Reading, Massachusetts: Addison-Wesley.

Moulton, R. (1980) 'Anxiety and new feminism', in I.L. Kutash, L.B. Schlesinger and Associates (eds) *Handbook on Stress and Anxiety*, San Francisco: Jossey-Bass.

Mount, M. and Muchinsky, P. (1978) 'P-E congruence and employee satisfaction: a test of Holland's theory', *Journal of Vocational Behavior*, 13: 84–100.

Mulligan, J. (1989) *The Personal Management Handbook*, London: Sphere.

Nelson, D.L. and Quick, J.C. (1985) 'Professional women: are distress and disease inevitable?', *Academy of Management Review*, 10(2): 206–18.

NFER-Nelson (1992) *OSI Norm Tables*, Windsor: NFER-Nelson.

Niven, N. and Johnson, D. (1989) 'Does stress management work?', *Management Services*, 33(11): 18–21.

Nugent, W.C. (1988) 'When employees seek workers' compensation for stress', *Employee Relations Law Journal* 14(2): 239–52.

Oborne, D.J. (1985) *Computers at Work – A Behavioural Approach*, Chichester: Wiley.

OPCS (Office of Population Census and Surveys) (1986) London: HMSO.

Ortega, D.F. and Pipal, J.E. (1984) 'Challenge seeking and Type A coronary-prone behavior pattern', *Journal of Personality and Social Psychology*, 46: 1328–34.

Osipow, S.H. and Davis, A.S. (1988) 'The relationship of coping resources to occupational stress and strain', *Journal of Vocational Behavior*, 32(1): 1–15.

Ostell, A. (1988) 'The perils of ignoring stress', *The Sunday Times*, 31 July, E15.

Payne, R. (1988) 'Individual differences in the study of occupational stress', in C.L. Cooper and R. Payne (eds) *Causes, Coping and Consequences of Stress at Work*, Chichester: Wiley.

Payne, R.L. (1979) 'Stress and cognition in organisations', in V. Hamilton and D.M. Warburton (eds) *Human Stress and Cognition*, Chichester: Wiley.

Payne, R.L. and Jones, J.G. (1987) 'Measurement and methodological issues in social support', in S.V. Kasl and C.L. Cooper (eds) *Stress and Health: Issues in Research Methodology*, Chichester: Wiley.

Pearlin, L.I. and Turner, H.A. (1987) 'The family as a context of the stress process', in S.V. Kasl and C.L. Cooper (eds) *Stress and Health: Issues in Research Methodology*, Chichester: Wiley.

Perrewe, P.L. and Ganster, D.C. (1989) 'The impact of job demands and behavioral control on experienced job stress', *Journal of Occupational Behavior*, 10: 213–29.

Phillips, T. (1989) 'Stress and train', *IT Training*, October/November, 41–3.

Pittner, M.S., Houston, B.K. and Spiridigliozzi, G. (1983) 'Control over stress, Type A behavior pattern, and response to stress', *Journal of Personality and Social Psychology*, 44: 627–36.

Pleck, J.H., Staines, G.L. and Lang, L. (1980) 'Conflicts between work and family life', *Monthly Labor Review*, 29–32.

Powers, R.J. and Kutash, I.L. (1980) 'Alcohol abuse and anxiety', in I.L. Kutash, L.B. Schlesinger and Associates (eds) *Handbook on Stress and Anxiety*, San Francisco: Jossey-Bass.

Quayle, D. (1983) 'American productivity: The devastating effect of alcoholism and drug abuse', *American Psychologist*, 38: 454–8.

Quick, J.C. and Quick, J.D. (1984) *Organisational Stress and Preventative Management*, New York: McGraw-Hill.

Quick, J.D., Horn, R.S. and Quick, J.C. (1986) 'Health consequences of stress', *Journal of Behavioral Medicine*, 8(2): 19–36.

Rabkin, J.G. and Struening, E.L. (1976) 'Life events, stress, and illness', *Science*, 194: 1013–20.

Reid, M. (1988) *All-Change in the City*, London: Macmillan.

Revicki, D.A. and Max, H.J. (1985) 'Occupational stress, social support, and depression', *Health Psychology*, 4(1): 61–77.

Reynolds, B. (1989) *The 100 Best Companies to Work for in the UK*, London: Fontana.

Rime, B., Ucros, C.G., Bestgen, Y. and Jeanjean, M. (1989) 'Type A behaviour pattern: Specific coronary risk factor or general disease-prone condition', *British Journal of Medical Psychology*, 62: 229–40.

Robbins, S.P. (1987) *Organisation Theory*, Englewood Cliffs, New Jersey: Prentice-Hall International.

Robertson, I.T. and Cooper, C.L. (1983) *Human Behaviour in Organisations*, Plymouth: MacDonald & Evans.

Rodahl, K. (1989) *The Physiology of Work*, London: Taylor & Francis.

Roden, R.J. (1985) *Stress in the Inland Revenue: Tax Officers (Higher Grade)* (unpublished Masters Dissertation) University of Manchester.

Rodgers, D.P. (1984) 'Helping employees cope with burnout issues', *Business*, December, 3–7.

Rogers, R.E. (1983) 'Perceptions of stress among Canadian and American managers: A cross-cultural analysis', in H. Selye (ed.) *Selye's Guide to Stress Research*, Vol. 2, New York: Van Nostrand.

Rohmert, W. and Luczak, H. (1979) 'Stress, work and productivity', in V. Hamilton and D.M. Warburton (eds) *Human Stress and Cognition*, Chichester: Wiley.

Romano, J.L. (1988) 'Stress management counselling: From crisis to prevention', *Counselling Psychology Quarterly*, 1(2 and 3): 211–19.

Rose, R.M., Jenkins, C.D. and Hurst, H.M. (1978) *Air Traffic Controller Health Change Study: A prospective investigation of physical, psychological, and work related changes*, Austin: University of Texas Press.

Rosenman, R.H., Brank, R.J., Jenkins, C.D., Friedman, M. and Wurm, M. (1975) 'Coronary heart disease in the Western Collaborative Group study: Final follow-up experience of 8.5 years', *Journal of the American Medical Association*, 223: 872–7.

Rosenman, R.H. and Friedman, M. (1983) 'Relationship of Type A behavior pattern to coronary heart disease', in H. Selye (ed.) *Selye's Guide to Stress Research*, Vol. 2, New York: Van Nostrand.

Rotter, J.B. (1966) 'Generalized expectancies for internal versus external control of reinforcement', *Psychological Monographs*, 80(1): 609.

Russek, H.I. and Zohman, B.L. (1958) 'Relative significance of heredity diet and occupational stress in C.H.D. of young adults', *American Journal of Medical Sciences*, 235: 266–75.

Saal, F.E. and Knight, P.A. (1988) *Industrial/Organisational Psychology*, California: Brooks/Cole Publishing Company.

Sadri, G., Cooper, C. and Allison, T. (1989) 'A Post Office initiative to stamp out stress', *Personnel Management*, 21(8): 40–5.

Sales, S.M. (1969) 'Organisational role as a risk factor in coronary disease', *Administrative Science Quarterly*, 14: 325–36.

Savery, L.K. (1988) 'The influence of social support on the reactions of an employee', *Journal of Managerial Psychology*, 3(1): 27–31.

Scheier, M.F. and Carver, C.S. (1985) 'Optimism, coping and health: Assessment and implications of generalised outcome expectancies', *Health Psychology*, 4(3): 219–47.

Schein, E.H. (1985) *Organisational Culture and Leadership*, San Francisco: Jossey-Bass.

Schneiderman, B. (1986) 'Seven plus or minus two central issues in human-computer interaction', *Proceedings of CHI '86 Conference on Human Factors in Computing Systems*, Boston.

Seers, A., McGee, T.T., Serey, T.T. and Graen, G.B. (1983) 'The interaction of job stress and social support: A strong inference investigation', *Academy of Management Journal*, 26: 273–84.

Seltzer, J. and Numerof, R.E. (1988) 'Supervisory leadership and subordinate burnout', *Academy of Management Journal*, 31(2): 439–46.

Selye, H. (1936) 'A syndrome produced by diverse nocuous agents', *Nature*, 138: 32.

—— (1956) *The Stress of Life*, New York: McGraw-Hill.

—— (1980) 'The stress concept today', in I.L. Kutash, L.B. Schlesinger and

Associates (eds) *Handbook on Stress and Anxiety*, San Francisco: Jossey-Bass.

—— (1983) 'The stress concept: past, present and future', in C.L. Cooper (ed.) *Stress Research, Issues for the Eighties*, Chichester: Wiley.

Shirom, A., Eden, D., Silberwasser, S. and Kellerman, J.J. (1973) 'Job stress and risk factors in coronary heart disease among occupational categories in Kibbutzim', *Social Science & Medicine*, 7: 875–92.

Shotton, M.A. (1989) *Computer Addiction? A study of computer dependency*, London: Taylor & Francis.

Sloan, S.J. and Cooper, C.L. (1986) *Pilots under Stress*, London: Routledge and Kegan Paul.

—— (1987) 'Sources of stress in the modern office', in A. Gale and B. Christie (eds) *Psychophysiology and the Electronic Workplace*, Chichester: Wiley.

Smith, M.J. (1984) 'Health issues in VDU work', in J. Bennett, D. Case, J. Sandelin and M. Smith (eds) *Visual Display Terminals: Usability Issues and Health Concerns*, Englewood Cliffs: Prentice-Hall.

Smith, M.J., Cohen, B.G., Stammerjohn, L.W. and Happ, A. (1981) 'An investigation of health complaints and job stress in video display operations', *Human Factors*, 23: 389–400.

Smithers, R.D. (1988) *The Psychology of Work and Human Performance*, New York: Harper and Row.

Spector, P.E. (1982) 'Behaviour in organisations as a function of employees' locus of control', *Psychological Bulletin*, 91, 482–99.

—— (1988) 'Development of the work locus of control scale', *Journal of Occupational Psychology*, 61(4): 335–40.

Spruell, G. (1987) 'Work fever', *Training and Development Journal*, 41(1): 41–5.

Staw, B.M. (1984) 'Organisational behavior: A review and reformulation of the field's outcome variables', *Annual Review of Psychology*, 35: 627–66.

Steers, R.M. and Rhodes, S.R. (1978) 'Major influences on employee attendance: A process model', *Journal of Applied Psychology*, 63: 391–407.

Stiles, W.B., Shapiro, D.A. and Elliot, R.K. (1986) 'Are all psychotherapies equivalent?', *American Psychologist*, 41: 165–80.

Sutherland, V.J. (1988) *Stress and Accidents in the Offshore Oil and Gas Industry* (unpublished Doctoral Thesis) University of Manchester.

Sutherland, V.J. and Cooper, C.L. (1986) *Man and Accidents Offshore: The Costs of Stress Among Workers on Oil and Gas Rigs*, London: Lloyd's List/Dietsmann (International) NV.

—— (1988) 'Sources of work stress', in J.J. Hurrell, Jnr., L.R. Murphy, S.L. Sauter and C.L. Cooper (eds) *Occupational Stress: Issues and Developments in Research*, London: Taylor & Francis.

Sutton, R.I. and Kahn, R.L. (1987) 'Prediction, understanding and control as antidotes to organisational stress', in J. Lorsch (ed.) *Handbook of Organisational Behavior*, Englewood Cliffs, New Jersey: Prentice-Hall.

Sutton, R.I. and Rafaeli, A. (1987) 'Characteristics of work stations as potential occupational stressors', *Academy of Management Journal*, 30(2): 260–76.

Syme, S.L., Borhani, N.O. and Buechley, R.W. (1966) 'Cultural mobility and coronary heart disease in an urban area', *American Journal of Epidemiology*, 82: 334–46.

Szilagyi, A.D., Sims, H.P. and Keller, R.T. (1976) 'Role dynamics, locus of control and employee attitudes and behavior', *Academy of Management Journal*, 19(2): 259–76.

Tannenbaum, R. and Massarik, F. (1989) 'Participation by subordinates in the managerial decision-making process', in M.T. Matteson and J.M. Ivancevich (eds) *Management and Organisational Behaviour Classics*, Homewood, Illinois: Irwin.

Taylor, S.J.L. and Chave, S. (1964) *Mental Health and the Environment*, London: Longman.

Taylor, W.L. and Cangemi, J.P. (1988) 'The effect of occupational stress on health and illness: A model', *Psychology: A Journal of Human Behavior*, 25(3–4): 53–64.

Taylor Made Films (1992) *Time Management: MORI Poll*, London.

Terkel, S. (1972) *Working*, New York: Pantheon Books.

Thompson, S.C. (1981) 'Will it hurt less if I can control it? A complex answer to a simple question', *Psychological Bulletin*, 90, 89–101.

Van Harrison, R. (1978) 'Person-environment fit and job stress', in C.L. Cooper and R.L. Payne (eds) *Stress at Work*, Chichester: Wiley.

Vecchio, R.P. (1991) *Organisational Behavior*, Chicago: Dryden Press.

Wahlund, I. and Nurell, G. (1978) 'Stress factors in the working environment of white collar workers', in A. McLean (ed.) *Reducing Occupational Stress*, DHEW (NIOSH) Pub. No. 78–140, Washington D.C.: US Government Printing Office.

Wall, T.D. and Martin, R. (1987) 'Job and work design', in C.L. Cooper and I.T. Robertson (eds) *International Review of Industrial and Organisational Psychology 1987*, Chichester: Wiley.

Warr, P., Cook, J. and Wall, T. (1979) 'Scales for the measurement of some work attitudes and aspects of psychological well-being', *Journal of Occupational Psychology*, 52: 129–48.

Webb, G.H. (1987) *The Bigger Bang*, London: Waterlow.

Weiss, H.M., Ilgen, D.R. and Sharbaugh, M.E. (1982) 'Effects of life and job stress on information search behaviors of organisation members', *Journal of Applied Psychology*, 67: 60–6.

Whitmore, R., Tatham, A. and Coletta, V. (undated) 'Anxiety. What it is, and how to control it', *Manchester Area Department of Clinical Psychology*.

Wilby, J. (1985) *Good Career Guide*, London: Sunday Times.

Willcocks, L. and Mason, D. (1987) *Computerising Work*, London: Paradigm.

Williams, A.P.O. (1985) 'The neglected process of self-selection', *City University Business School, Working Paper Series*, 71.

Wineman, J.D. (1982) 'The office environment as a source of stress', in G.W. Evans (ed.) *Environmental Stress*, Cambridge: Cambridge University Press.

Wolpin, J. and Burke, R.J. (1986) 'Occupational locking-in: some correlates and consequences', *International Review of Applied Psychology*, 35: 327–46.

Zuboff, S. (1988) *In the Age of the Smart Machine*, Oxford: Heinemann.

INDEX